ACKNOWLEDGEMENTS

I would like to thank everyone who contributed to the successful publication of this book, including numerous retirees for their invaluable thoughts on retiring to Spain and countless staff at government offices and local councils for their help with queries. I would also like to thank Peter Read for the editing, Grania Rogers for proof-reading, Joe and Kerry Laredo for the page design and indexing, Jim Watson for the illustrations, cartoons and maps, and everyone else who provided information or contributed in any way.

WITI

D0726732

FROM STOCK

TITLES BY SURVIVAL BOOKS

Alien's Guides
Britain; France

The Best Places To Buy A Home
France; Spain

Buying a Home
Abroad; Australia & New Zealand;
Bulgaria, Cyprus; Florida; France;
Greece; Ireland, Italy, Portugal;
South Africa; Spain;
Buying, Selling & Letting Property (UK)

Buying and Renting a Home
London; New York

**Foreigners Abroad: Triumphs
& Disasters**
France; Spain

Lifeline Regional Guides
Brittany; Costa Blanca;
Costa del Sol; Dordogne/Lot;
Normandy; Poitou-Charentes;
Provence/Côte d'Azur

Living and Working
Abroad; America;
Australia; Britain; Canada;
The European Union;
The Far East; France; Germany;
The Gulf States & Saudi Arabia; Holland,
Belgium & Luxembourg; Ireland;
Italy; London; New Zealand;
Spain; Switzerland

Earning Money from Your Home
France; Spain

Making a Living
France; Spain

Other Titles
Renovating & Maintaining
Your French Home; Retiring Abroad;
Retiring in Spain;
Rural Living in France;
Shooting Caterpillars in Spain;
Surprised by France

Order forms are on page 383.

WHAT READERS & REVIEWERS

When you buy a model plane for your child, a video recorder, or some new computer gizmo, you get with it a leaflet or booklet pleading 'Read Me First', or bearing large friendly letters or bold type saying 'IMPORTANT – follow the instructions carefully'. This book should be similarly supplied to all those entering France with anything more durable than a 5-day return ticket. It is worth reading even if you are just visiting briefly, or if you have lived here for years and feel totally knowledgeable and secure. But if you need to find out how France works then it is indispensable. Native French people probably have a less thorough understanding of how their country functions. – Where it is most essential, the book is most up to the minute.

LIVING FRANCE

Rarely has a 'survival guide' contained such useful advice. This book dispels doubts for first-time travellers, yet is also useful for seasoned globetrotters – In a word, if you're planning to move to the USA or go there for a long-term stay, then buy this book both for general reading and as a ready-reference.

AMERICAN CITIZENS ABROAD

It is everything you always wanted to ask but didn't for fear of the contemptuous put down – The best English-language guide – Its pages are stuffed with practical information on everyday subjects and are designed to complement the traditional guidebook.

SWISS NEWS

A complete revelation to me – I found it both enlightening and interesting, not to mention amusing.

CAROLE CLARK

Let's say it at once. David Hampshire's **Living and Working in France** is the best handbook ever produced for visitors and foreign residents in this country; indeed, my discussion with locals showed that it has much to teach even those born and bred in l'Hexagone. – It is Hampshire's meticulous detail which lifts his work way beyond the range of other books with similar titles. Often you think of a supplementary question and search for the answer in vain. With Hampshire this is rarely the case. – He writes with great clarity (and gives French equivalents of all key terms), a touch of humour and a ready eye for the odd (and often illuminating) fact. – This book is absolutely indispensable.

THE RIVIERA REPORTER

A mine of information – I may have avoided some embarrassments and frights if I had read it prior to my first Swiss encounters – Deserves an honoured place on any newcomer's bookshelf.

ENGLISH TEACHERS ASSOCIATION, SWITZERLAND

Have Said About Survival Books

What a great work, wealth of useful information, well-balanced wording and accuracy in details. My compliments!

THOMAS MÜLLER

This handbook has all the practical information one needs to set up home in the UK – The sheer volume of information is almost daunting – Highly recommended for anyone moving to the UK.

AMERICAN CITIZENS ABROAD

A very good book which has answered so many questions and even some I hadn't thought of – I would certainly recommend it.

BRIAN FAIRMAN

We would like to congratulate you on this work: it is really super! We hand it out to our expatriates and they read it with great interest and pleasure.

ICI (SWITZERLAND) AG

Covers just about all the things you want to know on the subject – In answer to the desert island question about the one how-to book on France, this book would be it – Almost 500 pages of solid accurate reading – This book is about enjoyment as much as survival.

THE RECORDER

It's so funny – I love it and definitely need a copy of my own – Thanks very much for having written such a humorous and helpful book.

HEIDI GUILIANI

A must for all foreigners coming to Switzerland.

ANTOINETTE O'DONOGHUE

A comprehensive guide to all things French, written in a highly readable and amusing style, for anyone planning to live, work or retire in France.

THE TIMES

A concise, thorough account of the DOs and DON'Ts for a foreigner in Switzerland – Crammed with useful information and lightened with humorous quips which make the facts more readable.

AMERICAN CITIZENS ABROAD

Covers every conceivable question that may be asked concerning everyday life – I know of no other book that could take the place of this one.

FRANCE IN PRINT

Hats off to *Living and Working in Switzerland*!

RONNIE ALMEIDA

Contents

IMPORTANT NOTE

Readers should note that the laws and regulations regarding retirement and buying property in Spain aren't the same as in other countries and are liable to change periodically. Those who aren't nationals of an EU country will need to obtain a residence permit to retire permanently in Spain. **I cannot recommend too strongly that you always check with an official and reliable source (not necessarily the same) and obtain expert legal advice before making plans to retire in Spain or buying or renting a home there.** Don't, however, believe everything you're told or read – even, dare I say it, herein!

To help you obtain further information and verify data with official sources, useful addresses and references to other sources of information have been included in all chapters and in **Appendices A to C**. Important points have been emphasised throughout the book in **bold** print, some of which it would be expensive or foolish to disregard. **Ignore them at your peril or cost!** Unless specifically stated, the reference to any company, organisation, product or publication in this book doesn't constitute an endorsement or recommendation.

THE AUTHOR

Joanna Styles was born in London but has lived and worked for many years on the Costa del Sol, Spain. She is a freelance writer and the author of several books, including **The Best Places to Buy a Home in Spain**, **Buying a Home in Greece**, **Living & Working in the European Union**, **Costa Blanca Lifeline** and **Costa del Sol Lifeline**, all published by Survival Books. She also regularly contributes to and updates a number of other Survival Books publications. Joanna is married with two daughters.

Author's Notes

- Frequent references are made in this book to the European Union (EU), which comprises Austria, Belgium, Cyprus, the Czech Republic, Denmark, Estonia, Finland, France, Germany, Greece, Hungary, Ireland, Italy, Latvia, Lithuania, Luxembourg, Malta, the Netherlands, Poland, Portugal, Slovakia, Slovenia, Spain, Sweden and the United Kingdom, and the European Economic Area (EEA), which includes the EU countries plus Iceland, Liechtenstein and Norway.

- **Prices quoted should be taken only as estimates**, although they were correct when going to print and fortunately don't usually change greatly overnight. Most prices in Spain are quoted inclusive of value added tax (*IVA incluido*), which is the method used in this book unless a price is specified as being exclusive of tax (*más IVA*).

- Times are shown using am (Latin *ante meridiem*) for before noon and pm (*post meridiem*) for after noon. Most Spaniards don't use the 24-hour clock. All times are local, and you should check the time difference when making international calls.

- His/he/him/man/men (etc.) also mean her/she/her/woman/ women. This is done simply to make life easier for the reader and, in particular, the author, and **isn't** intended to be sexist.

- British English is used throughout, but American English equivalents are given where appropriate.

- The Spanish translation of key words and phrases is shown in brackets in *italics*.

- Warnings and important points are shown in **bold** type.

- The following symbols are used in this book: ☎ (telephone), 🖨 (fax), 💻 (internet) and ✉ (email).

- **Appendices** at the back of the book contain lists of useful addresses and websites, suggestions for further reading, imperial/metric conversion tables, maps of the regions and provinces and transport networks, and tables of scheduled airline services between the British Isles and Spain.

INTRODUCTION

Millions of people dream of retiring to a home in the sun where they can enjoy a 'summer' lifestyle all year round. A numbers of surveys conducted in recent years concluded that as many as one in five Britons aged over 50 are planning to retire abroad by 2015-2020, and there are signs of similar trends in Germany and other northern Europeans countries. Europe's most popular retirement destination is Spain, which is already home to hundreds of thousands of foreign retirees whose favourite retirement spots include the Costa Blanca, the Costa del Sol, and the islands of Majorca and Tenerife.

Among Spain's many attractions are its year-round, sunny climate; beautiful beaches and countryside and vibrant cities; high standard and low cost of living; world-class healthcare; excellent food and wine; spectacular natural surroundings; and excellent (low-cost) air connections, particularly with northern European countries. Many retirees find that a move to Spain results in a much-improved quality of life and most claim they feel fitter and younger, boasting that retirement to Spain has not only taken years off their life but also helped them to live longer!

However, retiring to Spain isn't always a bed of roses and obstacles such as the bureaucracy, language difficulties (although this isn't generally a problem in popular tourist destinations), poor social services for the elderly, a lack of nursing homes and boredom are all potential barriers to a happy and fulfilling retirement.

However, as with all life-changing decisions, the key to a successful retirement in Spain is planning ahead and doing as much research as possible before you go. This is where this book will prove invaluable. Written specifically for retirees (and prospective retirees) in Spain, *Retiring in Spain* is worth its weight in sunshine.

General information about Spain isn't difficult to find, but **reliable** and **up-to-date** information in English especially intended for retirees planning to live in Spain isn't easy to find, least of all in one volume. Our aim in publishing this book is to help fill this void and provide the comprehensive, practical information necessary for a relatively trouble-free retirement. You may have visited Spain on holiday and may even own a holiday-home there, but retiring there (whether seasonally or permanently) is a different matter altogether. Adjusting to a different environment, culture and language can be a traumatic and stressful experience, and Spain is no exception.

However, with a copy of **Retiring in Spain** to hand you'll have a wealth of information at your fingertips. Information is derived from a variety of sources, both official and unofficial, not least the hard won personal experiences of the author and her researchers, friends, colleagues and many foreigners already enjoying their retirement in Spain. **Retiring in Spain** is a comprehensive handbook on a wide range of everyday subjects and represents the most up-to-date and comprehensive source of essential information for anyone planning to retire in Spain.

Within these pages you will find vital information and advice on topics such as the cost of living, retirement hot spots, getting to and from Spain, public transport and driving, buying a home, healthcare and financial matters. Suggestions are also provided to help smooth your 'settling-in' period and help you make the best use of your new-found leisure time. In short, everything you need to help make your retirement in Spain as fulfilling and successful as possible.

Most retirees to Spain would agree that, all things considered, they love living there – and wild horses couldn't drag them away. Retiring in Spain, even for just part of the year, is a wonderful way to enrich and revitalise your life, and it may even help you live longer. I trust this book will help you to avoid the pitfalls of retirement in Spain and smooth your way to a happy and rewarding future in your golden years.

Good luck!

Joanna Styles
September 2006

1.

WHY RETIRE TO SPAIN?

Retiring to Spain, whether permanently or for just part of the year (so-called 'seasonal retirement'), is an increasingly popular choice, particularly among retirees from countries with 'poor' (cold, wet, etc.) climates, high taxes or soaring property prices. For many people, the dream of spending their golden years in the sun has become an affordable option, although retiring in Spain (even for part of the year) isn't without its pitfalls and shouldn't be attempted without careful consideration and planning. Before deciding where, when or indeed, whether to retire to Spain, it's important to do your homework thoroughly and investigate the myriad implications and possibilities. Recognising and preparing for potential difficulties in advance is much easier than dealing with disappointment, or even a crisis, later.

However, if you do decide to take the plunge, you will be in good company. Tens of thousands of people have successfully retired to Spain: the latest official statistics showed that in 2004 there were over 150,000 foreign residents aged over 65, including some 40,000 Britons, 28,000 Germans and many other northern Europeans (notably Dutch and Scandinavians). **Unofficial figures are at least triple these.** Other foreigners (particularly Scandinavians) regularly spend the winter months in Spain and return to their home country for the warmer summer months.

As when making all major life decisions, it isn't wise to be in too much of a hurry. Many people make expensive (even catastrophic) errors when retiring in Spain, often because they don't do sufficient research or take into account the circumstances of their partners and family members. It isn't unusual for people to uproot themselves and after some time wish they had chosen a different part of Spain – or even that they had stayed at home! It's worth bearing in mind that a significant number of people who retire abroad return home within a relatively short period.

WHY DO YOU WANT TO RETIRE TO SPAIN?

The first question to ask yourself is **exactly** why you want to retire to Spain. Do you wish to live there permanently or spend only part of the year there? For example, many retirees spend the winter on the Spanish Mediterranean coast or in the Canaries and return to their home country for the summer. If you're planning to retire abroad for health reasons, the climate will be an important consideration. Do you primarily wish to live somewhere with a lower cost of living? Do you want to make frequent return trips to your home country, to visit your family and friends? What do your family and friends think about your plans to live in Spain? Can you afford to retire there? What of the future? Is your income secure and protected against inflation?

You will need to take into account the availability and cost of accommodation, communications, travelling times (and cost), security, health facilities, leisure and sports opportunities, culture shock, the cost of living and local taxes, among other things. Many retirees wishing to retire to Spain are North Americans or northern Europeans, who can often buy a home abroad for much less than the value of their family home. The difference between the money raised on the sale of your family home and the cost of a home in Spain can be invested to supplement your pension, allowing you to live comfortably in retirement, particularly when the lower cost of living is taken into consideration. However, if you plan to buy a second home in Spain, you will need to maintain two homes, although the running costs can usually be offset by letting your home(s) when you're absent.

ADVANTAGES & DISADVANTAGES

Before planning to live abroad permanently, you must take into account many considerations. There are both advantages and disadvantages to retiring abroad, although for most people the benefits far outweigh the drawbacks.

Advantages

The following are the main benefits (in alphabetical order) of retirement in Spain:

Climate

Spain's main selling point to its millions of annual visitors and hundreds of thousands of retirees is its weather. Several regions such as the Costa Blanca and Tenerife enjoy what the World Health Organisation (WHO) considers to be the healthiest climate in the world, and most of the Mediterranean coast offers warm, sunny weather for much of the year. For most people, one of the principal benefits is improved health as a result of living in a warmer climate and a more relaxing environment. Your general sense of well-being is greatly enhanced when you live in a warm and sunny climate.

Those who suffer from arthritis, colds, influenza and other illnesses exacerbated by cold and damp generally live longer and enjoy a better quality of life in a warm climate, while those who are prone to stress benefit from the relaxed lifestyle in most hot countries. However, if you're planning to retire abroad for health reasons, you should ask your doctor for his advice regarding suitable locations (see also **Keeping Healthy in Spain** on page 205).

Living in a warmer climate often results in an increased life expectancy for retirees (Spain has one of the world's highest life expectancies – 80 years according to the WHO's Health Report of 2005). A warm climate also provides ample opportunities to enjoy outdoor activities, such as gardening, golf, tennis or walking, during your increased leisure time. On the financial side, you'll save a considerable sum on heating bills, although you shouldn't automatically assume that because your retirement destination is hot in the summer it will also be warm in winter. For example, in most of Spain (including the Costa Blanca and Costa del Sol) it can be surprisingly cool in winter (particularly at night) when you will need some form of heating and the hot, humid summers in some areas mean costly air-conditioning is essential. It's wise to visit the region of your choice at different times of the year before making your decision, to find out exactly how cold and hot it **really** is in the winter and summer.

Friendly People

The Spanish are one of Europe's most gregarious and welcoming people with a well-deserved reputation for hospitality and tolerance. In rural areas, foreigners tend to stick out like sore thumbs initially, but are soon accepted into the local community. Many large towns and cities, particularly on the coast, are cosmopolitan and some, e.g. Barcelona and Madrid, are international melting-pots. There's generally little racial violence or tension in Spain.

Good International Communications

Almost all regions have international airports and those situated in popular retirement destinations (e.g. the Balearics, the Canaries, the Costa Blanca, the Costa del Sol and the Costa Brava) are served by inexpensive flights from numerous European destinations. Some airports such as Alicante and Malaga have daily flights to and from most large UK airports.

Higher Standard of Living

The combination of favourable tax rates and a low cost of living, means that there's a high chance that your standard of living will rise proportionately.

When this is added to the benefits of a warmer, year-round, climate, your quality of life will also improve significantly.

Increased Leisure & Sports Options

The availability of a wide range of leisure and sports activities at an affordable cost is an added attraction of retiring in Spain. Most resort areas have excellent leisure facilities, such as golf and tennis clubs, with reasonably priced membership. If you retire to an area with a mild climate, you will also have more time and opportunities to practise your chosen sport or activity, which will rarely be interrupted by rain!

Lack of Crime

Although the crime rate, particularly petty crime, has risen in many Spanish cities, overall statistics are generally lower than other western countries. In many small towns and villages, you can still leave your property unlocked and unattended. As well as a lower crime rate, many retirees choose Spain for the lack of the so-called 'yob culture', prevalent in many cities in northern Europe. See **Crime** on page 306.

Lower Cost of Living

Although the cost of living in Spain has risen over the last few years, prices of everyday goods are still lower than most northern European countries and many items are still relatively cheap. Among the things that retirees consider to be particularly good value are food (with the exception of imported goods), alcohol (a reasonable bottle of wine needn't cost more than €5), eating out (you can get a good three-course meal including wine for under €10) and transportation (public transport is among the cheapest in Western Europe).

Barcelona and Madrid are Spain's most expensive places to live, ranked 35 and 29 respectively in the 71 world cities featured in the UBS 'Prices and Earnings Survey' published in 2005. However, they compare favourably with other major European cities such as Oslo (the world's most expensive city), London (ranked 5), Stockholm (6), Paris (8), Dublin (13), Brussels (17) and Frankfurt (19). For further information on prices and a guide to a weekly shopping basket see **Chapter 3**.

Spanish tax rates also compare well with those in northern European countries, particularly the Scandinavian countries, and there are generous deductions. See **Taxation** on page 243 for further information.

Lower Property Prices

Property prices in North America and northern Europe (and in most of the world's capital cities) have risen considerably in recent years, and many people find themselves trapped in a spiralling property-price web, unable to buy a home that represents good value for money. Prices have also risen sharply in Spain, but many areas still offer affordable homes and in some lesser-known regions real bargains can be found. In 2006, there were signs that the previous buoyant market was starting to slow down a little. However, experts generally agree that a property in Spain, particularly in popular resort areas, will always be a good investment. See **Cost of Property** on page 151.

Quality Healthcare

The World Health Organisation's most recent report into worldwide health and healthcare standards (2000) found that Spain has the sixth-highest level of health and the seventh-best healthcare in the world (the UK ranked at 24 and 18 respectively). While the Spanish health service isn't without its shortcomings, most expatriate residents agree that the standards of care and expertise are excellent.

Well-established Expatriate Communities

Spain is already home to thousands of foreigners, concentrated mainly on the islands, the Costa Blanca and the Costa del Sol, where there are well-established expatriate communities, particularly British and German. In these areas, it's relatively easy to find your feet as there are numerous clubs, associations and activities where you can feel at home. If, however, your aim is to integrate into Spanish culture and society and 'become' as Spanish as possible, you will find this difficult in popular resort areas.

Wide Open Spaces

Spain is Europe's second-largest country and compared to the UK and the Netherlands, for example, it's relatively sparsely populated with vast areas of unspoilt countryside. Just over 10 per cent of Spain's land is protected and it has over 140 national parks, while several regions have 'protected' vast areas of their territory from development (e.g. almost one-third in Andalusia).

Disadvantages

As with all major life decisions, there are also disadvantages to retiring in Spain and you should consider these and their implications carefully before making a decision. However, it's worth noting that the majority are avoidable or easily surmountable, provided you do your homework before retiring there.

Boredom & Isolation

Although most people look forward to retirement, many find the reality of not working difficult and the prospect of full-time leisure daunting. The question of 'what are you going to do all day?' can be difficult to answer – even more so in Spain, where there may not be the same facilities and familiar leisure activities that you have in your home country. You may miss your social life back home and find it difficult to be accepted into (or to accept) your new expatriate or 'native' community. It's wise to visit your prospective retirement destination a number of times at different times of the year and to rent a property (see page 89) before buying a home and making a long-term commitment.

Bureaucracy

Spain is notorious for its bureaucracy and red tape, which, if you aren't prepared for it, can be frustrating and daunting. The situation is improving, but until the Spanish finally shake off their obsession with endless paperwork, employ a translator or *gestor* (a licensed professional who acts as an intermediary between individuals and official organisations – see page 311) under Legal System to stand in queues for you or make the most of the waiting time getting through all those books you never had time to read.

Communication Problems

For many, the main disadvantage of retiring abroad is the separation from family and loved ones, particularly from grandchildren who have a habit of growing up fast. This barrier can be reduced by keeping in touch regularly by phone (many companies offer inexpensive international calls), by e-mail (broadband internet access is available throughout most of Spain) – see

Keeping in Touch on page 58 – or by choosing to live in an area with easy access to your home country (see **Getting There** on page 33).

Culture Shock & Language Problems

Many retirees underestimate the cultural isolation that you can feel living abroad, particularly if you plan to move to a part of Spain where you will have few compatriots. Many people find that coping with retirement and the lack of structure to life without a daily work regime is made doubly stressful by the sense of isolation (and possible frustration) created by a new culture and language. Are you prepared to be in a minority and to be treated as a foreigner? Are you open to different ways of doing things? Do you make friends easily? Can you cope with a slower pace of life and a high level of bureaucracy?

It's also generally accepted that the older you are, the more difficult it is to learn a new language, although Spanish is classed as one of the easier foreign languages to learn. See **Learning the Language** on page 62. A new culture and language don't, however, have to make your life more frustrating and can do much to enrich it, although it's important to be aware of the potential difficulties. Culture shock (see page 307) can be significantly reduced if you retire to an area of Spain with an established expatriate community.

On the plus side, you can buy most British newspapers (many are printed in Spain) and many other foreign newspapers in cities and resort areas throughout Spain and thanks to Sky satellite television reception you can also enjoy your favourite British TV programmes (all British terresstrial channels are available via Sky).

Financial Problems

Without careful planning, retirement to Spain can involve financial problems, such as those caused by exchange rate fluctuations and poor investments. Tax and cost of living benefits may also turn out to be lower than originally thought. Consult financial experts to help you do your sums before you make a final decision. See **Chapter 3** and **Chapter 4** for further information about the financial implications of retiring in Spain.

Old Age & Infirmity

Before making plans to live in Spain, you should consider how you would cope if your mobility was restricted. Spain's facilities and support for those with disabilities are improving, but are still inadequate compared to many other countries. For example, it's common to find no lifts in buildings with a number of floors, disabled parking spaces (if available) are frequently occupied by non-disabled drivers' cars (see page 221) and social services often provide little or no help for the elderly and infirm. Another consideration is the poor provision of retirement homes or sheltered accommodation (see page 148) which are non-existent in many parts of Spain and, when available, places are in short supply.

OTHER CONSIDERATIONS

The following points should also be taken into account when considering whether or where to retire to in Spain:

● Decide whether you would like to move permanently to Spain or just for part of the year. This decision is important as it will influence where you decide to live in Spain and your finances, particularly taxation.

● If you're planning to retire to Spain with your partner, ask yourselves if you **both** want to go. It's vitally important that the decision should be a joint one and one that you're both happy with. While it isn't a happy subject, you should both think ahead and consider what you will do if one of you becomes ill or dies.

● Consider whether you will need to return regularly to your home country, e.g. for visits to relatives and grandchildren, medical appointments or keeping your affairs in order. If you're required to go 'home' frequently, choose a location near an airport with easy access to your home country.

● Think carefully about how you will feel being separated from your loved ones. Most of Spain is within two to three hours of northern Europe – a relatively easy distance – but even this means you won't be able to meet your best friend for coffee or a round of golf, or have the family round for Sunday lunch. One of the main reasons retirees move back to their home country after relocating to Spain is that they cannot cope with the separation from family and friends.

● Ask yourself 'why' you're considering retiring in Spain and write a list of the precise reasons. Make sure most or (preferably) all of the reasons are positive – an abundance of negative reasons may mean you're running away from problems in your home country. Bear in mind that a change of country doesn't necessarily mean that the problems will go away or disappear. It may be better to stay in your home country and sort out your problems before making a decision about retirement in Spain.

● Think about the 'pleasantness' of your chosen retirement location. You should be aware that an area can change considerably over a period; for example a village may be quiet and undeveloped when you buy a property and retire there, but it could rapidly become a major tourist spot or property investment target. This is particularly true of much of the Mediterranean coastline where previously unspoilt and 'undiscovered' resorts are now bustling concrete jungles. Before committing yourself to a location, make sure that you're aware of the regional and local authorities' plans for it.

● Be cautious about choosing your favourite holiday destination as your place of retirement. Holiday memories tend to be recalled through rose-tinted spectacles, but the reality of daily life can be very different, and your perspective and requirements as a resident are quite different from those of a tourist. Before buying a home you should visit an area at different times of the year and rent a property for an extended period (up to six months) before taking the plunge (see page 89).

● Investigate local public transport thoroughly. This is particularly important if you're elderly, as you may not always be able (or wish) to drive. There's little point in choosing an isolated spot or somewhere with a limited public transport system, when in a few years' time you may have to rely on local bus and train services for your transportation. You should also consider the terrain of your chosen home, as a location with lots of hills or steps can become an insurmountable problem if you have mobility problems or become disabled. It's advisable to avoid property situated in hilly areas (many parts of the Spanish coastline are steep), as although hillside homes offer wonderful panoramic views, you'll need a car for everything and the climb will become much more difficult as you get older!

● Do as much research as possible on your prospective retirement destination, preferably by visiting the area several times before making a decision. If you're planning to retire to Spain with a partner, you should do the research together, so that both of you're aware of the benefits and drawbacks. Survival Books publish many other best-selling publications for foreigners in Spain, including *Buying a Home in Spain*, *Living and Working in Spain* and *The Best Places to Buy a Home in Spain* (see page 383).

- Most importantly – <u>and it bears repeating often</u> – don't sell your home abroad but rent for a period in Spain (up to six months) so that you can become familiar with a region or town. Don't burn your bridges before you're <u>absolutely certain</u> you want to retire to Spain!

2.

Practicalities

Once you've decided you would like to retire to Spain, you need to consider the practical aspects of the move. This chapter contains information about permits and visas; getting to Spain by air (including a guide to airports in Spain), bus, train and ferry; getting around by public transport and car (including information on road rules); keeping in touch (telephone, internet and media); and learning Spanish.

PERMITS & VISAS

Before making any concrete plans to retire to Spain, you must check whether you need a visa or residence permit (*permiso de residencia*). If you need a visa in order to retire to Spain, find out how difficult (easy) it will be to obtain one and how long it usually takes. Foreigners aren't allowed to remain longer than three months in succession without obtaining a 90-day extension or a residence permit – see page 31.

When in Spain you should always carry your foreign identity card, passport or residence permit (or a copy certified by a Spanish police station). You can be asked to produce your identification papers at any time by the police or other officials, and if you don't have them with you, you can be fined (although this is unlikely). A residence permit constitutes an identity card for foreigners, which Spaniards must carry by law. Spain has a reputation for its notoriously lax immigration controls and registration of EU residents, many of whom live in Spain unofficially for years without becoming residents or paying taxes or social security. Needless to say, this is illegal and even dangerous.

The Spanish authorites take permit infringements by non-EU nationals seriously. If you're discovered living illegally in Spain there are severe penalties, including fines and even deportation for flagrant abuses, which means being excluded from Spain for a number of years.

Visitors & Visas

Visitors with a permanent address in Spain, can remain for a maximum of 90 days in succession and a total of six months in a calendar year (the exception is visitors who are touring and staying in different places for short periods, who can remain in Spain for six months in succession).

Most visitors require a full passport to visit Spain, although nationals of countries in the European Economic Area (EEA), Andorra, Monaco and Switzerland can enter Spain with a national identity card only. Visitors from EEA countries, North and South America, Andorra, Australia, Brunei, Bulgaria, Canada, Costa Rica, Croatia, Gibraltar, Grenada, Israel, Hong Kong, Japan, South Korea, Malaysia, Monaco, New Zealand, Romania, San Marino, Singapore and Switzerland **don't** need a visa for stays of up to 90 days. All other nationalities require a visa to visit Spain. Spanish immigration officials may require non-EEA nationals to produce a return ticket and proof of accommodation, health insurance and financial resources.

A non-EEA visitor wishing to remain in Spain longer than 90 days must obtain a special entry visa (*visado especial de entrada*) at a Spanish consulate **before** coming to Spain. If you're a non-EEA national, it isn't possible to enter Spain as a tourist and change your status to that of an employee, student or resident. Usually, you must return to your country of residence and apply for a visa, although it's possible to obtain an exemption from the civil governor of the local province.

Ninety-day Extension

EEA citizens who entered Spain as a visitor can apply for a 90-day extension (*prórroga de estancia/permanencia*), which permits them to remain for another 90 days. An extension should be applied for at a local police station (*comisaría de policía*) with a foreigners' department (*departamento/oficina de extranjeros*) at least two weeks before the first 90-day period has expired. A visitor can also leave Spain briefly before the 90-day period has expired, e.g. by crossing to a neighbouring country, and return again for another 90 days. This is legal, although your total stay **mustn't** exceed six months in a calendar year. However, if you wish to prove you've left, you must have your passport stamped – this may be difficult as some border posts between Spain and Portugal, and Spain and France are unmanned. After six months you **must** leave the country or apply for a residence permit (see below), although if you aren't legally employed in Spain or have insufficient financial means, your application will probably be refused.

Residents

Foreigners residing in Spain for longer than six months must apply for a residence permit (*permiso de residencia*) unless they're an EEA or Swiss national working (as an employee or self-employed) or studying full time (see the note below). If you come to Spain with the intention of remaining longer than six months (e.g. as an employee, student or a non-employed resident), you must apply for a residence permit within 15 days of your arrival. However, if you don't have a regular income or adequate financial resources, your application will be refused.

 Failure to apply for a residence permit within the specified time is a serious offence and can result in a heavy fine and even deportation.

Citizens of non-EEA countries must obtain a residence visa (*visado de residencia*) from a Spanish consulate in their home country before coming to Spain to work, study or live. There are various categories of visa, including employees, retired pensioners, investors, employees of multi-national companies (transferees), students, extended holidays over 90 days, and those engaged in cultural or sporting activities. The visa is stamped in your passport, which must be valid for a minimum of six months after the proposed date of arrival.

Retirees

Retired and non-active EEA nationals don't require a long-stay visa before moving to Spain, but a residence permit (*residencia*) is necessary and an application should be made within one week of your arrival. Non-EEA nationals require a residence visa (*visado de residencia*) to live in Spain for longer than three months and should make a visa application at their local Spanish Consulate well before their planned move.

All non-employed residents must provide proof that they have an adequate income or financial resources to live in Spain without working. The minimum income necessary for EU nationals is roughly equivalent to the Spanish statutory minimum wage (*salario mínimo interprofesional*), which is €540.90 (€600 by 2008) per month or €7,572 (€8,400 by 2008) a year (salaries in Spain are paid 14 times a year), although there's no official figure and the recipient of an EU state pension qualifies. Proof that you receive a state pension can be shown in monthly bank statements (if your pension is paid into your Spanish bank account) or receipts of the transfer from your bank in your home country.

Non-EU retirees can apply for a special residential visa (*visado de residencia sin finalidad lucrativa*), introduced with non-active residents in mind. Applicants mustn't have a criminal record and must have sufficient funds or income for accommodation, living expenses and healthcare for their family. Pensioners must show proof of an annual income in the form of a pension, in addition to owning a home in Spain. Non-EU nationals who aren't pensioners must be able to show an annual income of US$75,000 and proof of accommodation in Spain.

GETTING THERE

Even if you're planning to retire permanently to Spain, you're likely to want to be able to visit your family and friends (and for them to visit you) in your home country a number of times a year, therefore one of your major considerations will be the cost of getting to and from Spain and how long it will take. In addition to flying or driving time, you need to take into account journeys to and from airports, ports and railway stations. How frequent are flights, ferries or trains at the time(s) of year when you plan to travel? Are direct flights or trains available? Is it feasible to travel by car? What is the cost of travel from your home country to the region where you're planning to retire? Are off-season discounts or inexpensive charter flights available? Are costs likely to rise or fall in the future?

If a long journey is involved, you should bear in mind that it may take you a day or two to recover (longer as you get older). If you plan to let your home for part of the year, it will be more popular if it's within easy reach of an airport with a range of flights, particularly budget and charter flights, from the UK.

SURVIVAL TIP
Always allow plenty of time to get to and from airports, ports and railway stations in Spain, particularly when travelling during peak hours and in July and August, when traffic congestion can be horrendous.

By Plane

Most major international airlines provide scheduled services to Madrid and many also fly to Barcelona and other major cities such as Valencia. Inexpensive charter and budget flights to Spain are common from many European countries, particularly the UK and Germany. In recent years, the number of so-called 'no-frills' budget airlines has increased greatly and competition is fierce – in the first six months of 2006 some 30 per cent of passengers arriving at Malaga airport did so on budget airlines.

The Spanish state-owned national airline, Iberia, is Spain's major international carrier. Although it isn't rated as one of the world's best airlines, Iberia has an excellent safety record and its standard of service has improved in recent years. Its fares have also become more competitive, although, along with the majority of airlines, Iberia no longer provides free in-flight meals and newspapers on its European flights.

Nowadays, there's a wide range of flights from airports in the UK (and Ireland to a lesser extent) to many airports in Spain, although some regions are less well-served than others (see **Appendix F** for a list of UK airlines serving Spanish airports). The Costa Blanca, Costa del Sol, Palma de Majorca and the Canaries are the best served with year-round flights from numerous airlines, while destinations such as the north of Spain (excluding Catalonia) and the Costa de la Luz have fewer flight options.

Note also that the instability of the airline business means that airlines can (and do) merge or go bankrupt, which often results in a cut-back of services or the disappearance of a route altogether. Budget airlines also frequently change their routes and prices. You should therefore think twice about retiring to an area that's accessible only via a single budget airline – ask yourself how you would get there if the flights were terminated. Bear in mind that it's relatively easy to reach regional airports in Spain via Madrid or Barcelona, but domestic flights are expensive and time consuming, although last-minute offers are available.

Fares

In general, the earlier you book a seat with any airline the cheaper it is. If you're able to book more than six months in advance, real bargains are available and many scheduled airlines (particularly budget airline) have ticket sales at certain times of the year. Cheap seats are also available if you book literally at the last minute, but you run the risk of not getting a seat at all.

The cheapest Spanish destinations from the UK include Alicante, Barcelona, Madrid, Malaga and Palma de Mallorca, with one-way fares from as little as £10 (€15) in the low season rising to between £100 to £300 (€150 to €450) in the peak season (mid-June to mid-September), but **note that prices quoted here don't include fees, taxes and fuel supplements**, which often vastly inflate prices.

Charter flights from New York to Madrid cost around $350 (€284). It may be cheaper for North Americans, and others travelling on intercontinental flights, to fly to London and take a budget or charter flight from there, particularly outside the summer season. Fares from other European cities to Spain are generally more expensive than those from the UK, Ireland and Germany, and may cost up to 50 per cent more, although several budget airlines now offer inexpensive inter-European flights (see page 302).

If you're buying your ticket online, before confirming your booking, make sure the quoted price includes everything – on most airline websites the final price isn't quoted until the end of the booking process, making it difficult to compare fares.

Scheduled Flights

Fares on scheduled flights to Spain have fallen dramatically in recent years due to increased competition, particularly from budget airlines (such as Easyjet) and domestic airlines such as Air Europa (Spanish owned). 'National' or major airlines (e.g. Aer Lingus, British Airways and Iberia) offer year-round scheduled flights to the larger Spanish airports and flights can be booked at travel agents, by telephone or online. An advantage of the major airlines is that they often allow changes in your flight details (e.g. dates or destination) free of charge, although you must usually pay for last-minute changes and cancellations. Major airlines also tend to have higher weight allowances for luggage and will transport large items, e.g. golf clubs, free of charge.

Budget airlines (e.g. Easyjet and Ryanair) tend to offer flights to and from smaller airports, and flights on these airlines can only be booked through the airline itself via their customer telephone service or online. Budget airlines charge (e.g. £30/€45) for changes to flight details and luggage allowances are generally lower and extra charges are levied for items such as golf clubs.

Almost all scheduled airlines operate a 'no-ticket' policy and your flight is identified by your name and possibly some form of identification (e.g. your passport) or by a code provided when you book your ticket.

Few scheduled airlines provide free in-flight services such as meals and newspapers on flights under four hours duration – Monarch are one of the few exceptions. Food and drink is available for purchase, but is expensive (e.g. £1.80 (€3) for an instant coffee and £4 (€6) for a sandwich) and the quality varies considerably. You can save money (and your tastebuds!) by taking your own food and drink.

Most transatlantic flights from North America are routed via Madrid. If you're unable to get a direct flight to Spain from North America or Asia, it's usually advisable to fly via London, from where there are inexpensive daily flights to airports throughout Spain.

British Airways & Iberia – Iberia, British Airways (BA) and its subsidiary, GB Airways, operate daily flights to the main Spanish airports from several destinations in the UK. Iberia provides good connections to Central and South America and throughout Europe, but few connections to North America (New York and Miami only) and the rest of the world apart from a few cities such as Cairo, Tangier, Tel Aviv, and a number of countries in North and West Africa. BA and Iberia are both members of the One World alliance along with several other major airlines such as American Airlines, Cathay Pacific and Qantas. This allows them to provide flights to most destinations in the world via other airlines in the alliance at competitive fares. Travel agents are the best sources of information for the cheapest seats on One World flights.

Budget Airlines – Budget airlines, e.g. Air Berlin, EasyJet and Ryanair, offer some advantages, including flights to and from smaller airports and no seat allocation. Fares are generally lower, although they've risen in recent months and are often no cheaper than scheduled flights (particularly if you're able to take advantage of special offers from BA and Iberia). Budget airlines often advertise very cheap seats, although these are usually limited and involve travelling at unsociable times or at short notice. Flights in the high season or on popular routes are generally as expensive as those offered by scheduled airlines, but you can save money by travelling out of the high season and by avoiding weekends. Budget airlines' advertised prices usually don't include airport taxes, which can be high (e.g. €20 one-way), plus a fuel surcharge and at least £3.50/€5 for using a credit card. Some budget airlines (e.g. Ryanair) have even started charging per item of luggage – as if you would travel without it!

SURVIVAL TIP
Shop around for tickets and don't assume travel to Spain is always cheaper by budget airline.

Charter Flights

With the advent of budget airlines, charter flights to Spain are now less common from the UK. Among the largest charter companies operating from the UK are Avro and Thomson Fly (two of the largest), Cosmos, First Choice, Monarch Charter and My Travel, which offer good flight deals to

Spain from a wide range of airports in the UK, particularly if you book well in advance. Tickets for flights and holidays and car hire deals can be purchased from travel agents, by telephone or online. Charter flights are available to most Spanish resorts, but tend to operate only from April to October (longer to the Canaries).

Avro (UK ☎ 0870-458 2841, ☐ http://www.avro.com) provides flights from many UK airports to most resorts in Spain, including the Balearics and Canaries. It also has a limited number of seats on regional flights within Spain. Avro operates an 'Avro Flying Club' scheme targeted at frequent flyers and property owners abroad, whereby members (who pay a membership fee of £19.99 a year) are entitled to a 5 per cent on flights booked with Avro as well as discounts on Monarch scheduled flights, car hire and travel insurance.

Thomsonfly (UK ☎ 0870-190 0737, Spain ☎ 914 141 481, ☐ http://www.thomsonfly.com) offers charter flights from many airports in the UK, particularly during the summer when flights are available from smaller airports such as Aberdeen, Doncaster Sheffield and Norwich.

Airports

This section contains a survey of Spain's major international airports (the airport name is followed by the flight information telephone number), plus a few in neighbouring countries convenient for Spain, and lists the UK airports serving them. A map showing the location of airports within Spain is shown in **Appendix E** and a table showing which airlines fly from the UK and Ireland to Spanish airports is shown in **Appendix F** Comprehensive information for all Spanish airports can be found on ☐ http://www.aena.es (click on 'English' and then the airport you want from the 'Choose Airport' menu). Aena also provides a 24-hour flight information service with details of arrivals and departures at all Spanish airports (☎ 902 404 704).

Andalusia:

● **Almería** (☎ 950 213 700): Almería at the eastern end of Andalusia has a small airport with a small number of flights, mainly from the UK and Germany, with budget airlines offering several flights weekly. There's also a limited domestic flight service from the major Spanish airports, although flights are expensive. Almería is served by regular flights from Dublin, Birmingham, London Gatwick, London Stansted and Manchester airports. Murcia airport (see page 42) is also an option for the Costa de Almería.

- **Faro** (☎ +351-289 800 800, 🖳 http://www.ana-aeroportos.pt): Situated on the Algarve Coast in Portugal, Faro airport is served by a wide range of flights (Aer Lingus, Bmibaby, EasyJet, Flybe, Flyglobespan, GB Airways, Monarch and Ryanair all have flights there) and provides good road communications to the western Costa de la Luz and the resorts in the Spanish Algarve. Note, however, that if you wish to reach the rest of the Costa de la Luz from Faro airport, you must make a lengthy detour inland via Seville.

- **Gibraltar** (☎ +350-73026 from abroad ☎ 956 773 026 from Spain): Gibraltar airport also serves the Costa del Sol, although there are few flights and they're almost exclusively to and from the UK. This may change in the near future if Spain and Gibraltar reach an agreement on air traffic control, in which case flights will be available from Spain to Gibraltar. Queues to leave Gibraltar are often long and customs checks lengthy. There's no public transport to Gibraltar from the Costa del Sol except taxis. Some non EEA nationals may require a visa to enter Spain from Gibraltar. Gibraltar airport is served by regular flights from the UK from London Gatwick, London Heathrow, London Luton and Manchester airports.

- **Jerez** (☎ 956 150 000): The small Jerez airport, situated just outside Jerez de la Frontera, is convenient for the Costa de la Luz. However, it offers only a limited number of flights and public transport is poor. Jerez airport is served by regular flights from the UK only from London Stansted.

- **Malaga** (☎ 952 048 804): The region's main airport is Malaga's Pablo Picasso (8km/5mi to the west of Malaga city), the third-busiest in Spain handling some 10m passengers a year. It's well served by domestic and international flights, particularly from the UK, Germany and Ireland, with between 50 and 100 flights daily. Scheduled flights operate from most major European destinations throughout the year and charter flights are also widely available. The airport was modernised in the '90s and is spacious and generally efficient. A new control tower was completed in 2001 and a second terminal and runway are under construction. Completion of the terminal is expected in 2007 and of the runway in 2010, so until then allow extra time for parking and checking-in. Bus and train services link the airport with Malaga and the rest of the Costa del Sol, and taxis and car hire companies are plentiful.

  Malaga airport is served by regular flights from the UK and Ireland from Aberdeen, Belfast, Birmingham, Blackpool, Bristol, Cardiff, Cork,

Dublin, East Midlands, Edinburgh, Exeter, Glasgow, Humberside, Leeds/Bradford, London Gatwick, London Heathrow, London Luton, London Stansted, Liverpool, Manchester, Newcastle, Shannon and Southampton airports.

● **Seville** (☎ 954 449 000): The city's San Pablo airport is small but modern, situated 12km/7.5mi from the city centre. Domestic flights are plentiful, but international flights are limited and are available from Liverpool, London Gatwick, London Heathrow and London Stansted airports. Seville has excellent public transport links with the rest of Andalusia and Spain, including high-speed trains (*AVE*) to Madrid.

Balearics: The three main islands have airports, which are among the busiest in Europe during the summer months.

● **Majorca** (☎ 971 789 681): San Juan airport in Majorca (situated 11km/7mi east of Palma) is Spain's second-busiest, handling around 20m passengers a year. Flights are available from most major European cities, particularly in the UK and Germany, most of which are charter flights. Flights from mainland Spain are also frequent, the least expensive being from Barcelona and Valencia.

Palma airport is served by regular flights from Aberdeen, Belfast, Birmingham, Blackpool, Bristol, Cardiff, Dublin, Durham Tees Valley, East Midlands, Edinburgh, Exeter, Glasgow, Leeds/Bradford, Liverpool, London Gatwick, London Heathrow, London Luton, London Stansted, Manchester and Newcastle airports.

● **Minorca** (☎ 971 157 000): Minorca has a small international airport situated just south of the capital, Mahon. There are charter flights from several European capitals, although they're concentrated during the high season, and in winter there are no direct flights from some destinations. Domestic flights to mainland Spain are also available, although fares are high. Mahon airport is served by regular flights from Birmingham, Bristol, Edinburgh, Glasgow, Leeds/Bradford, Liverpool, London Gatwick, Manchester and Newcastle airports.

● **Ibiza** (☎ 971 809 000): Ibiza airport mainly handles charter flights from the UK and Germany, which are greatly reduced in the winter. Flights to mainland Spain are mostly via Barcelona and Valencia, and are expensive. Ibiza airport is served by regular flights from the UK from East Midlands, Edinburgh, Glasgow, Leeds/Bradford, Liverpool, London Gatwick, London Stansted, Manchester and Newcastle airports.

Canary Islands: All the inhabited Canary islands have airports, but the smaller islands of El Hierro, La Gomera and La Palma are served by tiny airports with virtually no international flights and only a limited number of flights from Gran Canaria or Tenerife. Several budget airlines now fly to the Canaries and numerous charter flights are available.

● **Tenerife** (☎ 922 759 000 for Reina Sofía, ☎ 922 635 999 for Los Rodeos): Tenerife has two airports, Reina Sofía in the south near the Costa del Silencio and Los Rodeos in the north near the capital, which has recently been refurbished and has a new terminal. Los Rodeos handles mainly domestic and inter-island flights, while Reina Sofía handles most international traffic with an abundance of charter flights, mostly from the UK and Germany. Public transport to the capital and resort areas is generally good, and taxis and hire cars are plentiful.

Reina Sofía airport is served by regular flights from Belfast, Birmingham, Blackpool, Cardiff, Cork, Dublin, East Midlands, Edinburgh, Glasgow, Humberside, Leeds/Bradford, Liverpool, London Gatwick, London Heathrow, London Luton, London Stansted, Manchester and Newcastle airports.

● **Gran Canaria** (☎ 928 579 130): Gando airport on the east coast of the island is one of the busiest in Spain. It's served by frequent charter and scheduled flights from mainland Spain and Europe, particularly the UK and Germany. Flights are inexpensive and available all year round. There are also flights to the other Canary islands. The airport is well connected with the north and south of the island, and public transport to the capital and southern resorts is good. Taxis and hire cars are plentiful.

Gando airport is served by regular flights from Bristol, Cardiff, Dublin, East Midlands, Glasgow, London Gatwick, London Luton, Manchester and Newcastle airports.

● **Fuerteventura** (☎ 928 860 600): Fuerteventura has an international airport to the south of the capital. There are frequent flights from Barcelona, Madrid and many European cities during the summer, although flights are considerably reduced during the rest of the year. The airport is served by flights from Cardiff, Dublin, East Midlands, Glasgow, London Gatwick, Manchester and Newcastle.

● **Lanzarote** (☎ 928 846 001): Lanzarote's Guacimeta airport is situated just outside the capital and has frequent services to the other islands, mainland Spain and Europe, particularly the UK and Germany. Public transport links the airport with the capital and the main resorts. Lanzarote has flights from Birmingham, Cardiff, Dublin, East Midlands, Edinburgh, Exeter, Glasgow, Leeds/Bradford, London Gatwick, London Luton, Manchester and Newcastle airports.

Catalonia:

- **Barcelona** (☎ 932 983 838): The region's main airport is Barcelona's El Prat de Llobregat, located 14km/9mi from the city centre. It was extensively modernised for the 1992 Olympic Games and is one of the best in Spain. The airport is very busy and offers a wide range of chartered and scheduled flights to domestic and international destinations. Weekend flights to Barcelona from the UK are in high demand and can be expensive. Public transport from the airport to the city is quick and efficient, although getting to the Costa Brava and Costa Dorada from El Prat can be slow due to traffic congestion.

  Barcelona airport is served by regular flights from Belfast, Birmingham, Bristol, Dublin, Edinburgh, Glasgow, Leeds/Bradford, Liverpool, London Gatwick, London Heathrow, London Luton, London Stansted, Manchester and Newcastle airports.

- **Girona** (☎ 972 186 600): Girona has a small international airport (28km/17.5mi from Blanes), which serves as the gateway to the Costa Brava and is one of Spain's fastest growing airports, with passenger traffic up by 46 per cent in 2005. It offers charter and budget flights from the UK and Germany and is served by regular flights from Dublin, East Midlands, Glasgow, Glasgow Prestwick, Liverpool, London Luton, London Stansted, Manchester, Newcastle and Shannon airports. The northern resorts on the Costa Brava can also be reached easily from Montpellier and Perpignan airports across the border in France, both of which are served by budget airlines from the UK.

- **Reus** (☎ 977 779 832): Reus airport (near Tarragona) is one of Spain's smallest and it handles few scheduled and charter flights. However, it's handy for resorts on the Costa Dorada and is a good alternative to Barcelona. Flights operate from Dublin, Glasgow Prestwick, Liverpool, London Luton and London Stansted airports.

Costa Blanca:

- **Alicante** (☎ 966 919 100): The Costa Blanca is served by three airports: El Altet (Alicante), Manisses (Valencia) and San Javier (Murcia). The main one and the international gateway to the Costa

Blanca is El Altet (11km/7mi from Alicante city centre), which is one of Spain's busiest airports. It provides a wide range of flights (mostly charter) to over 20 countries, although most are from the UK and Germany, plus a range of domestic flights. Communications with the north and south regions of the Costa Blanca are good, and taxis and hire cars are plentiful.

Alicante airport is served by regular flights from Aberdeen, Belfast, Birmingham, Blackpool, Bristol, Cardiff, Cork, Dublin, Durham Tees Valley, East Midlands, Edinburgh, Exeter, Glasgow, Leeds/Bradford, Liverpool, London Gatwick, London Heathrow, London Luton, London Stansted, Manchester, Newcastle, Norwich and Southampton airports.

● **Valencia** (☎ 961 598 500): The second airport serving the Costa Blanca is Manisses, some 8km/5mi from Valencia city centre, which handles many regular domestic flights plus scheduled flights to some European cities. Manisses airport is the most convenient for the Costa del Azahar and is a good alternative to El Altet (Alicante) for the northern part of the Costa Blanca, although traffic congestion around Valencia tends to increase journey times. Valencia airport is served by regular flights from Bristol, Dublin, London Gatwick, London Stansted and Manchester airports.

● **Murcia** (☎ 968 172 000): The third airport serving the Costa Blanca, especially the southern resorts, is Murcia's San Javier airport, which also serves the Costa Cálida and is useful for reaching the northern region of Almería. San Javier is a small airport, although air traffic has increased considerably in recent years and it offers a growing number of charter and budget flights to airports in the UK and Germany, as well as Dublin. Murcia airport is served by regular flights from Belfast, Birmingham, Blackpool, Bristol, Dublin, Exeter, Glasgow Prestwick, Liverpool, London Gatwick, London Luton, London Stansted, Manchester, Norwich, Shannon and Southampton.

Madrid:

● **Madrid** (☎ 902 404 704): Madrid's Barajas airport is Spain's busiest, handling some 34m passengers a year, and the main Spanish airport for intercontinental flights as well as the hub of domestic flights. The airport (15km/9.3mi to the east of the city) has been extensively modernised and a new terminal (terminal 4/T4) opened in early 2006 and is expected to double the passenger capacity.

> **SURVIVAL TIP**
> **If your flight arrives or leaves from T4 and you have a connecting flight, allow plenty of extra time as the distance between T4 and other terminals is considerable.**

The city centre is easily accessible by public transport, including buses and the *metro*, although the *metro* doesn't serve T4. Madrid airport is served by regular flights from Birmingham, Bristol, Dublin, Liverpool, London Gatwick, London Heathrow, London Luton and Manchester airports.

Northern Spain: The Atlantic and Cantabrian coasts in the north of Spain are poorly served by international flights from mainland Europe, although budget airlines have recently 'discovered' Asturias and Santander airports and there are domestic flights from Madrid and Barcelona to the region's major airports at Santiago de Compostela, Asturias, Santander and Bilbao.

- **Asturias** (☎ 985 127 500): This small airport, situated outside Avilés, has flights from London Stansted, Barcelona and Madrid. Buses to Gijón and Oviedo and taxis are available.

- **Bilbao** (☎ 944 869 664): Bilbao is served by flights from Cork, Dublin, London Stansted and many Spanish airports. Road connections to the rest of the Basque Lands and Cantabria are good, although Asturias and Galicia are several hours away by car.

- **Santander** (☎ 942 202 100): The city's tiny airport, 5km/3mi to the south, has flights from London Stansted, Barcelona and Madrid. Public transport provisions are poor.

By Train

There are direct trains to Spain (Barcelona or Madrid) from many European cities, including Lisbon, Montpellier, Oporto, Paris, Milan and Zurich, although rail travel is slow and relatively expensive compared to air travel. At the Spanish border it may be necessary to change trains due to Spain's wider gauge than the rest of Europe (except on *Talgo* and *TEE* trains, which have adjustable axles). International trains usually have two classes, first (*gran clase*) and tourist (*turista*), plus sleeping cars (*coches camas*) with a choice of individual compartments or couchettes. Some international services operate only at night.

The Spanish high speed train service, known as *AVE* (*Alta Velocidad Española*), runs on special lines travelling at speeds of up to 300kph/185mph. It's currently being extended and when the network is completed (planned for 2007) it will eventually be part of a Europe-wide, high-speed rail network when the line connects with the French *TGV* service at the border in 2007.

By Bus

There are regular international bus services from many European cities to Spain's major cities and resorts. For example, Eurolines runs coach services from the UK to 45 destinations in Spain. Journeys are very long, e.g. from London, it's 26 hours to Barcelona and 28 to Madrid, and fares are often little cheaper than flying (it's worth comparing bus fares with the cheapest charter flights). Unless you have a fear of flying or a love of coach travel, you may find one or two days spent on a bus a nightmare. Buses are, however, comfortable, air-conditioned, and equipped with toilets and video entertainment. Most services operate daily during the summer and three or four times a week at other times. Discounts are provided for students and youths on some routes. Bookings can be made at travel agents in Spain and abroad. Typical return fares with Eurolines are Barcelona-London around €120 and Madrid-London around €140. Apex returns are considerably cheaper.

By Ferry

Regular car and international ferry services operate year round between Spain and the UK, and domestic ferries run between the mainland and the Balearics, the Canaries, and Spain's North African enclaves of Ceuta and Melilla (plus Morocco). Spain's most important ports are Algeciras, Almería, Barcelona, Bilbao, Cadiz, Las Palmas (Gran Canaria), Palma de Mallorca, Santander, Santa Cruz (Tenerife) and Valencia. Two companies, Brittany Ferries (☎ UK 0870-366 5333, Spain ☎ 942 360 611, (🖳 http://www.brittanyferries.co.uk or 🖳 http://www.brittanyferries.es) and P&O (☎ UK 0870-598 0333, Spain ☎ 902 020 461, 🖳 http://www.poferries.com), operate ferry services between the UK and Spain (to Santander and Bilbao respectively). There's little to choose between them for comfort, services and fares. Ships provide a variety of facilities and services, including a choice of bars and restaurants, swimming pool, cinema, shops, medical service and evening entertainment, including a nightclub, casino, discotheque and live music.

Travelling between the UK and Spain by ferry saves you around 1,200km (750mi) of driving compared with travelling by road via France. Ferries can also be a cheaper way to travel, particularly with children and a car, as you don't pay expensive air fares for children and, if you bring your car with you, you save on car rental. Travelling from the UK to southern Spain by road (via France) entails spending at least two full days driving and one or two overnight stops en route, plus meals and petrol costs, although it can work out cheaper than the ferry.

SURVIVAL TIP
The seas can be rough between Spain and the UK (the Bay of Biscay is famous for its storms) and travel isn't advisable during bad weather if you're a bad sailor.

When seas are rough, there's absolutely no respite from sea sickness and the journey is a nightmare (if you take a mini-cruise during bad weather you have just a few hours relief before having to endure the return journey!). Check the weather report and be prepared to travel via France or fly. If you do travel by ferry, keep a good supply of seasickness pills handy!

Fares are only published in brochures and although you can book via the internet, you don't have access to the full range of tickets and can only find the price by using the (time consuming) booking form or quote facility. Note also that when you book your ticket, you must also book some form of accommodation, which ranges from a reclining seat to a luxury exterior cabin. Food and drinks are quite expensive, particularly bar drinks and snacks.

SURVIVAL TIP
It's advisble not to buy duty-free alcohol or cigararettes on board ferries as they are much cheaper in Spain.

Driving to Spain

Driving from the UK to Spain through France involves a long journey. If you use motorways, it's around ten hours' driving – less from the Normandy ports, more from Calais or Boulogne – from the Channel to the Spanish border, plus a further ten hours to the south of Spain. You also need to consider the journey time from home to a UK port and the duration of the ferry crossing. You must also take into account the cost of a cross-Channel ferry (see below), and expense of toll fees (around €65 from Calais to the Spanish border) and at least one overnight stop. It's a practical option if you wish to bring a arge amount of luggage with you or wish to have the use of your car in Spain, and it may be quicker and cheaper than travelling by ferry to northern Spain. Some people like to turn the journey into a mini-holiday and take their time enjoying the delights of France and Spain on the way.

Once you reach Spain there are two main motorway routes. If you're travelling to the Coast Brava or Costa Blanca (Spain's east coast), you can cross the border at La Jonquera and take the A7, which runs along the coast as far as Alicante (extremely busy during the summer months). The route for the west and central Spain, Madrid and the Costa del Sol is along the Atlantic coast in France and via San Sebastian. **Traffic congestion is chronic around Madrid, especially at weekends (Sunday evenings should be avoided) and holiday periods.** Comprehensive route maps can be found on several websites including 🖳 http://www.viamichelin.co.uk and 🖳 http://www.theaa.com.

Motorway information in France (including toll fees) is available from 🖳 http://www.autoroutes.fr and general traffic information is available from 🖳 http://www.bison-fute.equipement.gouv.fr (in French only). Spanish motorway information (including toll fees) is available from 🖳 http://www.aseta.es and general traffic information can be found on 🖳 http://www.dgt.es (in Spanish only).

If you drive to Spain, you must ensure that your car insurance covers travel abroad (most do, although you may need to obtain a 'green card') and you should also have breakdown recovery insurance for France and Spain.

SURVIVAL TIP
If you choose to drive to Spain via France, you should take it easy and make regular rest stops or share the driving.

Due to the high cost of ferry and road travel and the long travelling time by road between the UK and Spain, you may be better off flying and hiring a car on arrival. Many people who visit Spain frequently or for long periods, leave a car at their Spanish home.

Crossing the Channel

There's a wide choice of routes for travellers between France and the UK, depending on where you live and the route intended. The ports/routes below are listed from east to west:

- **Dover/Dunkerque** – Norfolk Line (⌨ http://www.norfolkline.com)

- **Dover/Calais** – P&O Ferries (⌨ http://www.poferries.com), Sea France (⌨ http://www.seafrance.co.uk)

- **Dover/Boulogne** – Speed Ferries (⌨ http://www.speedferries.com), five-times daily fast ferry service with a crossing time of 50 minutes.

- **Folkestone/Calais** – Eurotunnel (⌨ http://www.eurotunnel.co.uk) rail car shuttle.

- **Newhaven/Dieppe** – Transmanche Ferries (⌨ http://www.transmancheferries.com).

- **Portsmouth/Le Havre** – LD Lines (⌨ http://www.ldlines.com)

- **Portsmouth/Caen** – Brittany Ferries (⌨ http://www.brittanyferries.co.uk)

- **Portsmouth/Cherbourg** – Brittany Ferries (⌨ http://www.brittanyferries.co.uk), Condor Ferries (⌨ http://www.condorferries.co.uk)

- **Portsmouth/Saint-Malo** – Brittany Ferries (⌨ http://www.brittanyferries.co.uk)

- **Poole/Cherbourg:** Brittany Ferries (⌨ http://www.brittanyferries.co.uk), Condor Ferries (⌨ http://www.condorferries.co.uk)

- **Poole/Saint-Malo via Guernsey and Jersey** – Condor Ferries (⌨ http://www.condorferries.co.uk)

- **Weymouth/Saint-Malo via Guernsey and Jersey** – Condor Ferries (⌨ http://www.condorferries.co.uk)

- **Plymouth/Roscoff** – Brittany Ferries (⌨ http://www.brittanyferries.co.uk)

The most scenic route is via western France (Brittany or Normandy), although a lack of motorways slows some parts of the journey. The ferry route which entails the least number of hours' driving (and on the best roads) is via St Malo, from where it's possible to reach the Spanish border in around eight hours.

Channel ferry fares have risen in recent years and except for special deals or last minute fares, they're no longer cheap on any routes. Fares vary greatly depending on the time of day and when you travel, with peak fares during July and August. Ferry companies offer special deals and discounts for advance bookings and most have loyalty schemes (usually based on points-allocation) and property owners' clubs.

Shop around for the best deal, which is probably best done by a travel agent who has access to fares from all companies or a company specialising in discount Channel crossings, e.g. Cross-Channel Ferry Tickets (🖥 http://www.cross-channel-ferry-tickets.co.uk) whose search engine provides a listing of the cheapest crossing for the dates and times you choose.

GETTING AROUND

Public Transport

Public transport (*transporte público*) services in Spain vary considerably depending on where you live. Public transport is usually good in cities, most of which have efficient urban bus and rail services, some of which are supplemented by *metros* and trams. Spanish railways (RENFE) provide an efficient and reasonably fast rail service, particularly between cities served by *AVE* high-speed trains. Spain has comprehensive intercity bus and domestic airline services and is also served by frequent international coaches, trains and excellent air links. On the negative side, rail services are non-existent in many areas and buses can be infrequent in coastal resorts and rural areas, where it's often essential to have your own transport. Taxis are common in resort areas and cities, and are a cheap form of transport, especially when there's a number of passengers.

Urban public transport in major cities (such as Madrid and Barcelona) is inexpensive and efficient, and rates among the best in the world. Services include comprehensive bus routes, *metros* and extensive suburban rail networks. Systems are totally integrated and the same ticket can be used for all services (a range of commuter and visitor tickets are also available). There are travel agencies (such as Viajes Marsans, Halcón Viajes and Viajes Meliá) in major cities and large towns, and several specialist online agencies such as Last Minute dot com (🖥 http://www.lastminute.com) and Viajar (🖥 http://www.viajar.com).

Domestic Flights

There are a number of airlines providing domestic flights in Spain, including Iberia, Air Europa, Spanair and various smaller airlines such as Binter Canarias and Air Nostrum (subsidiaries of Iberia). Air Europa and Spanair operate most of the same routes as Iberia and are generally cheaper, although the competition has forced Iberia to reduce its prices. Single flights are available to most domestic destinations from €65 (from €95 to the Canaries) and cheaper night (*nocturno*) flights are available to some cities. Flights to the Balearics from the mainland are only slightly more expensive than ferries, although you must reserve well in advance during the summer season.

Most domestic flights are routed via Madrid or Barcelona, so it can be difficult to get a direct flight between regional cities. There are frequent flights between Spain's international airports and regional airports, with Iberia operating flights from Barcelona and Madrid to around 20 domestic airports. There's a half-hourly or hourly 'air bridge' (*puente aéreo*) shuttle service between Barcelona and Madrid, carrying over 2m passengers a year. Tickets for Iberia domestic flights can be purchased from machines at airports (using a credit card) and all companies have telephone and internet booking facilities: Air Europa (☎ 902 410 501, 💻 http://www.air-europa.com – tickets can also be purchased at Halcón Viajes travel agencies); Air Nostrum (☎ 902 400 500, 💻 http://www.airnostrum.es); Binter Canarias (☎ 902 391 392, 💻 http://www.bintercanarias.es); Iberia (☎ 902 400 500, 💻 http://www.iberia.com) and Spanair (☎ 902 929 191, 💻 http://www.spanair.com). Residents in the Balearics and Canaries receive discounts (usually one-third) on flights between the islands and the mainland.

Domestic Rail Services

The Spanish rail network is operated by the state-owned company RENFE, taking in most major cities, although it doesn't run to many small towns, and is supplemented by a few suburban networks such as the FFCC city lines in Barcelona and private narrow-gauge railways. Spain's railway network is below average by European standards, particularly regarding punctuality, although it's also one of the continent's cheapest. However, RENFE has undergone a comprehensive modernisation programme in the last decade, during which journey times have been reduced by up to 50 per cent. The RENFE website (💻 http://www.renfe.es) provides information on fares and timetables, plus a wealth of other useful information. A map showing the railway network can be found in **Appendix E**.

Long-distance trains: The high speed *Tren de Alta Velocidad Española (AVE)* service currently runs between Madrid and Seville (2 hours 35 minutes), Madrid and Lleida, and Madrid and Toledo. The *AVE* network is being extended from Madrid to Barcelona (by 2006) and to Malaga, Valencia and Valladolid (by 2007), and will eventually comprise part of a Europe-wide, high-speed rail network. Other first-class, long-distance *(largo recorrido)* trains include the *Talgo 200*, which has first and tourist class seats and is similarly equipped to *AVE* trains (although slower), and *Grandes Líneas* trains.

Tickets: Tickets for long and medium-distance travel can be bought online (🖳 http://www.renfe.es) or by telephone (☎ 902 157 507) through RENFE's secure booking service, TIKNET. It involves online or telephone registration, a codename and password, which must be used in order to buy tickets. TIKNET is open from 7am to 11pm. The first time you buy tickets you must collect them in person from a RENFE station, where you must show some form of identification (passport or residence permit) and give the booking reference. Tickets for subsequent purchases can be printed from a computer; collected from your departure station (up to one hour before the train leaves); obtained on the train if you're travelling on a regional or *Grandes Líneas* train; or collected at the access point to *AVE*, *Talgo* and *Lanzadera* trains. Other tickets must be bought at a station.

Discounts for Seniors: Senior citizens over 60 and disabled passengers are eligible for a 'gold card' *(tarjeta dorada)*, offering discounts of 40 per cent on all trains except AVE and Talgo 200 long-distance trains, where the discount is 40 per cent from Monday to Thursday (inclusive) and 25 per cent on Fridays, Saturdays and Sundays. The *tarjeta dorada* is obtainable from any RENFE station for €3 and is valid for one year.

Domestic Bus Services

There are excellent bus *(autobús)* services in major cities and towns in Spain and comprehensive long-distance coach *(autocar)* services between major cities. Buses are the cheapest and most common form of public transport and most coastal towns and rural villages are accessible by bus, but not by rail. The quality and age of buses varies considerably, from luxurious modern buses in major cities to old ramshackle museum pieces in some rural areas. Private bus services are often confusing and uncoordinated, and buses usually leave from different locations rather than a central bus station (*estación de autobúses*), e.g. Madrid has eight bus stations and most cities have two or more, possibly located on the outskirts of town.

Long-distance bus companies include Alsa-Enatcar (☎ 902 422 242, 💻 http://www.alsa.es), Auto Res (☎ 902 020 999, 💻 http://www.auto-res.net) and Continental-Auto (☎ 902 330 400, 💻 http://www.continental-auto.es). Fares on most routes are reasonable, with typical return fares from Madrid to Alicante around €40 and from Madrid to Barcelona around €55. Most major bus companies have telephone helplines and comprehensive websites with on-line booking.

Discounts for Seniors: Senior citizens are eligible for discounts on bus services in some parts of Spain. In large cities such as Alicante and Malaga, senior citizens over 65 who are registered as residents and in possession of a transport card, are usually entitled to unlimited free travel. The transport card is obtainable from the city council where you usually need to present a certificate of residence (*certificado de empadronamiento* – see **Local Council Registration** on page 192) and proof that you're aged over 65 (passport or residence permit). In other areas, senior citizens are entitled to substantial discounts, e.g. in Benalmádena (Costa del Sol) where over 65's are entitled to a 75 per cent discount or in Madrid where senior citizens are entitled to unlimited travel on city transport (*metro* and bus) for €9.90 per month.

Domestic Ferries

Domestic ferry services operate from mainland ports to the main Balearic and Canary Islands, supplemented by inter-island services. Services include Barcelona to Palma, Ibiza and Mahon; Dénia to Ibiza and Palma; Gandía to Ibiza and Formentera and Valencia to Palma, Ibiza and Mahon. Services operate from Cadiz to Tenerife, Las Palmas, Lanzarote and Fuerteventura in the Canaries. Tickets should be purchased in advance, particularly in summer, but can also be bought on board ferries, when a surcharge is payable. There are various tariffs depending on the type of seat required (couchettes are available on night trips) and tickets for high speed ferries can sometimes be twice the price. Ferries carry cars, boat-trailers, buses and trucks, and are equipped with restaurants and coffee shops, bar-lounges, TVs, discotheques and shops.

Ferries are very crowded in summer, with erratic schedules and a range of fares (shop around for the best deal).

There are regular inter-island ferries in the Balearics and Canaries, including a fast two-hour hydrojet service between Palma de Mallorca and

Ibiza, and a regular ferry service from Ibiza to Formentera. Frequent inter-island ferry services also operate in the Canaries, including a hydrofoil service between all the islands. For details of ferry companies in the Balearics see page 101 and for the Canaries see page 107.

Discounts for Seniors: Some ferry companies offer discounts to senior citizens aged over 60, e.g. Trasmediterranea 25 per cent, Fredolsen 15 per cent and Naviera Armas 12 per cent. Island residents are entitled to a 38 per cent discount on all inter-island ferries and ferries between islands and mainland Spain. You must present proof of residence when booking tickets.

Private Transport

Roads

Motoring in Spain has changed dramatically in the last few decades, during which the number of cars has increased considerably and the road network vastly extended. Spanish motorways are mostly toll roads built by private companies and are among Europe's finest roads. Unfortunately, they're also among the world's most expensive and consequently main trunk roads (*carreteras*) are jammed by drivers who are reluctant (or cannot afford) to pay the high motorway tolls. The road-building programme and provision of parking spaces has, however, failed to keep pace with the increasing number of cars on Spanish roads (it's hard to believe that Spain has a lower density of vehicles than most other European countries). In contrast to the excellent *autopistas* and fine trunk roads, roads in rural areas and small towns are often dreadful or even dangerous, and full of potholes.

Driving in Spain may be cheaper than using public transport, particularly when the costs are shared between a number of people and you avoid motorways. In any case, unless you're travelling between major cities you have little choice but to drive, as public transport is generally poor in rural areas. However, if you're travelling long distances, you'll find it quicker and certainly less stressful to take the train or fly. If you live in or near a city, particularly Madrid or Barcelona (where public transport services are excellent), a car is a liability, while in rural areas it's a necessity.

General road information can be obtained from ☎ 900 123 505 or via the internet (🖳 http://www.dgt.es), although at weekends and during peak holiday periods the phone lines and internet are overloaded and it can be impossible to get through. Road assistance is available from the Real Automobil Club de España/RACE (☎ 902 300 505, 🖳 http://www.race.es), Spain's largest and most famous motoring organisation, and the Real

Automobil Club de Catalunya/RACC (☎ 902 414 143, 🖳 http://www.racc.es). Services are similar and both have reciprocal agreements with foreign organisations such as the AA, AAA, ACI, ADAC, AvD, DTC, RAC and the TCI.

A map showing motorways and major roads is in **Appendix E**.

Road Rules: Spanish road rules were extensively revised in 2004 in an attempt to improve safety and the following is a summary of the most important regulations. Don't, however, expect other motorists to adhere to them – many Spanish drivers make up their own 'rules', which are infinitely variable!

● The Spanish drive on the right-hand side of the road and it saves confusion if you do likewise! If you aren't used to driving on the right, take it easy until you're accustomed to it. Be particularly alert when leaving lay-bys, T-junctions, one-way streets and petrol stations, as it's easy to lapse into driving on the left. It's helpful to have a reminder, e.g. a luminous sign saying 'Keep right!' on your car's dashboard.

● All cars must carry a reflective waistcoat (to be worn if you stop at the side of the road), two approved red warning triangles (to be placed around 10m in front of and behind the vehicle – or both behind on a dual-carriageway – if you're forced to stop at the side of the road), a full set of spare bulbs and fuses, a spare wheel and the tools for changing a wheel. There are fines for not carrying the above.

● Traffic flows anti-clockwise round roundabouts (traffic circles) and not clockwise, as in the UK and other countries where driving is on the left. When approaching a roundabout, you must give way to traffic on the roundabout (coming from your left). There's usually a give-way sign (which may be painted on the road) on all roads approaching roundabouts.

● The wearing of seat belts is compulsory on all roads at all times. Children aged under 12 or less than 150cm (5ft) tall must travel in the back seats of cars unless the front seat is fitted with an approved child seat. Failure to wear a seat belt can result in an on-the-spot fine and a two-point 'deduction' from your licence. If you have an accident and aren't wearing your seat belt, your insurance company can refuse to pay a claim for personal injury.

● Don't drive in bus, taxi or cycle lanes, identified by a continuous yellow line parallel to the kerb, unless it's necessary to avoid a stationary vehicle or an obstruction (you can be fined for doing so). Be sure to keep clear of tram lines, i.e. outside the restricted area shown by a line.

- For left-hand turns off a main road with traffic lights, there's often a marked filter lane to the right, where you wait to cross the main road at right angles.

- Headlights must be used when driving at night, in poor visibility during daylight and in tunnels at any time (you're reminded by a sign). Be extremely careful when driving in tunnels (remove your sunglasses!), some of which have very poor or no lighting. Your headlamps must be dipped (*luces de cruce*) at night when following a vehicle or when a vehicle is approaching from the opposite direction. Failure to dip your lights can result in a fine.

- A vehicle's hazard warning lights must be used to warn other drivers of an obstruction, e.g. an accident or a traffic jam, or if the vehicle is forced to drive at below the minimum speed. Warning triangles and reflective waistcoats must be used as appropriate (see above).

- Most traffic lights are situated on posts at the side of the road, although they may also be suspended above the road. The sequence of Spanish traffic lights (*semáforos*) is usually red, green, amber (yellow), red. Amber means stop at the stop line; you may proceed only if stopping may cause an accident. (Take care before stopping at an amber light when a vehicle is close behind you, as Spanish drivers routinely drive through amber – and even red – lights and may be taken by surprise if you stop!)

- Take care when approaching a railway crossing, indicated by a sign with a large 'X' or an engine in a triangle. You must take particular care at crossings without barriers, as several people are killed each year by trains at crossings without barriers. Approach a railway level crossing slowly and stop as soon as the barrier or half-barrier starts to fall, as soon as the red warning lights are illuminated or flashing or a warning bell rings, or when a train is approaching!

- Be particularly wary of mopeds (*ciclomotor*) and bicycles. It isn't always easy to see them, particularly when they're hidden by the blind spots of a car or are riding at night without lights. **Follow the example set by Spanish motorists, who, when overtaking mopeds and cyclists, always give them a WIDE berth.** It's also common to encounter tractors, horses, donkeys and sheep in rural areas. Keep an eye out for them and give them a wide berth also.

- Studded tyres and snow chains may be necessary in winter in mountainous areas. Snow chains are compulsory on some roads in winter, indicated by a sign.

- Drivers towing (*con remolque*) a caravan or trailer must display a sign of a yellow triangle on a blue background on the front of their vehicle. Note that towing a broken-down vehicle is permitted only by a tow truck.

- A dog must be restrained when carried in a car.

- The use of hand-held telephones and the wearing of audio headphones is illegal when driving, and you can be fined up to €300 and lose three points from your licence. 'Hands-free' sets are allowed, although they must be without earphones.

- When filling with fuel you must turn off the engine, all lights, electrical equipment (including the radio) and your mobile phone (?).

- All motorists in Spain must be familiar with the Spanish highway code (*Código de la Circulación*), available from bookshops throughout Spain.

Speed Limits: The following speed limits (*límites de velocidad*) apply to cars and motorcycles in Spain:

Type of Road	Speed Limit
Motorways (*autopistas*)	120kph (75mph)
Dual-carriageways (*autovías*)	100kph (62mph)
Other main roads (*carreteras*)	90kph (56mph)
Built-up areas (*vías urbanas*)	50kph (31mph) or as signposted, e.g. 20kph in some residential areas

Campervans, cars towing caravans and trailers up to 750kg are restricted to 90kph (56mph) on motorways and dual-carriageways, and 80kph (50mph) on other roads (unless a lower speed limit is in force). Cars towing loads of over 750kg are restricted to 80kph on motorways and dual carriageways, and 70kph (43mph) on other roads (unless a lower speed limit is in force). Obligatory speed restrictions are shown on round signs in black figures on a white background with a red rim. Recommended speed limits, e.g. on sharp bends, are shown on square signs in white figures on a blue background.

Driving Licences

The minimum age for driving in Spain is 14 for a motorcycle (moped) up to 50cc, 16 for a motorcycle up to 125cc and 18 for a motorcycle with an engine capacity over 125cc or for a car. There's also a maximum age of 65 for obtaining your first licence, although this doesn't apply to foreigners aged over 65, who can exchange a valid foreign licence for a Spanish licence (*permiso de conducción*).

The validity period of a Spanish licence depends on your age and the type of licence held, e.g. a motorcycle (A-1/A-2) or car (B-1) licence is valid for five years if you're aged between 45 and 70. **A driver aged over 70 must renew his licence every two years.**

Many foreign driving licences are recognised in Spain under reciprocal agreements, including all EU licences and some US state licences, in which case you can drive on the licence of your home country and aren't required to obtain a Spanish driving licence. Motorists from some countries require an International Driving Permit (IDP). Nevertheless, if you're a resident you must take your foreign licence to your local provincial traffic department to be stamped and registered. You must also undergo the same medical exams and eye tests as holders of Spanish licences.

Note, however, that the above rule isn't always known or recognised by the local police, and there have been cases of EU nationals resident in Spain driving Spanish-registered vehicles and being fined for not having a Spanish licence.

For this reason, many residents find it's simpler to exchange their foreign licence for a Spanish one! Holders of licences issued by countries without a reciprocal agreement with Spain must take a Spanish written and/or practical driving test. For further information, consult a Spanish consulate abroad or your country's embassy or consulate in Spain.

A Spanish driving licence is a plastic-coated card, the same size as a credit card, with personal information (including a photograph) printed on one side and driving information on the other. The card is similar to those issued in many EU countries such as Germany, Sweden and the UK.

You must carry your foreign or Spanish driving licence at all times when driving in Spain.

Points System: In an attempt to reduce the high accident and mortality rate on Spain's roads, the government introduced a points system, similar to that used in France, Germany and Italy, in July 2006. Under the system, most drivers are given an initial quota of 12 points on their driving licence. Drivers with under 30 months' driving experience or who have committed a serious driving offence within the previous three years receive eight points. When a driver commits an offence, a number of points are deducted from the licence depending on the seriousness of the offence. For example drunk driving leads to a six-point deduction, ignoring a red light loses four points and using a mobile phone while driving three points.

Drivers who lose all their points automatically lose their licence for a period. To regain their licence, drivers must retake the driving test and take a driving course of around 30 hours. These tests cannot be taken until at least six months after the last driving offence. Those who lose points, but still have credit on their driving licence regain their points two or three years after their last offence.

Driving a Car on Foreign Registration Plates

Residents: A Spanish resident isn't permitted to operate a car on foreign registration plates. Vehicles registered outside the EU cannot generally be operated in Spain or any other EU country by EU residents, although there are a few exceptions. The importation of right-hand drive (RHD) cars isn't permitted unless you're a new resident to Spain.

Non-residents: The regulations for non-residents depend on whether you're an EU national:

- **EU nationals** – Non-residents of Spain who are resident in another EU country can bring a vehicle registered in another EU country to Spain and can use it (for up to 182 days per year) without paying Spanish taxes. The vehicle must be legal in its country of registration, meaning that it must be inspected (for roadworthiness) as appropriate and taxed there.

- **Non-EU nationals** – A person resident outside the EU may temporarily import a vehicle registered outside the EU for a total period of six months (which needn't be continuous) within a calendar year. In certain circumstances, the six-month period can be extended. This applies, for example, to those regularly crossing into EU territory to work, full-time students from outside the EU, and people from outside the EU on a special mission for a specified period. The vehicle can be used only by the owner, his spouse, parents and children (who must also be non-residents). Note, however, that it's necessary for non-EU citizens to have a foreign-registered vehicle 'sealed' (*precintado*) by customs during periods of absence from Spain.

Comprehensive information about motoring in Spain is provided in out best-selling sister publication **Living and Working in Spain** by David Hampshire (see page 383). Details of the costs of running a car in Spain can be found on page 76.

KEEPING IN TOUCH

An important consideration when thinking about retiring in Spain is how easy it is to keep in touch with your friends and loved ones, and current affairs back in your home country.

Telecommunications

The telecommunications network in Spain is on a par with most EU countries and numerous companies offer telephone services, although few provide a complete service including line installation. For a list of the main companies, see page 81.

Landlines

Landlines are available in most of Spain with the exception of some rural areas. If your property doesn't have an existing telephone line and you wish to have one installed, contact Telefónica (☎ 1004 in Spanish, ☎ 902 118 247 in English, 🖳 http://www.telefonica.es or 🖳 http://www.telefonica inenglish.com). Installation takes from a few days to several weeks, depending on the location of the property.

If you live in a rural area with no landline infrastructure, you may wish to investigate radio or satellite lines (or alternatively use a mobile phone if this is an option). Installation is more expensive than a landline and the quality of reception can be poor at times, but it may be better than no connection at all. Contact Telefónica to find out what's available in an area, preferably **before** buying a home.

Line rental and call charges are among the highest in Europe, but significant savings can be made by shopping around different companies for the lowest rates (see page 81 for further information).

Mobile Phones

Mobile phones are hugely popular in Spain and the three digital networks (Amena, Movistar and Vodafone) cover around 90 per cent of the country – only the remotest rural areas have no reception. Mobile phones from the UK and most other EU countries (on the GSM network) can usually be operated in Spain, but calls are routed via your home country and are therefore **very** expensive. It's advisable to buy a Spanish mobile or have a Spanish SIM card fitted to your existing phone. For a listing of mobile phone companies, see page 82.

Internet

The internet provides an ideal and economical way of keeping in touch, particularly if you install a broadband (ADSL) connection when internet telephony is also possible – MSN Messenger (🖥 http://messenger.msn.com) and Skype (🖥 http://www.skype.com) are two of the most popular. All you need is broadband access and a headset or a special phone, and you're in business. Calls to other computers anywhere in the world are free, while calls from your computer to landlines are charged at a few cents a minute.

Broadband is now available in most urban areas and some rural areas. If it isn't available in your area, it may be worth considering satellite internet, provided by companies such as Avonline (🖥 http://www.avonlinebroadband. co.uk), BusinessCom (🖥 http://www.bcsatellite.net) and Global Telephone and Telecommunication (🖥 http://www.globaltt.com).

For a listing of the main internet service providers see page 82.

Postal Services

There's a post office (*oficina de correos*) in most towns and at main railway stations, major airports and ports in Spain. In addition to postal services, a limited range of other services are provided, including banking and savings accounts through Deutschebank. The post office produces few leaflets and brochures, and you may even have difficulty obtaining a tariff, but their website provides comprehensive information (🖥 http://www.correos.es). You shouldn't expect post office staff to speak English or other foreign languages, although main post offices in major cities may have an information desk with multi-lingual staff.

It's probably best not to rely on the Spanish postal service for keeping in touch as it has the reputation of being one of the slowest and least efficient in Europe! Never rely on any important post being delivered in less than ten days (even within Spain), as instances of letters taking much longer to arrive at any destination are fairly commonplace. Even sending letters by express (*urgente*) post isn't the answer, as there's no guarantee that it will arrive earlier than ordinary post. The only way to ensure express delivery within Spain or from Spain to another country is to use a courier or to send letters by fax or email.

Newspapers & Magazines

Foreign newspapers and magazines are readily available in most popular resort areas and many of the UK dailies (e.g. *Daily Mail*, *The Guardian* and *The Times*) are printed in Spain and available on the morning of publication (including Sunday editions). Many other English-language daily newspapers are widely available on the day of publication, including *USA Today*, *International Herald Tribune* and the *Wall Street Journal Europe*. French, German and Scandinavian newspapers are also easily obtainable. **Foreign newspapers cost around three times more than the price in their country of origin.**

Many English-language newspapers are published in Spain, including the *Costa Blanca News*, *Costa del Sol News*, *Sur in English*, *Majorcan Daily Bulletin* and the *Tenerife News*. Free local English-language newspapers and magazines are published in many areas and contain a wealth of information about local events, restaurants, bars, entertainment, services and shops. Other free newspapers and magazines are published in Dutch, Finnish, French, German and Swedish.

See **Appendix B** for a listing of English-language newspapers and magazines published in Spain.

Television

The standards for TV reception in Spain **aren't the same as in some other countries**. Due to the differences in transmission standards, TVs and video recorders operating on the British (PAL-I), French (SECAM) or US (NTSC) systems won't function in Spain, which, along with most other continental European countries, uses the PAL B/G standard. It's possible to buy a multi-standard European TV (and VCR) containing automatic circuitry that switches between different systems. Some multi-standard TVs also include the NTSC standard and have an NTSC-in jack plug connection allowing you to watch American videos. A standard British, French or US TV won't work in Spain, although they can be modified. The same applies to 'foreign' video recorders, which won't operate with a Spanish TV unless they're dual-standard.

Most furnished rental property comes equipped with a television. Spanish TV broadcasts little in English (the occasional film), but Spain is well served by satellite TV, popular among expatriates. The two main providers are:

● **Sky Television** – To receive most English-language channels, you must subscribe to Sky and you need a Sky Digital receiver and dish (total cost around €600 plus monthly subscription), supplied by a number of companies in Spain. Information about installation in the UK and viewing packages can be found on Sky's website (🖳 http://www.sky.com).

● **BBC** – The BBC's commercial subsidiary, BBC Worldwide Television, broadcasts two 24-hour channels: BBC Prime (general entertainment) and BBC World (24-hour news and information). BBC World is free-to-air, while BBC Prime is encrypted and requires a D2-MAC decoder and a smartcard, available on subscription from BBC Prime, PO Box 5054, London W12 0ZY (☎ 020-8433 2221, 🖳 http://www.bbcprime.com).

Radio

There are English and other foreign-language commercial stations in major cities and resort areas, where the emphasis is on music and chat with some news and traffic bulletins. The main English-language stations are as follows:

Canaries

● Oasisfm (Tenerife, 101FM)

● Power FM (all islands except El Hierro and La Palma, 91-92FM)

Costa Blanca

● Costa Blanca FM (south only, on 106FM)

● Holiday FM (102.6FM and 102.8FM)

● Onda Cero International/OCI (94.6FM)

● REM (88.2FM, 105.1FM)

● Spectrum FM (106.7FM)

● Sunshine FM (102.6FM, 102.8FM)

Costa de Almería

- REM (92.7FM)
- Spectrum (92.6FM)

Costa del Sol

- Central FM (98.6FM, 103.8FM)
- Coastline Radio (97.6FM)
- Onda Cero International/OCI (101.6FM)
- REM (91.9FM, 104.8FM)
- Spectrum FM (105.5FM)

English-language radio programmes are listed in the local expatriate press and on the stations' websites where many can be heard online.

BBC

The BBC World Service is broadcast on short wave on several frequencies (e.g. 12095, 9760, 9410, 7325, 6195, 5975 and 3955Khz) simultaneously and you can usually receive a good signal on one of them. The signal strength varies depending on where you live, the time of day and year, the power and positioning of your receiver, and atmospheric conditions. All BBC radio stations, including the World Service, are also available via Sky. The BBC publishes a monthly magazine, *BBC On Air*, containing comprehensive information about BBC world service radio and television programmes. It's available on subscription from the BBC (On Air Magazine, Room 207 NW, Bush House, Strand, London WC2B 4PH, ☎ 020-7557 2211, ⊠ on.air. magazine@bbc.co.uk) and from some newsagents in Spain.

LEARNING THE LANGUAGE

Spanish

What most foreigners refer to as Spanish is actually Castilian (*castellano*) – **the** Spanish language and the official language everywhere in Spain and understood by the vast majority of Spaniards. All references to Spanish throughout this book are to Castilian, spoken by 65 per cent of Spaniards as their first and only language. The other 35 per cent speak Spanish and a regional language (see below).

It isn't always **essential** for retired residents who live among the expatriate community to learn Spanish and in resort areas with large foreign populations (e.g. Torrevieja in the southern Costa Blanca and Benalmádena on the Costa del Sol you may hear hardly any Spanish at all!). However, learning some Spanish certainly makes life easier and less frustrating. Unfortunately, many residents (particularly British retirees) make little effort to learn Spanish beyond the few words necessary to buy the weekly groceries and order a cup of coffee, and live as if they were on a short holiday. Some even assume that everybody, whether Spaniards or other foreigners, speak their national language and don't even bother to ask before launching into their native tongue!

If you're a retiree, you should make an effort to learn at least the rudiments of Spanish so that you can understand your bills, use the telephone, deal with servicemen, and communicate with your local town hall. If you don't learn Spanish, you will be continually frustrated in your communications and will be constantly calling on friends and acquaintances to assist you, or even paying people (such as *gestores*) to do jobs you could quite easily do yourself.

SURVIVAL TIP
For anyone living in Spain permanently, learning Spanish shouldn't be seen as an option, but a necessity. The most important and serious purpose of learning the language is that in an emergency it could save your life or that of a loved one!

Learning Spanish also helps you to appreciate the Spanish way of life and make the most of your time in Spain, and opens many doors that remain firmly closed to resident 'tourists'.

Although it isn't easy, even the most non-linguistic (and oldest) person can acquire a working knowledge of Spanish. All that's required is a little hard work and some help and perseverance, particularly if you have only English-speaking colleagues and friends. You won't just 'pick it up' (apart from a few words), but must make a real effort to learn. Although learning any language isn't easy, learning basic Spanish is simpler than learning many other languages because it's written phonetically with all letters pronounced.

If you don't speak Spanish, it's advisable to take language classes **before you leave home**, as you will probably be too busy for the first few weeks after your move when you most need the language. Knowing how to ask for things and understanding something of what's said to you will also make settling in easier and less stressful. If you're moving to an area in Spain where English is widely spoken, basic Spanish will probably be sufficient to start with, but if your chosen retirement spot is essentially Spanish, you should consider doing an intensive language course before you arrive.

Options include evening classes (Spanish is the most popular evening class language in the UK), online courses (💻 http://www.bbc.co.uk/languages, 💻 http://www.parlo.com and 💻 http://www.vistawide.com are some of the best) and joining an Spanish expatriate group in your home country – these often run social and cultural activities, giving you the opportunity to practise your Spanish and learn more about Spain. The Instituto Cervantes, the official Spanish cultural representative abroad, also runs language courses at its centres, e.g. in Leeds, London and Manchester in the UK (💻 http://www.cervantes.org).

Once you arrive in Spain, you should enrol in a course at a local language school as soon as possible. Many town councils in resort areas run Spanish courses for residents. Courses are usually good value and offer the chance to meet other local people, but they're often over-subscribed, so book early. Many universities also run intensive Spanish for foreigners (*español para extranjeros*) courses, e.g. Alicante University (☎ 965 903 793, 💻 http://www.ua.es – go to 'International Programs' on the English-language page) and Malaga University (☎ 952 278 211, 💻 http://www.uma.es/estudios/extraj/extranjeros.htm). Private classes are another option, although they're the most expensive way of learning Spanish, but you will learn more, and private teachers are available throughout Spain. Expect to pay from €20 an hour for a qualified teacher. A 'language exchange' whereby you meet someone regularly and spend half the time speaking English and the other half speaking Spanish, is a cheaper alternative to private lessons and also a good social opportunity.

You should be aware that medical staff at some health centres and hospitals may refuse to treat patients who don't speak Spanish or who don't have an interpreter. Staff at government offices (local, provincial and regional) may also refuse to deal with those who cannot speak Spanish and have no interpreter.

Regional Languages

Spain also has three official regional languages: Basque (*euskera*), Catalan (*catalán*) and Galician (*gallego*), which share equal status with Spanish in the regions where they're spoken. This means that road signs, street and buildings names, notices and official documents are in the regional language rather than Spanish, causing considerable problems for foreigners and Spaniards from other regions of Spain. It's an important consideration if you're planning to live in the Basque Country, Catalonia (e.g. the Costa Brava, Barcelona), the Balearics, Galicia or Valencia (Costa del Azahar and the Costa Blanca). In these regions, communications from the authorities may be in the local language only and officials may be reluctant to speak any other language. In rural areas, it may be difficult to settle in socially if you don't speak the regional language. Ask yourself if you want to learn another language (e.g. Catalan) as well as Spanish?

For details about which regional languages are spoken in which popular retirement spots see the area profiles on page 100.

Catalan

Of the three official regional languages, Catalan is the most widely-spoken and some 6.5m people in Catalonia, the Balearics, Valencia (including the Costa del Azahar and Costa Blanca), Andorra and parts of the French Pyrenees speak it. Catalan has several dialects, e.g. *Mallorquín* (spoken on Majorca), *Menorquín* (spoken on Minorca) and *Valenciano* (spoken in Valencia). The degree to which Catalan is spoken depends very much on the area: in some places Spanish is more widely-spoken than Catalan, e.g. in Barcelona where less than half the population speaks fluent Catalan and the southern area of the Costa Blanca where *Valenciano* is hardly heard at all (although state schools teach almost all subjects in *Valenciano*). In other areas Catalan dominates speech and some people may rarely speak anything else or may even refuse to.

If you choose to retire to an area where Catalan shares official language status with Spanish it isn't essential to learn it, but it's a good idea to master a few key phrases as a way of integrating into local society.

Galician

Some 2.5m Galician inhabitants speak Galician and a surprising number (mostly in rural areas) don't speak any Spanish. If you plan to move to an urban area in Galicia, it probably won't be necessary to learn Galician, but if your chosen retirement spot is in a village, it may be essential if you wish to have any contact with your neighbours!

Basque

Basque is the least-spoken of the three regional languages and by far the most difficult – it's cluttered with consonants and unfathomable to anyone but regional speakers (at least with Catalan and Galician, Spanish speakers can get an idea of what's being said). Basque has had a revival over the last few years, but is mainly spoken in rural areas and few Basques don't speak Spanish, so it probably isn't essential to learn it.

Regional Accents

In common with most countries, Spain has an infinite number of regional accents, which also vary from one province to another and often even within the province itself. Regional accents not only involve different pronunciation, but also variations in vocabulary and grammar. For example, 'small' is '*pequeño*' in Castilian Spanish, but '*chico*' is used instead throughout Andalusia. The Canary islanders rarely use the informal '*tú*' and '*vosotros*' forms of address and prefer the '*usted*' or '*ustedes*' even when talking to relatives or people they know well.

It's generally accepted that the easiest accent to understand is the Spanish spoken in central Spain, namely Madrid and the two Castiles, where Spaniards have the reputation of speaking clearly or 'listening to themselves as they speak'.

Regional accents in Andalusia are among the most difficult to understand – 'c's are often pronounced as 's's and plural endings not pronounced at all – and in some rural areas, even native speakers find deciphering the local accent a challenge. This can be a shock to a foreigner who believes he has a reasonable level of Spanish to find he cannot understand a word. However, perseverance pays off and it doesn't take long to 'tune into' a regional accent and understand the essentials of what's being said.

3.

CAN YOU AFFORD IT?

A prime consideration when considering retiring in Spain is whether you can afford it! It's important to do your sums carefully and consider **all** the financial implications. It isn't uncommon to hear tales of expatriates forced to return to their home country because they didn't do their homework and found out later that they couldn't afford to live in Spain. Not only do you need to consider the day-to-day living expenses but also your long-term financial prospects. If your income is generated in a currency other than euros (e.g. you receive a pension from the UK or the USA), you must take into account currency fluctuations and allow for periodic gains and losses. Sound financial advice from an expert familiar with the Spanish tax system **and** your home country's tax system is essential. It's important to plan ahead, invest wisely and make the most of any legal opportunities to save or avoid tax.

This chapter contains essential information about the cost of living, money-saving measures, and your entitlement to pensions and benefits when resident in Spain. Information about Spanish currency, banking and taxation can be found in **Chapter 8**.

SPAIN'S ECONOMY

Spain currently has one of the strongest economies in Europe and has been transformed in the last few decades from a rural, backward agricultural country into a nation with a diversified economy and strong manufacturing and service sectors. After joining the European Union (EU) in 1986, Spain had one of the world's fastest-growing economies with annual growth averaging over 4 per cent until the country was hit hard by recession in the early '90s. A vastly improved balance of payments and economic reforms initiated a strong recovery and since 1997 Spain has had one of the highest growth rates in the EU. Growth continues apace and remains higher than the EU average (3.4 per cent in 2005 compared to the EU average of 1.7 per cent) and the Economist Intelligence Unit forecasts similar figures for both 2006 and 2007, considerably higher than those for the UK, France, Germany and Italy.

Inflation, although higher than the EU average, was relatively low at 3.7 per cent in 2005 (3.9 per cent in March 2006) and in 2005, for the first time in recent years, Spain had a budget surplus – compared to a 7.5 per cent budget deficit in 1993. Unemployment reached an all-time low in 2005 when figures dropped below 10 per cent for the first time since 1979 and the rate for March 2006 (8.7 per cent) is below the EU average for the first time.

In spite of these encouraging economic figures, Spain remains one of the poorest countries in the EU-15 (i.e. excluding the ten new members who joined in 2004) where only Greece and Portugal are poorer. Even when the new poorer members of the EU are taken into account, Spain's GDP per head of €20,838 is considerably below the EU-25 average of €23,400. Only four regions have higher GDPs (the Basque Country, Catalonia, Madrid – Spain's richest region, and Navarra), while in others, such as Extremadura and Andalusia, GDP per head stands at a mere €14,051 and €16,100 respectively.

COST OF LIVING

As far as the cost of living is concerned, Spain is no longer the El Dorado that it once was and costs have risen considerably in recent years with many goods and services now costing on a par with those in most other European countries. However, many things remain cheaper than in northern European countries, including property (with the exception of the Balearics, Costa del Sol, Barcelona and Madrid), property taxes, motoring, food, alcohol, hotels, restaurants and general entertainment.

It's difficult to calculate an average cost of living, as it depends on each individual's circumstances and lifestyle. The actual difference in your monthly bills depends on what you eat, where you shop and where you lived before coming to Spain, but in general terms the cost of living is lower than in the UK, France and Germany, and around the same as North America. The following section provides a rough guide to day-to-day costs.

Regional Variations

Not surprisingly, Madrid and Barcelona are Spain's most expensive places to live, although up-market resort areas such as Marbella and Palma de Mallorca provide close competition. In general, prices are higher in resort areas where savvy locals inflate prices for tourists and resident foreigners, and cheaper inland and in coastal areas that aren't popular with foreigners. For example, the cost of living is lower in the city of Malaga than in the neighbouring resort of Fuengirola, and prices in Alicante city are cheaper than in Jávea. Similarly, prices vary within a locality depending on the location – you can expect to pay at least €3 for a coffee or beer at a seafront café whereas you would only pay €1 at a local bar. Note, however, than even in the major cities and popular resorts, the cost of dining out is generally very reasonable by international standards and you can have a meal with wine anywhere for €15-20.

Prices on the islands are often higher than the mainland to cover importation costs, although the Canaries have favourable tax rates (the equivalent of VAT is levied at 7 per cent instead of 16 per cent) and car fuel is considerably cheaper.

Food

It's difficult to calculate the cost of your food bill in Spain, which is generally cheaper than in most northern European countries, particularly items such as fruit and vegetables and alcohol. Around €150 should feed two adults for a month, including inexpensive wine (you can buy a reasonable bottle of wine for less than €5), but excluding fillet steak, caviar and expensive imported foods. Eating out is also considerably cheaper than other European countries and in many areas the *menú del día* (three courses, plus a drink and bread) costs between €7 and €10, providing excellent value for money. You can save money on food costs by:

- buying Spanish products rather than imported ones – imported items cost at least 50 per cent more than a similar Spanish product, e.g. a litre of local fresh milk costs around €0.75 while a litre of Irish fresh milk costs €1.40; a packet of Spanish chocolate digestives costs €1.20 and an imported packet costs €1.90.

- shopping at indoor and street markets where fresh produce (especially fruit and vegetables) costs less than in supermarkets and the quality is usually better. Small specialist shops are also usually cheaper. You can also often find bargains at the end of the morning or day when stalls are closing.

- shopping at hypermarkets and/or low-cost supermarkets such as Día, Lidl and Plus. Spain's cheapest supermarket chain in 2005 was Dani and the most expensive was Hipercor. A survey carried out in early 2006 by the national consumer organisation, Organización de Consumidores y Usuarios (OCU), found that the cheapest cities for supermarket shopping were Almería, Cuenca, Ourense, Pontevedra, Teruel and Vigo, while the most expensive were Bilbao, Las Palmas de Gran Canaria, Pamplona and San Sebastián.

Shopping Basket

The following table is a rough guide to the lowest price of specific food items (own-brand included) in an average supermarket in a resort in Spain. The prices don't take into account special offers, bulk buying or seasonal variations (e.g. oranges are more expensive in the summer when they're imported). Imported items are up to three times more expensive than local foodstuffs.

Item	Amount	Cost (from)
Beverages		
Beer	6 x 250ml	€1.50
Coffee (ground)	250g	€1.50
Coffee (instant)	100g	€1.50
Fizzy drink	2 litres	€0.60
Milk	litre	€0.75
Tea	40 bags	€2.25
Water	2 litres	€0.75
Wine	75ml	€2.00
Fresh Fish		
Salmon	1kg	€6.00
Sardines	1kg	€4.00
White fish	1kg	€8.00
Meat		
Beef	1kg	€6.00
Chicken	1kg	€2.75
Pork	1kg	€2.50
Cooked meats	1kg	€4.00
Bread & Dairy Produce		
Bread	baguette	€0.60
Bread	loaf	€0.80

Butter	250g	€1.90
Cheese	1kg	€6.00
Eggs	6	€0.70
Margarine	500g	€0.70
Yoghurt	4x125g	€0.70

Fruit & Vegetables

Apples	1kg	€1.50
Bananas	1kg	€1.50
Carrots	1kg	€0.60
Green beans	1kg	€2.00
Oranges	1kg	€0.75
Potatoes	1kg	€0.60
Tomatoes	1kg	€0.80

Store Cupboard

Beans	tin	€0.75
Biscuits	packet	€0.50
Cereal	375g	€2.00
Cooking oil (olive)	1 litre	€4.50
Cooking (sunflower)	1 litre	€0.80
Crisps	250g	€0.75
Flour	1kg	€0.50
Jam	350g jar	€1.20
Pasta	500g	€0.30
Rice	1kg	€0.50
Sardines	tin	€0.50
Sugar	1kg	€0.95

Tuna	3 pack	€1.30
Toiletries & Cleaning		
Shampoo	250ml	€1.60
Shower gel	750ml	€1.20
Toilet paper	4 rolls	€0.50
Toothpaste	tube	€0.80
Washing powder	18 washes	€3.00
Washing-up liquid	250ml	€0.90

Leisure & Sport

Prices for leisure and sporting activities are generally reasonable in Spain. The following list is a general guide to the cost of some activities:

Leisure

Tickets	
Entertainment	**Cost**
Cinema	from €5
Concert	from €15
Musical	from €20
Theatre	from €12
Theme park or zoo	from €20

Discounts are often available for the over 65's.

Miscellaneous Items

Newspaper	€1 (Spanish), from €1.80 (foreign)
CD	from €12

DVD	from €15
DVD Rental	from €2

Second-hand books can be purchased from numerous shops and markets in resort areas, while new books are best purchased from 🖳 http://www.amazon.com.

Sports

Month's gym membership	from €20
One-day ski pass	from €25
Round of golf (18-hole)	from €50 (from €60 on the Costa del Sol)
Tennis court per hour	from €5

Motoring

Buying a Car

New cars are more expensive in Spain than in many other European countries owing to taxes (up to 12 per cent registration tax and 16 per cent IVA), although dealers compete in offering discounts, guarantees, financing terms and special deals, therefore it pays to shop around. A small family car costs from €15,000. Second-hand cars are also more expensive, but they hold their value better. It often pays to buy a used car that's around two years old – high mileage cars, particularly ex-rental cars, are good value.

Insurance

Most insurance policies are reasonably priced in Spain and similar to other European countries, although the actual price depends on the cover and policy. Third-party car insurance (the minimum legal requirement) is inexpensive for those with a no-claims bonus or if you choose to pay an excess, and costs from around €300. For further information see **Car Insurance** on page 267.

Fuel

In common with other European countries, fuel prices have increased considerably in recent years and the days of cheap petrol are long-gone. Even so, fuel prices in Spain are lower than many other EU countries, including the UK. Diesel is slightly cheaper than petrol, but only by a few cents (although fuel consumption is **much** better). Fuel is significantly cheaper in the Canaries than the mainland. Prices are set by individual petrol stations, so it's worthwhile shopping around for the lowest price. Some petrol companies have introduced energy-saving fuel, e.g. BP's *Ultimate* fuels, Cepsa's *Optima* range and Repsol's *Diesel e+10*, which are more expensive than conventional fuel, but companies claim they are better for the engine and as a result you get better fuel consumption.

Information on fuel prices by province is available from http://http://www6.mityc.es/energia/hidrocarburos/carburantes/index.asp – click on the province and the type of fuel for a list of local prices.

Road Tax

Road tax is levied annually by the local council and rates vary from town to town depending on the vehicle and its fiscal horsepower (*potencia fiscal* or *caballos fiscales*). Among the cheapest cities are Madrid, Valencia and Zaragoza, while Barcelona, Bilbao and Córdoba are the most expensive. As a general guide, expect to pay between €80 and €150 a year for a family car (e.g. a Renault Scenic).

Eco Motoring

With world oil supplies already on the countdown to running dry (some experts warn supplies won't last beyond 2045), global warming a stark reality and fuel prices rising almost daily, it's no wonder consumers are starting to investigate alternatives. Technology is still very much in its infancy and there are few options currently on the market, but progress is being made almost daily and it's only a matter of time before most cars on the road are hybrid (able to run on more than one type of fuel) or run on an alternative to oil.

Some countries have already made significant advances. Bioethanol instead of petrol is widely used in Brazil which has been converting its surplus sugar cane into bioethanol for more than 30 years. Sweden has set itself the ambitious target of reducing its dependency on petrol to zero by

2020. To this end, the government has introduced generous concessions and discounts to motorists who buy ecologically-friendly cars.

In other countries, however, biofuels and 'green' cars have yet to make an impact. Within the EU, biofuels currently account for less than 1 per cent of fuel consumption, but the EU has set its 25 member states the target of raising this figure to 6 per cent by 2010. In Germany (where there are more than 1,700 petrol stations selling biodiesel) the target seems attainable, but in other countries such as Spain, with around only 200 stations selling biodiesel, it appears less likely.

Types of 'Eco-cars': In some countries, such as Brazil and the US, the consumer has a reasonable selection of hybrid cars and nearly three-quarters of new Brazilian cars can run on either bioethanol or petrol. Elsewhere, however, there's currently little choice, although this is expected to change significantly in the next decade when numerous car manufacturers launch new 'bio-cars', e.g. BMW plans to launch its 745H with a hybrid engine (petrol and hydrogen) in 2008 and Honda, Mercedes and Opel all plan to market bio-cars by 2010.

Spain: In mid-2006 there were only three hybrid models available in Spain: the Ford Focus Flexi-Fuel, the Honda Civic Hybrid and the Toyota Prius. The Ford Focus Flexi-Fuel, reasonably priced at around €17,500, is the only car available in Spain that runs on petrol and bioethanol. The Honda Civic Hybrid and Toyota Prius run on petrol and electricity generated by the car itself via a battery. Pollution is considerably reduced, e.g. the Prius stops its engine when you're in a traffic jam – and therefore fuel consumption is economical in urban areas. On the other hand, both cars still rely on petrol and are considerably more expensive than similar sized models (the Honda Civic costs from €24,200 and the Prius from €26,000). There are currently no state concessions or discounts for buyers of ecologically-friendly cars, although this may change in the future. Saab and Volvo also manufacture biocars, but these aren't yet available in Spain.

Biofuels:

- **Biodiesel** – Biodiesel is manufactured from vegetable oils (e.g. sunflower and palm), recycled oils (collected mostly from bars and restaurants) and animal fats. Biodiesel is expected to become the main biofuel in Spain where 65 per cent of new car sales are diesel models. Most cars manufactured since 1995 can run on biodiesel without problems (but check with your dealer first) and those that cannot run on biodiesel require only a basic modification costing around €400. A litre of biodiesel costs around €1, the same as conventional diesel.

The benefits of biodiesel include zero sulphur emissions, the fuel is biodegradable and few cars need engine modifications. On the other hand, biodiesel is less stable than petrol and freezes at a higher temperature. In Spain, the main disadvantage is its limited availability – around 200 petrol stations stock it, although as consumer demand increases it's expected to become more widely available. The majority of petrol stations with biodiesel pumps are found in Catalonia with a scattering of others around Spain. For a list see 💻 http://www.energias-renovables.com/paginas/combustible.asp and click on a province.

- **Bioethanol** – Bioethanol for fuel consumption is manufactured by the fermentation of grain, sugar cane or sugar beet. Vehicles that currently run on bioethanol usually use E85 (85 per cent bioethanol and 15 per cent petrol), although soon cars will be able to run on E100 (100 per cent bioethanol). Benefits include considerably lower fuel consumption, better engine performance and a significant reduction in carbon monoxide emissions. However, bioethanol is a volatile and corrosive substance and most conventional cars require costly engine modification in order to use fuel with more than 15 per cent ethanol. Although Spain is one of Europe's largest manufacturers of bioethanol, most is exported because there's no consumer demand. As a result, no petrol stations in Spain currently sell bioethanol.

- **Hydrogen** – Hydrogen is currently the world's best hope as the answer to the dwindling fuel supply, although manufacturers have yet to find an ecological and economical way of producing it on a large scale – production currently involves a costly and highly polluting process. Hydrogen has two outstanding advantages over other types of fuel (conventional and biofuel): it has a very high energy content, which means a little goes a long way, and its only emission is water vapour (experts claim that the vapour is so pure you can drink it!). However, until scientists discover a way of producing hydrogen via solar or wind power, hydrogen-powered cars still belong to the future.

Property

Despite huge price increases over the last five years, property in Spain remains good value and is an excellent investment – many buyers have seen huge returns. In some areas of Spain, bargains are still available, although these are usually found only in rural areas or relatively 'undiscovered' regions such as Aragon and Extremadura. On the other hand, fees and taxes payable when buying a property are high and are around 10-11 per cent of the purchase price. For further information on property prices and what you can buy for your money, see **Chapter 5**.

Property taxes aren't expensive in Spain and the annual total is often much lower than the equivalent monthly taxes in some countries, e.g. the UK. Maintenance costs may be high if you buy a property with a pool or large garden or if you need someone to look after your property when you're away, or you let it.

Transport

Public transport is generally inexpensive in Spain and if you purchase a season ticket (*bono*), savings are considerable. You can also save money by travelling at off-peak times (usually outside weekends) and by booking at the last minute. Pensioners are usually entitled to discounts, e.g. one-third on RENFE train journeys. See **Getting Around** on page 48 for information about public transport.

Utilities

Electricity

Spain has the EU's second-cheapest electricity, although prices have risen over the last few years. Actual charges depend on your local electricity company and include a monthly standing charge, e.g. around €5 in Andalusia (payable irrespective of consumption); consumption charged per KW, e.g. €0.08 in Andalusia; an electricity tax of 4.9 per cent; and VAT (*IVA*) at 16 per cent. Bills are usually levied bi-monthly. See **Utilities** on page 80 for a list of electricity companies and contact details.

You can save on electricity bills by using the night tariff (*tarifa nocturna*) which offers savings of over 50 per cent on electricity used between 11pm and 7am (midnight and 8am in the summer); installing solar power (for heat and electricity production); and using low-consumption appliances (look for those with the 'A' classification).

Gas

Gas is generally cheap in Spain and usually available only in bottles unless you live in a city with mains gas such as Alicante, Barcelona or Malaga. A

12.5kg bottle costs around €12.50 (the cost fluctuates wildly) and used for cooking and water heating should last around a month. Gas heaters are a popular and economical way of heating a home, but be aware that they can create damp conditions.

Water

For a country that frequently suffers from drought, the price of water is surprisingly low in Spain and among the cheapest in Europe. Actual charges depend on your local water company and vary from €1 to €2.50 per m³ plus a monthly standing charge. In many community properties, particularly apartment blocks, properties don't have individual water meters and the cost of water is included in the community fees. Water bills include VAT at 7 per cent – they are usually sent out quarterly and usually include sewerage.

You can reduce your water consumption by installing a 'water saver' that mixes air with water (available from hypermarkets and DIY stores).

Telephone

Landlines: Since the introduction of competition in the market several years ago, telephone costs have fallen sharply, although they are still among the highest in the EU. Installation costs around €100 (there are periodic free or discount deals) and monthly line rental around €13.50. Local calls typically cost from €0.01 per minute (plus connection charge), national calls from €0.02 (plus connection charge) and international calls from €0.06. VAT at 16 per cent is levied on all telephone charges. Bills are payable monthly.

You can save money on telephone bills by shopping around the different companies to find the cheapest calls and services – many people use different companies for different types of calls. Tariffs are continually changing, so keep an eye on the latest deals. The major telephone companies include:

- Jazztel – ☎ 1565, 🖥 http://www.jazztel.com

- ONO – ☎ 902 500 060, 🖥 http://www.auna.es

- Spantel – ☎ 902 020 202, 🖥 http://www.spantel.es

- Tele2 – ☎ 800 760 790, 🖥 http://www.tele2.es

- Telefónica – ☎ 1004, 🖥 http://www.telefonica.es

- Uni2 – ☎ 912 521 200, 🖥 http://www.uni2.es

Mobile phones: Mobile phone rates vary hugely depending on the company and who and when you're calling. The best deals are available on contract arrangements, although you must usually pay a minimum monthly amount (e.g. €9), but 'pay as you talk' options are better value if you don't use the mobile much. It's usually cheaper to make a mobile to mobile call than a mobile to landline or vice versa. Spain's mobile phone companies are:

● Amena – 🖳 http://www.amena.com

● Movistar – 🖳 http://www.movistar.com

● Vodafone – 🖳 http://www.vodafone.es

Internet: A price war is raging with internet tariffs and it's worth comparing prices to find the cheapest provider for your needs. Dial-up internet connections generally cost the same as local calls, but most companies offer discount services which allow you to buy a fixed number of access hours per month at a discount. Broadband is similarly competitive, although as yet there are no 'free' deals as in the UK, and unlimited 24-hour access with a speed of a minimum of 512/128 kbps costs at least €20 per month. Internet services are provided by most telephone companies (see above). The top five broadband providers are:

● Telefónica – 🖳 http://www.telefonicaonline.com

● Terra – 🖳 http://www.terra.es

● Tiscali – 🖳 http://www.tiscali.es

● Wanadoo – 🖳 http://www.wanadoo.es

● Ya.com – 🖳 http://www.ya.com

PENSIONS & BENEFITS

Pensions

If you're entitled to a state retirement pension in your home country you'll probably be able to receive it in Spain. You should inform the pension authorities in your home country well in advances of your plans to move to Spain and provide details of your Spanish bank account so that your pension can be paid directly in Spain (if desirable).

Contributions

Under EU law, social security contributions made towards a state pension scheme in any EU country count towards a state pension in another EU country. If you qualify for a state pension you can claim it from any EU country where you have made contributions or from the EU country you're living in when you retire. All EU countries have different regulations regarding the qualifying age, the number of contributions and the amount paid. If you apply for your pension in Spain, the authorities will consult your social security contributions record in other EU countries and you may qualify for a higher pension than is normally paid in Spain. This process takes considerable time and you're advised to start the application process at least six months before you retire.

UK Pensioners

If you're entitled to a UK-state pension, payments can be made to you in Spain and your pension payments are index-linked and subject to annual increases in line with inflation rates in the UK (but not those in Spain). In January 2006 there were nearly 73,000 British state pension claimants in Spain (figures from the Department of Work and Pensions).

You can choose to have payments made by cheque and sent by post or transferred directly to a Spanish bank account. The latter method is cheaper and more efficient and you don't lay yourself open to the mercies of the Spanish postal system. For payment via bank transfer, you must provide the authorities with the name and address of your bank, your account number (20 digits) and IBAN. Payments are made every four or 13 weeks (you can choose) unless your pension payment is very small, in which case payment is made once a year.

UK nationals planning to move to Spain before the retirement age, should apply for a State Pension Forecast (Form BR19). Contact the International Pension Service, Tyneview Park, Newcastle, NE98 1BA, UK (☎ 0191-218 7777, 🖥 http://www.thepensionservice.gov.uk) for further information.

Benefits for UK pensioners

Depending on your status, you may be entitled to additional benefits from the UK government when you move to Spain.

Bereavement Benefit: A lump sum of £2,000 is paid to help at the time of your partner or spouse's death. If you're over state pension age you're unlikely to receive this benefit and it's usually only paid if your partner or spouse wasn't in receipt of a state pension.

Long-term Incapacity Benefit: If you qualify for this in the UK, you will continue to receive it in Spain, but the amount is calculated on the same rate as the Spanish authorities pay to Spanish nationals, so you may find the benefit significantly reduced.

Winter Fuel Allowance: If you qualify for this benefit in the UK and move to an EEA country, you may continue to receive the allowance when you move abroad. Contact the Winter Fuel Payment Centre, Southgate House, Cardiff Central, Cardiff CF91 1ZH (☎ 08459-151515, 💻 http://www.the pensionservice.gov.uk/winterfuel).

4.

LOCATION, LOCATION, LOCATION

Once you have decided to retire to Spain, one of your first tasks is to choose the area where you wish to settle and what sort of home to buy. **If you're unsure about where to live or what to buy, it's advisable to rent for a period.**

The secret of finding the right place to retire is research, research and more research – the right choice of location often makes the difference between a dream and nightmare retirement. You may be fortunate and love the first place you choose without doing any homework and live happily ever after. However, successful retirement is much more likely if you thoroughly investigate the towns and communities in your chosen area, compare the range of amenities and facilities available, and research property prices to ensure that you can afford to buy or rent there.

Where you choose to retire to will depend on a number of factors, including your personal preferences, whether you plan to buy or rent a property, whether you intend to retire to Spain permanently or for just part of the year, and, not least, your financial resources. When seeking a permanent home, don't be too influenced by where you have spent an enjoyable holiday or two. A town or area that was acceptable for a few weeks' holiday may be far from suitable for a retirement home, particularly regarding the proximity to shops, medical facilities and other amenities.

It's worth bearing in mind that Spain is a large country (the second-largest in Europe after France) and is home to a wealth of varying landscapes, climates and cultural backgrounds, some of which are so different they could almost be a separate country. Even within the same region it's common to find hugely differing locations, e.g. Andalusia is home to some of continental Europe's highest mountain ranges (the Sierra Nevada is permanently snow-capped), verdant pastures and barren deserts. Not for nothing do many people consider Spain to be a country made up of numerous little 'countries'.

It consists of 17 regions, which enjoy a huge degree of autonomy from the central government. Regional governments are responsible for most issues regarding education, health and infrastructure within the region as well as numerous other areas affecting everyday life in the area. This is one of the reasons why standards vary from region to region, e.g. some regions spend more on healthcare than others, and it's worth taking this into account when choosing your retirement location.

The 'best' area to retire to depends on a range of considerations, including the proximity to a town, shops (e.g. a supermarket), public transport, sports facilities, beach, etc. When looking for a home, bear in mind the travelling time and costs to shops and local amenities such as the health centre, restaurants, and sports and social facilities. If you buy a remote country property, the distance to local amenities and services could become a problem, particularly as you get older and less mobile. If you live in a remote rural area you'll need to be much more self-sufficient than if you live in a town and will need to use a car for everything, which can add significantly to the cost of living.

This chapter contains information about short-term accommodation options, general advice about location and a comprehensive guide to the most popular retirement spots in Spain, including all the *costas*, and main islands and Barcelona and Madrid.

SHORT-TERM ACCOMMODATION OPTIONS

Renting

If you haven't decided on your retirement destination or cannot decide between several locations, it's advisable to rent a furnished property for a period. This will allow you time to become familiar with the weather (try to make your rental period coincide with the height of summer or the depths of winter so that you get a good idea what the weather is **really** like); the amenities and the local people, meet other foreigners who have retired to Spain and share their experiences; and, not least, to discover the cost of living at first hand.

If you plan to retire to Spain permanently or for long periods, it's advisable to rent for at least six months and preferably a year. An area that's quiet and relaxing between November and March can become noisy, congested and stressful between April and October, particularly in popular holiday areas. Conversely, somewhere that's attractive in the summer can virtually 'close' in winter. If you cannot rent long term, try to visit an area for two-week periods in each of the four seasons.

Provided you still find Spain alluring, renting buys you time to find your dream retirement location at your leisure. You may even wish to consider renting a home long term (or even permanently) as an alternative to buying, as it saves tying up your capital and can be surprisingly inexpensive in many regions. You also save on the fees associated with buying and selling (see page 153). Some people let their property in their home country and rent one in Spain, when it's even possible to make a profit.

SURVIVAL TIP
**If you plan to let your property in your home country,
make sure that you choose a reputable management
company to look after both the property and the rentals,
and take expert advice on the tax implications.**

If you're looking for a rental property for a few months, e.g. three to six months, it's best not to rent unseen, but to rent a holiday apartment for a week or two to allow yourself time to look around for a longer-term rental. Properties for rent are advertised in local newspapers and magazines, particularly expatriate publications, and can also be found through property publications in many countries (see **Appendix B)** and numerous websites (see **Appendix C**). Many estate agents offer short and long-term rentals and developers may also rent properties to potential buyers. A rental contract (*contrato de arrendamiento*) is necessary when renting a property, whether long or short-term. Standard, state-sponsored rental contracts are available from tobacconists' (*estancos*).

Long-term Rentals

Spain doesn't have a flourishing long-term (i.e. one year or longer) rental market in resort areas, where it's more common for people to buy, and it can be difficult to find good long-term rentals for a reasonable rent. Most rental properties in resort areas, whether long or short-term, are let furnished (*amueblado*) and long-term unfurnished (*sin amueblar*) properties are difficult to find. However, in major cities, long-term rental properties are usually let unfurnished and furnished properties are in short supply. Rental costs vary considerably depending on the size (number of bedrooms) and quality of a property, its age and the facilities provided. However, the most significant factor affecting rents is the region, the city and the particular neighbourhood.

A small, one or two-bedroom, unfurnished apartment (e.g. 50 to 75m^2) which rents for up to €1,200 per month in Madrid or Barcelona, costs around 50 per cent less in most rural and resort areas outside the main tourist season. Many homeowners are reluctant to sign long-term rental contracts, as a contract for a primary residence (*contrato de arrendamiento de vivienda*) is for a minimum of five years (although it can be terminated earlier by a tenant as specified in the contract) and provides tenants with much more security than a short-term contract.

Short-term Rentals

Short-term rentals are always furnished and are usually for holiday lets or periods of up to a year. A short-term or temporary contract (*contrato de arrendamiento de vivienda por temporada*) is necessary, which provides tenants with fewer rights than a long-term contract. There's an abundance of self-catering properties to rent, including apartments, cottages, farmhouses, townhouses and villas. Rents for short-term rentals are usually higher than for longer lets, particularly in popular holiday areas where many properties are let as self-catering holiday accommodation. However, many agents let self-catering properties in resort areas at a considerable reduction (except for the Canaries) during the low season, which may extend from October to May. Some holiday letting agents divide the rental year into three seasons, e.g. low (October to March), medium (April to June) and high (July to September).

The rent for an average one- or two-bedroom furnished apartment or townhouse during the low season is usually between €500 and €800 a month for a minimum one- or two-month let. Rent is usually paid one month in advance with one month's rent as a deposit. Lets of less than a month are more expensive, e.g. €300 a week for a two-bedroom apartment in the low season, which is some 50 per cent (or less) than the rent charged in the high season. Many hotels and hostels also offer special low rates for long stays during the low season (see below). However, when the rental period includes the peak letting months of July and August, the rent can be prohibitively high.

Standards vary considerably, from dilapidated, ill-equipped apartments to luxury villas with every modern convenience. Always check whether a property is fully equipped (which should mean whatever you want it to mean) and whether it has central heating if you're planning to rent in winter. You may also wish to check whether a property has a telephone line, internet connection and a satellite TV dish. Rentals can be found by contacting owners advertising in the publications listed in **Appendix B** and through estate agents in most areas, many of whom handle rentals as well as sales.

Hotels & Motels

Hotel rates vary depending on the time of year, the exact location and the individual establishment, although you may be able to haggle over rates outside the high season and for long stays (many hotels have special low rates in winter). Hotels located in large towns and cities, coastal resorts and spa towns are the most expensive, and rates in cities such as Madrid and Barcelona are similar to other major European cities. However, inexpensive hotels can be found in most towns, where a single room (*habitación individual*) can usually be found for €20 to €30 and a double (*habitación doble*) for €30 to €40 (usually without a private bath or shower).

Minimum and maximum rates are fixed according to the facilities and the season, although there's no season in the major cities or in the Canaries, and in ski resorts the low season is the summer. Rates are considerably higher in tourist areas during the high season (*temporada alta*) of July and

August, when rooms at any price are hard to find. On the other hand, many hotels have low half or full board rates outside the main season, particularly in winter, when a double room with a bath can be had for around €50 for two, including dinner (buffet) and breakfast – even lower rates may be available for stays of a week or longer. Bed and breakfast accommodation is also available, although it isn't usually budget accommodation when you need to choose a hostel.

Further information about hotels and budget accommodation can be found on page 300.

Home Exchange

An alternative to renting is to exchange your home abroad with one in Spain for a period. This way you can experience home living in Spain for a relatively small cost and may save yourself the expense of a long-term rental. Although there's always an element of risk involved in exchanging your home with another family, most agencies thoroughly vet clients and have a track record of successful swaps. HomeLink International claims 99 per cent of its clients enjoy successful swaps. There are home exchange agencies in most countries, many of which are members of the International Home Exchange Association (IHEA). There are many home exchange companies in the US, including HomeLink International with over 12,500 members in around 50 countries (☐ http://www.swapnow.com). Two long-established home exchange companies in the UK are HomeLink International (☎ 01962-886882, ☐ http://www.homelink.org.uk), which publishes a directory of homes and holiday homes for exchange, and Home Base Holidays (☎ 020-8886 8752, ☐ http://www.homebase-hols.com). *The Home Exchange Guide* by M. Simon and T. Baker (Poyeen Publishing) provides comprehensive information and advice.

GENERAL LOCATION CONSIDERATIONS

Accessibility

Is the proximity to public transport, e.g. an international airport, port or railway station, or access to a motorway important? Don't believe all you're told about the distance or travelling times to the nearest airport, railway station, motorway junction, beach or town, but check for yourself. Note that travelling times to and from airports in resort areas are always longer in the summer months.

Amenities

What local health and social services are provided? How far is the nearest hospital with an emergency department? Are there any English-speaking doctors, dentists and private clinics or hospitals in the area? These are particularly important considerations for older retirees and need thinking about for any long-term retirement plans. What shopping facilities are available in the neighbourhood? How far is it to the nearest sizeable town with good shopping facilities, e.g. a supermarket? How would you get there if your car was off the road or you were unable to drive?

SURVIVAL TIP
Many rural villages are dying and have few shops or facilities so they aren't usually a good choice for a retirement home.

Climate

For most people the climate is probably the most important factor when choosing where to retire. **Bear in mind both the winter and summer climates**: while much of the Spanish coastline enjoys a pleasant climate for most of the year, winters can be cold and summers hot almost anywhere, and the only destination with guaranteed winter sunshine is the Canaries. Consider the aspect of a home – west-facing properties are the hottest in the summer, while north-facing properties receive practically no sun at all except in the height of summer. A home facing south has the best prospect of morning and afternoon sun.

If you're retiring to Spain from northern Europe, it might be one of your priorities to escape wet weather – rainfall is a scarce commodity in many parts of Spain, where drought is common and water shortages frequent. On the other hand, many coastal regions experience torrential rain in the winter, often lasting for days and causing flash flooding. As the Spanish saying goes, 'it never rains to everyone's taste' (*nunca llueve al gusto de todos*)! Many areas also experience frequent high winds, e.g. the easterly *Levante* on the Costa de la Luz and the northerly *Tramontana* in Catalonia and the Balearics.

Community

Do you wish to live in an area with many other expatriates from your home country or as far away from them as possible (practically impossible in many areas)? If you wish to integrate with the local community, avoid the foreign 'ghettos' and choose a Spanish village or an area or development with mainly local inhabitants. However, unless you speak fluent Spanish or intend to learn it, you should think twice before buying a property in a village, although residents in rural areas who take the time and trouble to integrate into the local community are invariably warmly welcomed. If you're buying a property, it's important to check on your prospective neighbours, particularly when buying an apartment. For example, are they noisy, sociable or absent for long periods? Do you think you will get on with them? **Good neighbours are invaluable.**

On the other hand, if you wish to mix only with your compatriots and don't plan to learn Spanish, then living in a predominantly foreign community may be ideal. Many developments and towns are inhabited largely by second homeowners and are like ghost towns for most of the year. In these areas many facilities, businesses and shops are closed outside the main tourist season, when even local services such as public transport and postal collections may be severely curtailed. Visit the development during the winter (November and January are the months when fewest people visit Spain) to check how quiet it is.

Construction

As recent visitors to Spain will have noticed in many regions, the sky-line is often littered with cranes and thousands of new homes are under construction. This is particularly true of the Mediterranean coast – it's estimated that over 1m new homes will be built on the Costa Blanca alone over the next decade – and over a relatively short period of time the landscape in many areas has been changed completely. Previously small, quiet urbanisations have turned into busy, small towns and mountain sides are now covered in apartment blocks.

If you plan to rent or buy a property in an area where there's currently little construction, check the regional government's and local authority's plans for the area. If you're intent on buying off-plan, find out what the short and medium-term building plans are for the surrounding area – if further construction is in the pipeline, you may lose your views and/or privacy and will suffer months of dust and noise (builders start work at 8am).

Crime

What is the local crime rate? In many resort areas, the incidence of housebreaking and burglary is high, which also results in more expensive home insurance. Check the crime rate in the local area, e.g. burglaries, housebreaking, stolen cars and crimes of violence. Is crime increasing or decreasing?

 Professional crooks love isolated houses, particularly those full of expensive furniture and other belongings that they can strip bare at their leisure.

You're much less likely to be the victim of thieves if you live in a village, where crime is virtually unknown (strangers stand out like sore thumbs in villages, where their every move is monitored by the local populace). See also **Crime** on page 306.

Garden

If you're planning to buy a country property or villa with a large garden or a plot of land, bear in mind the high cost and amount of work involved in its upkeep. It's best to choose a property with a low-maintenance garden with little lawn (lawns need watering nearly all-year round in many parts of Spain), plenty of paved areas and drought-loving plants. Beware of buying land with fruit and olive trees – they involve a lot of work including pruning, weeding, watering and harvesting, as well as expertise. Even if you enjoy gardening and are looking forward to being able to spend extra time in the garden during your retirement, bear in mind that you won't always have the energy and may need to employ a gardener, which can be expensive (most charge at least €100 a month for basic maintenance).

Local Council

Is the local municipal council well run? Unfortunately, many are wasteful and simply use any extra income to hire a few more of their cronies or spend it on grandiose schemes. What are the views of other residents? If the municipality is efficiently run you can usually rely on good social and sports services and other facilities. In areas where there are many foreign residents, the town hall may have a foreign residents' department (*departamento de extranjeros*).

Enquire about the social services run by the council in the area you plan to retire to. All municipalities with a population over 20,000 are required by law to provide social services to their inhabitants, but the quality and quantity of services vary considerably from one town to another. Some councils provide excellent provision for pensioners, while others may provide little more than the occasional home visit.

Natural Disasters

Almost all areas of Spain are susceptible to some kind of natural disaster. Floods after torrential rainfall are commonplace in the autumn and winter months along most of the Mediterranean coast and in the Canaries. The south-east corner of the country is an earthquake zone and although most of the frequent earth tremors are barely perceptible, occasionally there's a strong quake causing damage to property. In January 2005, an earthquake of 4.7 on the Richter scale damaged over 200 homes in Murcia. Forest fires are also a common threat to property and lives – 2005 was a particularly 'black' year and nearly 180,000 hectares of forest was burnt in over 26,000 fires and 24 people died.

Noise

Spain is the world's second-noisiest country (after Japan) so if you're planning on a peaceful retirement choose your location carefully. This means making sure your home isn't next to a busy road, industrial plant, commercial area, discotheque or bars. If you plan to live in an apartment block (where the walls are likely to be paper-thin) check whether there are noisy permanent neighbours – visit at lunchtime and in the evening – or properties let to holidaymakers, who often have little respect for others' peace and quiet. Bear in mind that Spaniards generally keep later hours than northern Europeans and few go to bed before midnight.

Traffic noise is a major problem in Spain, particularly motorbikes that roar up and down streets all night. Beware of properties situated on sea-front promenades, which may be an oasis of calm and beautiful sea views most of the year, but can turn into noisy hell-holes in summer with non-stop tourist raves until the early hours.

Parking

If you're planning to buy in a town or city, is there adequate private or free on-street parking for your family and visitors? Is it safe to park in the street? In cities, it's important to have secure off-street parking if you value your car.

SURVIVAL TIP
Parking is a huge problem in most cities and large towns, and private garages or parking spaces may be unobtainable or prohibitively expensive. In out-of-town developments there may also be inadequate parking, particularly in summer, so it's advisable to ensure that you have a private garage or a reserved parking space close to your home.

Traffic congestion is a problem in many towns and resorts, particularly during the high season. Bear in mind that an apartment or townhouse in a town or community development may be some distance from the nearest road or car park. How do you feel about carrying heavy shopping hundreds of metres to your home and possibly up several flights of stairs? If you're planning to buy an apartment above the ground floor, you may wish to ensure that the building has a lift (that works!).

Sports & Leisure Facilities

What's the range and quality of local leisure, sports, community and cultural facilities? What's the proximity to sports facilities such as beaches, golf courses, ski resorts or waterways? Properties in or close to ski and coastal resorts are considerably more expensive, but they also have the best leisure facilities. If you're a keen skier you may want to be close to the Sierra Nevada (Granada) or the Pyrenees, although there are also smaller skiing areas in other regions.

Tourists

If you live in a popular tourist area, i.e. almost anywhere on the Mediterranean coast or the islands, you will be inundated with tourists in the summer. They won't only jam the roads and pack the beaches and shops, but may even occupy your favourite table at your local bar or restaurant! Bear in mind that while a 'front-line' property on the beach sounds attractive and may be ideal for short holidays, it isn't always the best solution for permanent residents.

Many beaches are hopelessly crowded in the peak season, streets may be smelly from restaurants and fast food outlets, parking may be impossible, services stretched to breaking point, and the incessant noise may drive you crazy. You may also have to tolerate water shortages, power cuts and sewage problems. Some people prefer to move inland to higher ground, where it's less humid, you're isolated from the noise and can also enjoy excellent views. On the other hand, getting to and from hillside properties is often precarious and the frequently poorly-maintained roads (usually narrow and unguarded) are definitely for sober, confident drivers only.

SPECIFIC LOCATION CONSIDERATIONS

If possible, you should visit an area a number of times over a period of a few weeks, both on weekdays and at weekends, in order to get a feel for the neighbourhood (walk, don't just drive around!). It's also advisable to visit an area at different times of the year, e.g. in both summer and winter, as somewhere that's wonderful in summer can be forbidding and inhospitable in winter. In any case, experts recommend you rent for a period before deciding to buy (see **Short-term Accommodation Options** on page 89), allowing you to get a good feel for an area without the expense and stress of buying and selling a property.

There are many points to consider regarding the location of a home, which can roughly be divided into the immediate surroundings, the neighbourhood and the general area or region. Take into account your present and future needs – you may be fit and active now, but may not be in a few years' time.

Costa or *Campo*?

Spain's long Mediterranean coastline, stretching from Gibraltar in the south to the French border in the north, is home to a large percentage of the Spanish population and favoured by the majority of foreign retirees – the Costa Blanca and Costa del Sol between them account for the bulk of retirees from the EU. In recent years, however, many foreign homebuyers have purchased property inland, away from the coastal areas. Both coastal and inland areas vary greatly, but in general the following advantages and disadvantages apply to the *costa* and *campo* the length of the coastline.

Costa

Advantages include a mild climate, generally excellent amenities, good airport access, established expatriate communities and often spectacular scenery offering wonderful views. On the other hand, property prices are much higher, the cost of living is generally inflated in most popular tourist resorts, over-crowding is a problem in the summer months when many areas are literally heaving and it can be difficult to escape the 'expatriate bubble'.

Campo

Inland Spain offers beautiful countryside, generally peaceful surroundings, much cheaper property and the chance to discover the 'real' Spain. Disadvantages include a more extreme climate (expect temperatures to be at least five degrees warmer or colder than the coast), lack of amenities and infrastructure in some places, and long travelling times from the nearest airport. Many people who buy a remote country home find that the peace of the countryside palls after a time and they yearn for the more exciting city or coastal nightlife. If you've never lived in the country, it's advisable to rent before buying, and if you choose to retire in an inland area you should make learning Spanish one of your top priorities.

Island Living

Spain's two island groups, the Balearics and Canaries, are both popular retirement destinations and the main islands have good amenities and well-established expatriate communities. Communications between the islands and mainland Spain and Europe are generally good, although ferry services are suspended in bad weather. All the islands are small – even the largest, Majorca, can easily be covered in a day. Living on an island can be claustrophobic, particularly if you plan to live there permanently. Life on an island is more restricted and remote, e.g. you cannot jump into your car and drive to Barcelona or Madrid or 'pop' over the border into Andorra, France, Gibraltar or Portugal. Bear in mind that the Canaries are over two-hours by air from mainland Spain, which means that a change of scenery (apart from a trip to another island) involves more than a day-trip.

POPULAR RETIREMENT HOT-SPOTS

The following section contains information about the most popular areas in Spain with foreign retirees. This book's sister publication, **The Best Places to Buy a Home in Spain** by Joanna Styles (see page 383) contains comprehensive surveys of most regions of Spain and a wealth of information about the facilities and amenities in each area.

The following sources of information have been used in this section:

- **Population** figures are from local or regional censuses, although the figures for foreign residents only reflect those who have registered with the local council and actual figures are considerably higher.

- **Property** price increases in 2005 and the prices quoted per square metre are from the Ministry of Housing's report (🖳 http://www.mviv.es) on house prices during 2005, published in February 2006. The average national price rise in 2005 was 12.6 per cent.

- **Weather** statistics are from the National Weather Centre's website (Instituto Nacional de Meteorología: 🖳 http://www.inm.es).

Balearics

Overview

The Balearics lie some 200km (124mi) south-east of Barcelona and consist of four inhabited islands, Formentera (off the south coast of Ibiza and virtually undeveloped), Ibiza, Majorca and Minorca. Popular with the rich and famous since the 19th century, the Balearics continue to attract thousands of tourists each year.

Climate

The islands generally have a mild and pleasant climate, but winters can be cold (snow isn't uncommon on the mountains in Majorca) and it's generally windy, particularly on Minorca, famous for its more or less permanently windswept conditions.

Getting There by Ferry

Ferries are the main means of getting to and around the Balearics, and the only way of getting to Formentera. Services are efficient, but may be suspended in bad weather. Residents are entitled to discounts (usually one-third) on all fares (paid for by the Spanish government). Ferry services are run by the following companies:

● Balearia – Routes from Barcelona to the three main islands; Denia and Valencia to Ibiza and Majorca; and inter-island services (☎ 902 160 180, 💻 http://www.balearia.net).

● Iscomar – Barcelona and Valencia to Majorca; Denia to Ibiza; and inter-island services (☎ 902 119 128, 💻 http://www.iscomarferrys.com).

● Trasmediterránea – Barcelona and Valencia to the three main islands (☎ 902 454 645, 💻 http://www.trasmediterranea.es).

Health

Regional health authority information is available from ☎ 971 175 600 and 💻 http://portalsalut.caib.es.

Language

The Balearics have two official languages, Spanish and Catalan, spoken as regional dialects, which differ according to the island (i.e. *ibicenco* on Ibiza, *mallorquín* on Majorca and *minorquín* on Minorca). English and German are widely spoken.

Property Market

The islands are home to some of Europe's most expensive real estate (most villas cost in excess of €1m) and witnessed price rises of over 250 per cent from 2000 to 2004! The property market has since shown signs of slowing down, with prices rising by 10.5 per cent during 2005 – less than the national average. Nevertheless, the islands have some of the country's most expensive property with an average price per m² of over €2,000.

Ibiza and Majorca have the most expensive property and a good variety of resale properties ranging from luxury apartments to country mansions (*masías*). Minorca is around 25 to 30 per cent cheaper than the other islands and there's less property for sale. All islands have drastically reduced new development and strict building regulations are in force.

Ibiza

Overview: Ibiza is the closest island to mainland Spain and offers mostly unspoilt landscapes, with plunging cliffs, beautiful sandy coves, and typical Mediterranean olive and almond groves. Renowned for its bohemian atmosphere and nightlife (not for nothing is the island Europe's 'disco capital' during the summer), Ibiza is packed  to bursting point during the summer, but quiet otherwise (services often close during winter).

Main resorts: Popular retirement spots include Ibiza Town, the capital with its beautiful medieval walls and cobbled streets; Santa Eulalia del Río, home to a well-established expatriate community, excellent amenities and the island's cultural capital; Portinatx, in the north-east corner – one of the island's windiest spots; and the luxury villa developments of San Rafael, Cala Salada and Cala Vellada in the west near San Antonio.

Advantages: Stunning natural surroundings including many completely unspoilt bays and good flight connections from many UK airports.

Disadvantages: Overcrowding in the summer months and limited services outside the high season.

Population: 106,250

Expatriate population: 18,500

Average annual hours of sunshine: 2,732

Average annual days of rain: 46

Average January temperature: 11.8°C (53°F)

Average July temperature: 25°C (77°F)

Getting there: Ibiza airport (information ☎ 971 809 000) is well-served by year-round flights from mainly the UK and Germany. Daily flights are also available to Barcelona and Madrid.

Public transport: The main population centres have an efficient bus service, but otherwise private transport is essential. See ▣ http://www. ibizabus.com for details of timetables and routes.

Private transport: Good main roads run from the airport to Ibiza Town and on to San Antonio and Santa Eulalia. The regional government has advanced plans to convert the Ibiza Town-San Antonio highway into a motorway, but vociferous local opposition has delayed work.

Property prices: Average two-bedroom apartment from €200,000, three-bedroom villa with pool from €500,000.

Rental prices (per month): Two-bedroom apartment from €900, three-bedroom villa from €1,500. Long-term rental properties are in short supply in Ibiza and most contracts are for four to six months only.

Retirement developments: Private nursing homes are the only option.

Health facilities: Generally good. The island's public hospital is located in Ibiza Town and there are also private clinics in Ibiza Town and Santa Eulalia.

Amenities: Generally good, although limited outside the high season in many areas.

Leisure activities: Ibiza is essentially an outdoor leisure destination and a water sports paradise. There's a well-established network of expatriate clubs and activities, but some retirees may find the choice of leisure activities somewhat limited.

Language: Spanish and the island's dialect of Catalan, *ibicenco*. English is widely-spoken. The annual invasion of British and German tourists in summer almost eradicates the island's Spanish identity.

Useful websites:

💻 http://www.illesbalears.es – official tourist site for the Balearics

💻 http://www.ibiza-spotlight.com – useful holiday and long-stay information

Majorca

Overview: Majorca is by far the largest island in the group and offers the most varied scenery and the best choice of amenities and leisure activities. The north-west is dominated by the Sierra de Tramontana peaks and inland consists mostly of flat agricultural plains.

Main resorts: Palma, the island's elegant capital and home to half the island's population, is a lively cosmopolitan city with plenty of cultural and social activities. The south-west is the most popular region with foreign residents, mainly based in exclusive developments such as Bendinat, Costa d'en Blanes, Santa Ponsa and

Algaida, where there are good amenities. Nearby villages such as Algaida, Bunyola and Estellencs are also popular with foreigners seeking rural tranquillity, but within easy reach of the capital.

In the north-west the most popular areas include the town of Sóller and its surrounding villages, Pollença and Alcudia, both attractive small towns. The south-east of the island is the quietest, where some areas are peaceful even during the summer. The main towns here are Felanitx, Manacor and Santanyi, all of which have good amenities.

Advantages: A wider choice of amenities and activities than the other islands, beautiful natural surroundings, and the opportunity to enjoy both tranquil rural surroundings and cosmopolitan city life.

Disadvantages: Many areas are overcrowded in the summer, particularly the resorts close to Palma, and Majorca is expensive with among the highest cost of living in Spain.

Population: 758,900

Expatriate population: 98,200

Average annual hours of sunshine: 2,763

Average annual days of rain: 52

Average January temperature: 11.7°C (53°F)

Average July temperature: 25.1°C (77°F)

Getting there: Majorca airport (information ☎ 971 789 681) is Spain's third-busiest and facilities are extremely crowded in the summer. The island has a good choice of flights, particularly from the UK, Germany and mainland Spain.

Public transport: Bus services are excellent in Palma and to and from resorts to the west and east of the city. Other routes are less efficient and often time-consuming. For information on timetables and routes, see 🖳 http://tib.caib.es. Train services run from Palma to Inca and Manacor. There are plans to extend the railway to the north and east coasts.

Private transport: The road network is generally good, particularly around Palma and the southern resorts. Traffic congestion is a problem in the capital. Roads to the north-west (Sóller area) are mountainous.

Property prices: An average two-bedroom apartment costs from €200,000 and a three-bedroom villa with pool from €600,000.

Rental prices (per month): A two-bedroom apartment costs from €750 and a three-bedroom villa from €1,500.

Retirement developments: Private nursing homes are the only option.

Health facilities: Excellent. Majorca has three public hospitals (two in Palma and one in Manacor) and a good network of health centres around the island. Private clinics are plentiful.

Amenities: Generally good, particularly in and around Palma. The east coast of the island is less well-served and many services close in the winter.

Leisure activities: A good choice is available, particularly in Palma where the cultural scene is lively, and the island has a well-established network of expatriate clubs, which tend to be based in the south-east and Palma.

Sports facilities: Majorca is one of the world's top sailing destinations and boasts several world-class marinas. Golf enthusiasts have a choice of 12 courses and racket sports are also popular.

Language: Spanish and the island's dialect of Catalan, *mallorquín*. Outside the resort areas, Majorca has retained much of its local identity and in some rural areas the influence of tourism has been minimal. English and German are widely-spoken.

Useful websites:

🖳 http://www.illesbalears.es – official tourist site for the Balearics

🖳 http://www.majorcadailybulletin.es – daily newspaper in English

Minorca

Overview: Minorca is the least developed of the Balearics and the island that has best retained its traditional way of life and landscape. The whole island is a Biosphere Reserve and famous for its windswept hills, numerous secluded coves and hundreds of prehistoric stone structures dotted almost everywhere. Minorca was under British rule  for most of the eighteenth century and British influences still prevail. Minorca is very much a seasonal tourist destination and quiet for most of the year.

Main resorts: The main towns are Mahón, the capital and one of the Mediterranean's finest harbour towns with Georgian architecture dominating; Ciutadella in the west, which also boasts an elegant harbour; and Fornells, an upmarket resort in the north. The main resort areas are concentrated around Ciutadella, such as Cala en Blanes and Cala 'n Bosch.

Advantages: Virtually unspoilt and stunningly beautiful surroundings, with cheaper property and a lower cost of living than Ibiza and Majorca.

Disadvantages: Limited amenities for most of the year (with the exception of Mahón) and few activities and windy conditions almost year-round.

Population: 82,900
Expatriate population: 7,800 (around half British)
Average annual hours of sunshine: 2,694
Average annual days of rain: 66
Average January temperature: 10.7°C (51°F)
Average July temperature: 24.3°C (75°F)

Getting there: Minorca airport (information ☎ 971 157 000) has a limited number of flights and tickets can be difficult to obtain, particularly outside the high season.

Public transport: Bus services tend to be restricted to Mahón and Ciutadella, and private transport is essential.

Private transport: The road network is based around the main Ciutadella-Mahón road, which forms a backbone across the island.

Property prices: An average two-bedroom apartment costs from €160,000 and a three-bedroom villa with pool from €400,000.

Rental prices (per month): A two-bedroom apartment costs from €700 and a three-bedroom villa from €1,200. Long-term rental property is in short supply on the island.

Retirement developments: Private nursing homes are the only option.

Health facilities: Good. The island's only public hospital is in Mahón. Private health clinics are available in Mahón and Ciutadella.

Amenities: Good in Mahón and Ciutadella. Limited elsewhere.

Leisure activities: Tends to be limited to Mahón and Ciutadella, where there are expatriate clubs.

Sports facilities: Minorca is essentially a destination for water sports enthusiasts and nature lovers. Surfers are particularly well-catered for. There's a golf course near Fornells.

Language: Spanish and the island's dialect of Catalan, menorquín. Minorca has lost little of its island identity and remains very Spanish, although English is widely spoken.

Useful websites:

💻 http://www.illesbaleares.es – official tourist site for the Balearics

💻 http://www.visitmenorca.com – official tourist site for the island

Canaries

Overview

The Canary Islands (or Canaries) are located in the Atlantic, 95km (60mi) off the west coast of Africa and 1,150km (700mi) from the Spanish mainland. They consist of seven inhabited islands (in order of size, largest first): Tenerife, Fuerteventura,

Gran Canaria, Lanzarote, La Palma, La Gomera and Hierro, with a total population of around 1.9m. The Canaries are one of Spain's premier tourist spots (attracting over 7m visitors a year) and are also home to numerous foreign retirees. The *lingua franca* is English and the islands have strong historic ties with the UK.

Climate

The islands enjoy one of the world's best year-round climates (they're often referred to as the 'land of the eternal spring') with mild, warm winters and temperate summers, with daytime temperatures usually between 20°C and 27°C (68°F to 81°F) throughout the year. Rainfall (mostly between November and February) is low, although recent winters have seen some of the islands' wettest weather on record.

Getting There

The main islands of Tenerife, Lanzarote, Fuerteventura and Gran Canaria have international airports and are well served by inexpensive flights from the mainland, the UK, Germany and other European countries. Residents on the islands are entitled to discounts (usually one-third) on all airfares paid for by the Spanish government.

Airport Information

Gran Canaria (☎ 928 579 130), Tenerife (☎ 922 759 000), Lanzarote (☎ 928 846 001), Fuerteventura (☎ 928 860 600).

Ferries

Ferries are essential in the Canaries, particularly to the western islands that aren't served by international flights. Services are suspended during bad weather. Routes are operated by the following companies:

- Fred Olsen – Operates from Tenerife (Los Cristianos) to La Gomera, Agaete (Gran Canaria), El Hierro and La Palma (☎ 902 100 107, 🖳 http://www.fredolsen.es).

- Naviera Almas – ferries travel from Tenerife to the western islands and from Gran Canaria and the eastern islands (☎ 902 456 500, 🖳 http://www.navieraalmas.com).

- Trasmediterránea – weekly services between Cadiz (mainland Spain) and Gran Canaria, La Palma and Tenerife. Inter-island routes from Las Palmas to Santa Cruz, Fuerteventura and Lanzarote (☎ 902 454 645, 💻 http://www.trasmediterranea.es).

Health

Regional health authority information is available on 💻 http://www.gobiernocanarias.org/sanidad (GP appointments can be made online).

Advantages

Year-round pleasant climate, well-established expatriate communities, good choice of leisure activities, high standard of living, lower taxes than mainland Spain.

Disadvantages

Year-round tourism means some areas are permanently crowded, overdevelopment has spoilt some areas and island living can be claustrophobic, particularly on the smaller islands.

Gran Canaria

Overview: Gran Canaria is the third-largest island and has the most varied scenery with dramatic mountains, rugged cliffs and lush vegetation in the north, and rolling sand dunes and palm trees in  the south. The capital, Las Palmas (population 350,000), is the largest town in the islands, the seat of government and one of Europe's largest ports. This cosmopolitan city offers excellent leisure and cultural activities, good shopping and amenities.

Main resorts: The main resorts are found in the south and some areas are highly developed, although most construction is low-rise. Maspalomas (with its endless sandy beach), Playa del Inglés and San Agustín are the most popular areas. Further west is Puerto Mogán, an attractive marina development, and Puerto Rico, both more upmarket resorts.

Population: 802,240

Expatriate population: 60,500 (12 per cent German, 4 per cent British)
Average annual hours of sunshine: 2,851
Average annual days of rain: 25
Average January temperature: 17.9°C (64.4°F)
Average July temperature: 24.6°C (76°F)
Public transport: An excellent bus network connects population centres on the coast to Las Palmas and one another. Inland, bus services are less frequent, but taxis are inexpensive.

Private transport: The island's motorway runs north-south along the coast and is currently being expanded to provide three-lanes in each direction. Traffic congestion is common, particularly in and around Las Palmas. Elsewhere, roads are generally good, although the island's mountainous terrain means most are winding and progress can be slow.

Property prices: €1,746 per m². The average two-bedroom apartment costs from €130,000 and a small villa from €400,000. The property market is stable (prices rose by 10.7 per cent in 2005), although prices in the municipality of San Bartolomé de Tirajana (including Maspalomas and Playa del Inglés) and the Vega de San Mateo (west of Las Palmas) rose by 20 per cent. The buy-to-let market is currently saturated in the south of the island and competition for holiday lets is fierce.

Rental prices (per month): A two-bedroom apartment costs from €700 and a three-bedroom villa from €1,000.

Retirement developments: Construction is planned in Las Palmas and Maspalomas.

Health facilities: Excellent. The island has three large public hospitals in Las Palmas and there are numerous private clinics.

Amenities: Good in Las Palmas and the south. Limited elsewhere.

Leisure activities: Las Palmas has a good choice of cultural and social activities, which are more limited elsewhere.

Sports facilities: Gran Canaria has six golf courses (all in the south) and offers unique sailing opportunities round the island (some areas are only accessible by boat) and to the other Canary islands.

Language: Spanish. Germans and Scandinavians predominate in the southern resorts and English is also widely spoken. Las Palmas and most inland areas remain typically Spanish.

Useful websites:

💻 http://www.grancanaria.com – official tourist site

💻 http://www.canary-guide.com – tourist guide

Lanzarote

Overview: Lanzarote is the fourth-largest island and many claim it's the most spectacular with its famous Fire Mountains and their lunar landscapes, stark volcanic rocks and over 300 extinct volcanoes, which form the Timanfaya National Park (covering around a third of the island). It also has excellent fine white-sand beaches.

Main resorts: The island's resorts are mostly located in the east and include Arrecife (the island's capital), the Costa Teguise (a favourite with windsurfers), Playa de los Pocillos, El Puerto del Carmen, and Playa Blanca (on the southern coast), one of the fastest growing residential areas on the island.

Population: 123,040

Expatriate population: 27,740 (10 per cent German, 15 per cent British, although unofficial figures claim there are around 40,000 British residents on the island)

Average annual hours of sunshine: 2,944

Average annual days of rain: 20

Average January temperature: 17°C (63°F)

Average July temperature: 23.8°C (74°F)

Public transport: The bus service is good in the east of the island, but less frequent elsewhere.

Private transport: Driving on Lanzarote is generally safe – the roads are uncongested – and connections from the airport to the capital and nearby resort areas are good.

Property prices: €1,938 per m². An average two-bedroom apartment costs from €120,000 and a small villa from €300,000. The municipalities of Teguise and Tías have the most expensive property. The property market is currently booming (prices rose by 18 per cent in 2005 – one of the highest rises in the country), reflecting an increased interest in the island from foreign buyers.

Rental prices (per month): A two-bedroom apartment costs from €700 and a three-bedroom townhouse from €1,000. Long-term rental accommodation is difficult to find.

Retirement developments: None.

Health facilities: Limited, although the capital has a hospital.

Amenities: Limited outside the capital.

Leisure activities: Excellent for outdoor types.

Sports facilities: Lanzarote has one golf course, two marinas and excellent windsurfing conditions.

Language: Spanish. Lanzarote has preserved much of its traditional identity, although English is widely spoken.

Useful websites:

⌨ http://www.lanzarote.com

⌨ http://www.a-zpaperwork.com – both these sites contain useful information for property owners and residents

Tenerife

Overview: Tenerife is the largest and best known of the Canaries, and dominated by Spain's highest mountain (Mount Teide, which is often snow-capped), which splits the island in two. The south is arid with sandy beaches, while the north is lush with banana trees and a dramatic, rugged coastline, ancient woodland and black sandy beaches.

Main resorts: The main population centres include the capital, Santa Cruz de Tenerife, a lively cosmopolitan town with a recently renovated centre and good amenities. Santa Cruz regularly tops the list of the most desirable places to live in Spain, although few foreigners live here. Puerto de la Cruz in the north is a typical Canary town with a historic port, while La Laguna is home to the islands' university. Most foreigners favour the resorts in the highly developed south – Playa de las Américas and Los Cristianos are the largest and both have good amenities. Golf del Sur and Amarilla Golf are quieter resorts, while Fañabe and Los Gigantes are more up-market.

Population: 838,900

Expatriate population: 102,000 (16 per cent British, 13 per cent German)

Average annual hours of sunshine: 2,851

Average annual days of rain: 31

Average January temperature: 17.9°C (64°F)

Average July temperature: 24.6°C (76°F)

Public transport: Bus services are generally excellent between the capital and the main resorts in the north and south, but less efficient elsewhere.

Private transport: Motorways connect the capital to Puerto de la Cruz and the airport in the south as far as Playa de las Américas. Congestion is common around the capital. Elsewhere roads are good but winding due to the island's mountainous terrain, and progress can be slow.

Property prices: €1,451 per m². An average two-bedroom apartment costs from €150,000 and a small villa from €400,000. The property market in 2005 was slow with an average annual rise of around 7 per cent, with even lower rises in some areas, e.g. Adeje and Orotava. The most expensive property is found in the municipalities of Adeje and Puerto de la Cruz.

Rental prices (per month): Two-bedroom apartment from €500, three-bedroom villa from €900. Tenerife has a better choice of long-term rental accommodation than the other islands.

Retirement developments: There are a few including Florida Park (🖥 http://www.freedomretirements.co.uk) situated in San Eugenio Alto near Los Cristianos.

Health facilities: Very good. Public hospitals are located at Santa Cruz and La Laguna, and there are numerous private clinics in the south.

Amenities: Excellent.

Leisure activities: Generally a good choice – Santa Cruz offers a varied cultural calendar – and there's a well-established expatriate network of clubs and activities.

Sports facilities: The south has several golf courses and racket sports are popular. Tenerife has five marinas and excellent facilities for water sports.

Language: Spanish. The south of Tenerife is dominated by its English-speaking population, but Santa Cruz and towns in the north have preserved their local identity.

Useful websites:

🖥 http://www.etenerife.com – relocation site

🖥 http://www.sun4free.com– relocation site

Other Islands

Overview: Fuerteventura (pop. 86,650), La Palma (pop. 85,300), La Gomera (pop. 21,700) and El Hierro (pop. 10,500) are considerably smaller islands with limited amenities and facilities. Communications are generally poor and, apart from Fuerteventura airport, which has some international flights, airports provide flights to other islands and mainland Spain only. Outside the capitals, public transport is poor.

The property market is limited, although prices on all the islands have risen in recent years, particularly on El Hierro and La Gomera where annual increases in 2005 were 26 and 19 per cent respectively. Prices per square metre are still, however, some of the lowest in Spain with the exception of Fuerteventura (€1,758).

Useful websites:

- Canaries (⌨ http://www.canarias.org)

- Fuerteventura (⌨ http://www.fuerteventuraturismo.com)

- La Palma (⌨ http://www.lapalmaturismo.com)

- La Gomera (⌨ http://www.gomera-island.com)

- El Hierro (⌨ http://www.elhierro.es)

Costas

Costa Blanca

Overview: The Costa Blanca (Spain's White Coast) stretches from Pilar de la Horadada on the Mar Menor in the south to the bustling town of Denia in the north. The area, one of Europe's premier retirement destinations, consists of flat plains in the south with numerous salt-pans (home to flamingos) and dramatic rocky cliffs in the north. The coastline is generally less developed than the Costa del Sol, although development is currently intense in many  areas, but property is less expensive and the cost of living is lower.

Main resorts: The main residential areas in the south are Pilar de la Horadada, currently expanding and increasingly popular with foreign residents; Orihuela Costa, home to the Costa Blanca's main golf courses and with a large foreign population; Torrevieja, a busy and fast-expanding town with good amenities and services; Guardamar del Segura, which has one of Spain's best beaches; and La Marina and Ciudad Quesada, large inland urbanisations.

North of Alicante, the Costa Blanca is divided into the Marina Baja and Marina Alta. The Marina Baja coastline is home to Villajoyosa, an essentially Spanish resort with a large fishing fleet; Benidorm, Europe's quintessential package-holiday destination with a towering sky-line and excellent amenities and services; Alfaz del Pi inland and its coastal resort of Albir; and the pretty up-market town of Altea which has several luxury developments.

Marina Alta is the most picturesque part of the Costa Blanca with several impressive mountain ranges, sandy bays and cliffs. Resorts include Calpe, the busiest in the area with well-established resident British and German communities; Moraira, an up-market resort with an attractive marina; Jávea, 'the Pearl of the Costa Blanca' with its well-preserved old quarter, fishing port and marina; and Denia, the services centre of the area with good amenities and facilities. Inland is the beautiful Jalón Valley, with almond and orange groves surrounded by mountains.

Advantages: Year-round pleasant climate (Jávea has the best micro-climate in the area), excellent beaches, lively expatriate scene, good value property and good communications.

Disadvantages: Over-crowding in the summer months, over-development in some areas and a surfeit of foreigners in some areas – it can be difficult to get a taste of the 'real Spain'.

Population: Around 1.4m

Expatriate population: Official figures claim around 15 per cent are foreigners (the highest in Spain), although unofficial figures are considerably higher. Nearly half the foreign residents are British. In some municipalities, the foreign resident population has grown significantly over the last few years, e.g. Torrevieja where population figures have increased 65 per cent in the last decade!

Climate: The World Health Organisation considers the Costa Blanca to have one of the world's healthiest climates. The south is considerably warmer and drier than the north.

- **Average annual hours of sunshine:** 2,864

- **Average annual days of rain:** 37

- **Average January temperature:** 11.5°C (52°F)

- **Average July temperature:** 24.9°C (77°F)

Getting there: Alicante airport (information ☎ 966 919 100), situated in the centre of the Costa Blanca, is the main entry point for visitors to the area and offers one of the best choices of flights in Spain, particularly to the UK, with services to all main airports. The airport, which is currently undergoing a major expansion, has good services.

Murcia airport (information ☎ 968 172 000) is handy for resorts in the south and has an increasing number of flights, although it's small and often crowded.

Valencia airport (information ☎ 961 598 500) 10km/6mi to the west of the city, is an alternative for resorts on the Marina Alta, but the choice of flights is limited.

Public transport: Services vary from excellent within the large towns (e.g. Alicante and Benidorm) to almost non-existent in some areas. A (slow) train service connects Alicante and Denia, but buses are the main means of public transport.

Private transport: Private transport is essential unless you live in a large town. Roads are generally good, although often congested, particularly in the summer when tailbacks along the coast roads are almost a permanent feature. Some motorway stretches are toll roads.

Property prices: €1,614 per m². The average two-bedroom apartment costs from €130,000 and a small villa from €250,000. The property market is robust with prices rising by 13.4 per cent in 2005.

Rental prices: A two-bedroom apartment costs from €450 and a three-bedroom villa from €800 (per month).

Retirement developments: An increasingly wide choice: Euroresidencias (🖳 http://www.euroresidencias.es), Kei Retirement (🖳 http://www.kei-retirement.com) and Sanyres (🖳 http://www.sanyres.es) are the largest developers. A new development is under construction in Santa Pola, just south of Alicante, offering apartments and small villas (Santa Pola Life Resort: ☎ 965 147 109, 🖳 http://www.santapolaliferesort.com).

Health facilities: Generally excellent, although public services are over-stretched in many areas. Hospitals are located in Alicante, Denia, Orihuela and Villajoyosa. Private health treatment is widely available. Regional health authority information is available from 🖳 http://www.san.gva.es.

Amenities: Good and improving in most areas and operate year-round in the larger resorts. Alicante and Valencia are lively cities with excellent amenities and shopping.

Leisure activities: Excellent with something for everyone. Many areas have well-established expatriate clubs and societies. Alicante has a reasonable cultural calendar and Valencia has just opened a world-class auditorium.

Sports facilities: Excellent. Golf enthusiasts have a wide choice of courses; bowls teams play regularly; there are several good tennis clubs; marinas line the coast and Valencia hosts the America's Cup in 2007; and you can even play cricket! Valencia also has one of Spain's leading Primera Liga football teams.

Language: Spanish and the regional variation of Catalan, *valenciano*. English is widely-spoken almost everywhere and in many resorts foreign residents outnumber the Spanish, so it can often be difficult to believe you're in Spain. Others resorts, such as Guardamar del Segura and Villajoyosa, have preserved their Spanish identity.

Useful websites:

🖳 http://www.costablanca.org

🖳 http://www.info-costablanca.com

🖳 http://www.thisiscostablanca.com

Further reading: *Costa Blanca Lifeline* (see page 383).

Costa Brava

Overview: Spain's 'Wild Coast' runs from just north of Barcelona to the French border and is one of the country's most stunning coastal stretches. The Costa Brava is typically Mediterranean with tiny coves, fishing villages and pine-covered cliffs. The area is increasingly popular with foreign retirees, attracted by its  beautiful scenery and lack of high-rise development. This is one of Spain's most 'Spanish' coasts and one where English isn't widely spoken.

Main resorts: Main resorts in the south include Blanes, popular with Spanish holiday makers; Lloret de Mar, the birthplace of Spanish package-holidays and still a brash, developed resort; and Tossa de Mar, home to a large artist population.

Beyond Tossa de Mar is the area known as Baix Empordà, the region most favoured by foreign retirees. The main residential centres here includes Sant Feliu de Guixols, with a stunning old quarter and good amenities; nearby Santa Cristina and S'Agaró with small, up-market villa developments; Palamós, a busy and popular harbour town; Calonge with its medieval castle; and Palafrugell, the main services centre for the Baix Empordà. Inland lies the city of Girona, with a stunning old quarter and excellent amenities – Girona regularly tops the list of Spanish provincial capitals with the best quality of life.

The Alt Empordà area is the rockiest section of the Costa Brava and home to several small resorts such as Roses, the main tourist centre; L'Escala with a large fishing port; and the small village of Cadaqués, Dalí's birthplace and popular with artists.

Advantages: Stunning natural surroundings, proximity to Barcelona and France, good amenities and good value property.

Disadvantages: Some resorts are quiet out of season, poor winter weather and you may need to learn Catalan as well as Spanish.

Population: 384,000

Expatriate population: 29,600

Climate: Cooler and wetter than other Mediterranean coasts, although winters are generally mild on the coast. Inland temperatures are much lower in the winter, when snow is common in many parts. The weather on the Alt Empordà is considerably wilder and windier than the south, although high winds are common almost everywhere.

- **Average annual hours of sunshine:** 2,290

- **Average annual days of rain:** 67

- **Average January temperature:** 6.9°C (45°F)

- **Average July temperature:** 22.9°C (73°F)

Getting there: Girona airport (information ☎ 972 186 600) is the main entry point, although the choice of flights is somewhat limited. The airport is small with basic services.

Barcelona airport (information ☎ 932 983 838), Spain's second-busiest, has a much larger choice of destinations including many UK connections. Services are excellent and public transport to the city centre is good.

If you're travelling to the northern region of the Costa Brava, it may be worthwhile investigating flights to the French airports of Montpellier and Perpignan.

Public transport: Bus services are generally efficient between the main towns and to and from Girona and Barcelona. For details of routes and timetables, see 🖥 http://www.sarfa.com (available in English). A regional train service runs inland from Barcelona to the French border, with stops at Girona and Figueres.

Private transport: Private transport is essential in most parts of the Costa Brava. The roads in the south and Baix Empordà are generally good, but those in the Alt Empordà are winding and progress is slow. Roads around popular resorts are very congested in the summer and jams are a permanent feature in and around Barcelona.

Property prices: €1,814 per m². The area had one of Spain's strongest property markets in 2005, reflecting increased interest from foreign retirees, with prices rising by 13.5 per cent. The average two-bedroom apartment costs from €110,000 (south) and from €170,000 in the Baix Empordà. A three-bedroom villa costs from €400,000.

Rental prices (per month): A two-bedroom apartment costs from €600 and a three-bedroom villa from €1,100. There's a shortage of long-term rental accommodation in the area.

Retirement developments: Private nursing homes are the only option unless you live in Barcelona.

Health facilities: Generally very good. Girona's public hospital serves the area and there are also several in Barcelona. Regional health authority information is available from ☎ 934 824 220 and 🖥 http://www.gencat. es/ics. Private medical treatment is widely available and most large towns have clinics.

Amenities: Generally are good in the larger towns, such as Girona and Parafrugell, but limited in the Alt Empordà outside the tourist season.

Leisure activities: A good choice of amenities is provided throughout the Costa Brava and there are small expatriate circles in some areas. Barcelona offers year-round, world-class cultural activities.

Sports facilities: Excellent. There are six golf courses concentrated around the Baix Empordà, 17 marinas along the coast (ideal for exploring by boat as some of its coves are only accessible from the sea) and nearly 20 ski resorts within easy access of the Costa Brava.

Language: Spanish and Catalan. The area has retained much of its Spanish identity and, although English is spoken in the tourist resorts, outside these the ability to speak Spanish is essential. If you choose to live in a rural area or a small village, it's worthwhile learning to speak Catalan.

Useful websites:

🖥 http://www.costabrava.org – official tourist site

Costa Cálida

Overview: Spain's 'Warm Coast' encompasses the coastline in the region of Murcia, stretching from Aguilas in the west to the Mar Menor, south of the Costa Blanca. This is one of Spain's most up and coming *costas*, and its relatively cheap property has attracted foreign buyers in their droves over the last few years.

The coastline is a mixture of arid plains, rocky cliffs and beautiful sandy beaches. Inland Murcia is mostly agricultural with vast areas under plastic for early greenhouse produce. The Mar Menor is Europe's largest salt water lake, covering an area of 170km² (105mi²) and surrounded on all sides by residential developments, the main one being La Manga, a narrow wedge of land between the Mar Menor and the Mediterranean. The area is known for its excellent beaches, the variety of year-round water sports and the therapeutic benefits of its high salinity.

Main resorts: The main residential areas on the Costa Cálida are: Aguilas, a small but growing town but quiet outside the summer; the fishing port of Puerto de Mazarrón – known as the 'Cornwall of Spain' (but without the greenery!) – has miles of virtually beaches and coves; and Cartagena, a historic port and one of Spain's most over-looked cities, which offers good amenities and services. Around the Mar Menor are the attractive small towns of San Pedro de Pinatar, Santiago de la Ribera and Los Alcázares, all with good amenities and facilities, but quiet out of season. La Manga is packed almost to bursting point with high-rise apartments and hotel blocks, and is one of Spain's top tourist destinations. Inland from the Mar Menor are several small towns, such as Torre Pacheco, increasingly popular with foreign residents (mainly British and German) and home to several golf courses.

The Costa Cálida is currently one of the fastest developing areas on the Spanish coastline. There are huge construction plans in the pipeline, particularly for inland destinations, and Murcia's landscape is expected to change considerably over the next few years. Bear this in mind if you plan to retire here.

Advantages: Warm winter climate, good-value property and a relatively unspoilt coastline.

Disadvantages: Massive influx of tourists during the summer, excessive heat in summer and water shortages.

Population (Murcia province): 1.2m (Murcia province)

Expatriate population (Murcia province): Around 120,000 (around 25 per cent British)

Climate: This is Spain's driest area with plenty of sunshine and the country's lowest rainfall in winter. Some people find the summer heat too much and there's often little respite at night.

- **Average annual hours of sunshine:** 2,797

- **Average annual days of rain:** 33

- **Average January temperature:** 10.6°C (51°F)

- **Average July temperature:** 26.2°C (79°F)

Getting there: Communications have improved significantly in the area and Murcia's airport (information ☎ 968 172 000, see page 42), to the north of the Mar Menor, offers a good choice of budget-airline flights, mostly to the UK. The airport is small with over-crowded facilities and no public transport other than taxis.

Alicante airport (information ☎ 966 919 100), 75km/47mi north of Los Alcázares, also serves the eastern section of the Costa Cálida.

Public transport: Bus services around the Mar Menor resorts and La Manga are reasonable, although the frequency is reduced outside the high season. Buses also connect the larger towns with Cartagena and Murcia, otherwise private transport is essential.

Private transport: The road network in the eastern region has been improved greatly and motorways now connect Alicante, Murcia, Cartagena and La Manga (some stretches are toll roads), although they are heavily congested in summer. Outside the motorway network, roads are reasonable but progress can be slow, particularly on roads to Mazarrón.

Property prices: €1,392 per m². The property market continues to be strong in the area, although price rises in 2005 (11.3 per cent) were considerably lower than in previous years when buyers could expect gains of over 20 per cent. An average two-bedroom apartment costs from €150,000 and a small villa from €250,000.

Rental prices (per month): A two-bedroom apartment costs from €400 and a three-bedroom villa from €800.

Retirement developments: Polaris World (🖳 http://www.sainmo.com) is currently constructing five large gated developments centred around shopping centres and golf courses.

Health facilities: Generally good around the Mar Menor where there are four public health centres and a hospital at Santiago de la Ribera. Other public hospitals are located in Cartagena, Lorca and Murcia. Regional health authority information is available from 🖳 http://www.murciasalud.es. Private health treatment is available and clinics can be found in the large towns.

Amenities: Generally good, although the choice is reduced outside the summer season.

Leisure activities: A good choice is available in most large towns and Murcia has a year-round cultural calendar including concerts performed by the city symphony orchestra.

Sports facilities: The area is a paradise for water sport enthusiasts with sailing and diving activities at the top of the list – the marine reserve around Cabo de Palos is one of Europe's best locations. Golf is also popular in the area and there are several courses, mainly situated near the Mar Menor.

Language: Spanish. The area remains very Spanish and is one of the most popular destinations for Spanish holidaymakers in the summer. English is spoken in the main resorts, but the ability to speak Spanish is essential here.
Useful websites:

🖥 http://www.murciaturistica.es – official tourist site

Further reading: *Going Native in Murcia* by Debbie and Marcus Jenkins (Lean Marketing Press).

Costa de Almería

Overview: Situated in the eastern corner of Spain's Mediterranean coast, the Costa de Almería has been top of property investors' lists for the last few years and the trend looks set to continue, at least for the short-term. The landscape here is arid (Europe's only desert is found here) with miles of unspoilt coastline, including the unique and beautiful Cabo de Gata natural park. Vast areas are under plastic and greenhouse produce is the motor behind the area's buoyant economy.

Main resorts: In the west are the resorts of Almerimar with several good golf courses and marinas and increasingly better amenities, and Roquetas del Mar, the most developed resort on this stretch of the coastline offering mainly apartment accommodation. The city of Almería, host to the Mediterranean Games in 2005, has good services and amenities. On the eastern side of the coast, the main resort is Playa de Mojácar with the beautiful white town of Mojácar, home to a thriving artists' colony.

Advantages: Warm winter climate, relatively unspoilt coastline and good-value property.

Disadvantages: Lack of amenities and services outside the summer when some resorts practically close down, the virtually treeless landscape can be monotonous and Almería province has poor communications with the rest of Spain.

Population: 612,350 (provincial figure)

Expatriate population: Around 30,000 (some 7,000 Britons are officially resident in the province)

Climate: This is Spain's driest and hottest corner – an advantage in the winter when coastal temperatures are among southern Europe's warmest, but summers can be very hot.

- **Average annual hours of sunshine:** 2,965

- **Average annual days of rain:** 26

- **Average January temperature:** 12.5°C (55°F)

- **Average July temperature:** 25.7°C (76°F)

Getting there: Almería airport (information ☎ 950 213 700) situated to the north of Almería city, is small with limited facilities, but has a reasonable choice of flights from the UK and Germany. Murcia airport (see page 42) is a good alternative for Mojácar.

Public transport: Generally poor, although services are more efficient during the summer. Private transport is essential.

Private transport: The road network has improved considerably in the last few years and connections with the cities of Granada and Murcia are reasonable. Much of the coastal road to Malaga remains single-carriageway.

Property prices: €1,426 per m². The area's property market was one of the country's strongest in 2005 with price rises of 16 per cent, although you can still buy some of Spain's cheapest coastal properties here. An average two-bedroom apartment costs from €150,000 and a small villa from €270,000. Inland properties are considerably cheaper.

Rental prices (per month): A two-bedroom apartment costs from €400 and a three-bedroom villa from €800.

Retirement developments: The development at Turre (🖥 http://www. kei-retirement.com) and Palazzo Vivaldi situated in Roquetas del Mar (🖥 http://www.wpml.co.uk/palazzo_vivaldi) are currently the main options apart from private nursing homes.

Health facilities: Excellent. Regional health authority information is available from ☎ 902 505 060 and 🖥 http://www.juntadeandalucia.es/servicioandaluzdesalud.

Amenities: Good in the main population centres, although limited outside the high season.

Leisure activities: A reasonable choice and Almería city offers year-round cultural events.

Sports facilities: Generally good. The best choice of water sports and golf is centred around Almerimar. Almería has excellent athletics facilities.

Language: Spanish. The ability to speak Spanish is essential, although English is spoken in resort areas.

Useful websites:

⊟ http://www.andalucia.org – official regional tourist site

⊟ http://www.viva-almeria.com – useful relocation information

Costa de la Luz

Overview: Spain's 'Coast of Light' has one of the country's longest coastlines and runs for over 320km (200mi) along the Atlantic from the Portuguese border in the west to Tarifa on the Strait of Gibraltar, Europe's southernmost tip. The Costa do la Luz is one of tho least spoilt and developed coasts in Spain, although  in recent years its popularity with foreign property buyers and retirees has soared. Attractions here include vast sandy beaches, windswept marshes (including Europe's largest wetlands reserve, Doñana National Park), white villages and delicious seafood. The historic cities of Cadiz, Huelva and Seville are within easy reach, as is the world-famous 'sherry triangle' encompassing Jerez, Puerto de Santa María and Sanlúcar de Barrameda. Resorts are busy in the summer, but quiet otherwise and some of the smaller resorts shut down during the winter.

Geographically, the Costa de la Luz is divided into two by the Doñana National Park and the Guadalquivir River Estuary, which cannot be crossed by cars. Travel from one side of the coast to the other (e.g. from Huelva to Sanlúcar) involves a lengthy detour via Seville.

Main resorts: The western section is known as the 'Spanish Algarve' and is currently one of the country's property hot spots and increasingly popular with foreign residents. Ayamonte is the main town, with good services and amenities. Nearby resorts include Isla Canela, Isla Cristina and Islantilla, home to up-market villa and low-rise apartment developments, golf courses and some amenities. The small towns of Punta Umbría and Mazagón have stunning sandy beaches and pine forests, and good amenities.

South of Doñana is the province of Cadiz where the main resorts include Chiclana, one of the area's fastest growing towns and home to La Barrosa (one of Spain's most beautiful beaches), and Santi Petri, an up-market villa and golf development. Conil has excellent beaches, an interesting old quarter and good amenities, while El Palmar and Caños de Meca on Cape Trafalgar are small resorts with limited amenities. Barbate and its resort, Zahara de los Atunes, where tuna fishing is a prime activity, and Tarifa, Europe's wind-surfing capital, have limited services and are quiet in winter.

Advantages: Virtually unspoilt coastline, endless sandy beaches and proximity to some of Andalusia's most interesting towns and cities.

Disadvantages: Poor communications in the south, quiet out of season when in some areas there's very little happening and almost permanently windy conditions (particularly in Tarifa).

Population: Cadiz province – 1.18m, Huelva province – 490,000

Expatriate population: Around 21,500 foreigners are officially resident in Cadiz province (8,000 from the EU) and 14,500 in Huelva province (2,800 from the EU).

Climate: Generally mild with pleasant year-round temperatures, although it's considerably hotter in the north in the summer. The coast is wetter than the Mediterranean and often very windy.

- **Average annual hours of sunshine:** 2,768

- **Average annual days of rain:** 55

- **Average January temperature:** 12.4°C (55°F)

- **Average July temperature:** 23.4°C (73°F)

Getting there: The area is served by several airports: Faro (information ☎ +351-289 827 203), around 45 minutes drive from Ayamonte, has numerous flights from the UK and is a practical option for the western resorts.

Seville airport (information ☎ 954 449 000) offers only limited international flights.

Jerez airport (information ☎ 956 150 000) is small with few facilities and has a limited number of flights from Germany and the UK.

Gibraltar airport (information ☎ +350-73026) has some flights from the UK and is a good option for visitors to Tarifa and nearby resorts, but queues to leave Gibraltar can be long and you may need a visa to enter Spain.

Malaga airport (see page 38) has the best choice of international flights, but travel time to Tarifa is around two hours.

Public transport: Bus services are generally poor in most parts of the Costa de la Luz and private transport is essential almost everywhere.

Private transport: The western section has a good road network and the A49 motorway connects Seville and Huelva to the Portuguese border.

Communications along the coast in Cadiz province are slowly improving (there are plans to make the entire route dual-carriageway), but progress is slow and traffic congestion a problem.

Property prices: €1,609 per m² in Cadiz province where prices rose by 14 per cent in 2005 and €1,468 per m² in Huelva province where prices rose by 15.6 per cent in 2005. The property market is strong, particularly around Tarifa and the Spanish Algarve. An average two-bedroom apartment costs from €125,000 and a small villa from €300,000.

In recent months, numerous problems with property purchase have come to light in Cadiz province where it's estimated there are literally thousands of illegal properties (illegal construction, additions without planning permission and unregistered buildings). Ask your lawyer to check and double-check a property's status before parting with any money or committing yourself to a purchase.

Rental prices (per month): A two-bedroom apartment costs from €500 and a three-bedroom villa from €850.

Retirement developments: Private nursing homes are the only option.

Health facilities: Generally good, although there are no public hospitals between Algeciras and Cadiz. Public hospitals are located at Algeciras, Cadiz, Huelva, Jerez and La Línea. Regional health authority information is available from ☎ 902 505 060 and 💻 http://www.juntadeandalucia.es/servicioandaluzdesalud. Private health treatment is widely available and there are numerous private clinics

Amenities: Good in the main towns. Limited otherwise.

Leisure activities: This is essentially an 'outdoor destination' and cultural and social amenities are limited, although Seville and Jerez have year-round cultural calendars. The Maestranza Theatre In Seville stages world-class theatre and opera. Relatively few foreigners live in the area, so don't expect to find well-established expatriate networks. Chiclana has the largest British community.

Sports facilities: The Spanish Algarve is a golfer's paradise with eight courses set in stunning surroundings. In Cadiz province there are several courses, although none south of Conil. Water sports enthusiasts are also well catered for with sailing (there are several marinas), wind and kite-surfing, and diving the main activities.

Language: Spanish. The Costa de la Luz is typically Spanish (it's popular with Spanish holidaymakers) and English isn't widely spoken, therefore the ability to speak some Spanish is essential.

Useful websites:

💻 http://www.andalucia.org – official regional tourist site

Costa del Azahar

Overview: Spain's 'Orange Blossom Coast' stretches around 120km (75mi) along the Mediterranean coast from Vinarós in the north to the city of Valencia (Spain's third-largest city) in the south. This is currently one of the least developed coastlines, although increased interest in the area from foreigners, particularly retirees, means development is taking place in many resort areas. Most of the coastline boasts long sandy beaches flanked by vast stretches of flat orange groves, although the northern stretch is mountainous with pine-covered rocky cliffs and bays.

The Costa del Azahar is popular with Spanish holidaymakers in the summer and some resorts are quiet in the winter.

Main resorts: The northern section, known as Baix Maestrat, is the most popular area with foreign residents. The main residential areas include Vinarós, a large town and the main services centre, which has a sizeable expatriate community; Benicarló with an interesting medieval old quarter and large fishing port; Peñíscola, one of the country's most attractive seaside towns, with the largest expatriate community; and Alcossebre, which has up-market, low-rise housing and a modern marina.

Further south in the Plana Alta are Torreblanca, a quintessential package-holiday destination, offers good services; Oropesa del Mar, one of Spain's fastest growing resorts and home to the vast Marina d'Or development; and Benicàssim, a top tourist spot with numerous villa and townhouse developments nearby. South of the city of Castellón are several pleasant towns such as Almassora, Burriana, Moncofa and Nules, all of which have good services and amenities.

Advantages: A relatively unspoilt coastline with spectacular natural surroundings in the north, good-value property and a low cost of living.

Disadvantages: Many resorts are quiet out of season and over-crowded in the summer.

Population: Around 350,000

Expatriate population: Very small – fewer than 5,000 EU nationals are officially resident in the area, although this figure is expected to increase significantly over the next few years.

Climate: Pleasant year-round temperatures with mild winters. Inland, particularly in mountain villages, it can be considerably colder. Summer temperatures are lower than the Costa Blanca or Costa del Sol.

- **Average annual hours of sunshine:** 2,689

- **Average annual days of rain:** 45

- **Average January temperature:** 10.4°C (51°F)

- **Average July temperature:** 24.5°C (76°F)

Getting there: The area currently has no regional airport, but a small airport in Castellón (served by budget airlines only) is expected to open in early 2007. Valencia airport (see page 42) is the main entry point for travellers and Reus airport (see page 41) Costa Dorada section is convenient for those going to the northern part of the Costa del Azahar.

Public transport: Efficient bus services connect the larger towns and the cities of Castellón and Valencia. Valencia and Castellón are also served by a local train service which stops at the main towns on the way. Otherwise private transport is essential.

Private transport: The road network is excellent and the AP7 toll motorway runs along the length of the coast, linking Valencia with Barcelona and France.

Property prices: €1,554 per m². The area saw one of the highest price increases in Spain in 2005 (18.1 per cent), although property is now more expensive than in neighbouring Valencia province and the Costa Cálida. Many new developments are currently under construction, although not on the same scale as the Costa Blanca. The opening of Castellón airport and the celebration of the America's Cup in Valencia in summer 2007 are expected to continue to drive property prices higher over the next two years. An average two-bedroom apartment costs from €140,000 and a small villa from €350,000.

Rental prices (per month): A two-bedroom apartment costs from €600 and a three-bedroom villa from €850.

Retirement developments: Ciudad Senior (☎ 963 169 277, ▣ http://www.acciona-inmobiliaria.com) is under construction in Benicarló and comprises 400 apartments for the over 55s. Euroresidencias (▣ http://www.euroresidencias.es) have a development in Valencia city.

Health facilities: Generally good. Hospitals can be found in Castellón and Valencia. Regional health authority information is available from ▣ http://www.san.gva.es. Private health treatment is available at clinics in the main towns.

Amenities: Good in the larger towns. In some areas amenities are limited outside the summer season.

Leisure activities: A reasonable choice is available and Valencia has an excellent year-round cultural calendar. The expatriate scene is limited in most areas.

Sports facilities: Three golf courses are currently available, although more are planned. Water sports are popular and the area has six marinas.

Language: Spanish and the regional variation of Catalan, *valenciano*, which is widely spoken. English is spoken only in resort areas and foreign residents have had little impact on the area. The ability to speak Spanish (and *valenciano*) is essential.

Useful websites:

🖳 http://www.comunitatvalenciana.com

Costa del Sol

Overview: Along with the Costa Blanca, the Costa del Sol is the most popular area with foreign residents, including thousands of retirees, attracted by the area's year-round pleasant climate, good communications and excellent amenities. The Costa del Sol runs  for 160km (100mi) along the Mediterranean from Gibraltar in the west to Nerja in the east. The coast, mostly flanked by spectacular mountain ranges, offers long sandy beaches in the west, and rocky cliffs and coves in the east.

Main resorts: The western end of the Costa del Sol is the most up-market and most expensive, and includes a number of residential areas. Sotogrande is home to some of Spain's most exclusive properties (mainly villas) and several world-class golf courses and has increasingly better amenities, although it's quiet out of season. Estepona and its nearby coastal stretches is one of the coast's fastest developing areas, with good services and a large expatriate community, while Marbella and its world-famous marina, Puerto Banús, has mainly luxury developments, excellent year-round amenities and a lively expatriate scene.

The central Costa del Sol area is the most densely populated and home to the largest foreign community, which in several areas outnumbers the local populace. Main resorts here include Mijas Costa, an extensive urban sprawl including several developments popular with expatriates and providing good services; Fuengirola, a compact and busy resort, with excellent amenities and services; Benalmádena, one of the fastest growing areas, has good services and a large British population; and Torremolinos, **the** package-holiday destination and still popular with thousands of tourists, with good amenities.

The eastern side of the Costa del Sol is the least developed and still very Spanish (apart from a expatriate pockets). Large stretches remain agricultural and some resorts are quiet out of season and services aren't as comprehensive as the western side. Main resorts include Rincón de la Victoria, essentially a dormitory town for Malaga; Vélez-Málaga with its lively coastal resort, Torre del Mar with its much-improved amenities; and Nerja, one of Spain's most attractive seaside towns with good services.

Inland from the Costa del Sol is increasingly popular with foreign residents seeking cheaper property and quieter surroundings, yet within easy reach of the coast. Towns such as Alhaurín, Antequera, Coín, Colmenar, Monda and Ronda have good amenities and all have considerable expatriate communities.

Advantages: Pleasant year-round climate, well-established expatriate communities, excellent facilities and amenities, and easy access.

Disadvantages: Overdevelopment is rife in most coastal resorts and the infrastructure is over-stretched.

Population: Around 1.2m

Expatriate population: Around 100,000, although unofficial figures are up to four times this.

Climate: Pleasant year-round with the warmest winter temperatures found on the eastern stretch where it's also hotter in the summer. Marbella generally has the best climate. Inland, winters are cooler and summers hotter. It's often windy

- **Average annual hours of sunshine:** 2,815

- **Average annual days of rain:** 43

- **Average January temperature:** 11.9°C (54°F)

- **Average July temperature:** 24.8°C (76°F)

Getting there: Malaga airport (information ☎ 952 048 484), currently undergoing a huge expansion, is Spain's fourth-busiest with an excellent choice of flights to most UK and major European cities.

Gibraltar airport (information ☎ +350-73026, ☎ 956 773 026 from Spain) also serves the area, but only provides flights from the UK and queues to enter Spain can be long.

Public transport: Services vary from excellent in the larger population centres to poor in the coastal areas that aren't served by the Malaga to

Fuengirola train route (although by 2012 trains are expected to run from Estepona to Nerja). Public transport is improving, however, and bus services are more punctual and efficient.

Private transport: Roads are generally good, but traffic congestion is common.

Property prices: €2,049 per m². After several years of frenzied price rises, 2005 saw a rise of 8.2 per cent, one of the lowest in the country. The market is currently saturated with resale properties and some experts predict a fall in prices in the near future, making it an ideal market for buyers. The average two-bedroom apartment costs from €140,000 (€180,000 on the western side) and a small villa from €325,000 (€400,000 on the western side).

Numerous scandals have come to light recently regarding off-plan properties in Marbella, where it's estimated that some 30,000 properties have been built illegally! With several councillors in prison (including the mayor) and the city council virtually bankrupt, Marbella City Council was dissolved in April 2006. Until the legal and political situation is resolved, it's advisable not to buy off-plan or new resale properties in Marbella unless your lawyer obtains official confirmation from the regional government (Junta de Andalucía) that the property has been built legally.

Rental prices (per month): A two-bedroom apartment costs from €650 and a three-bedroom villa from €1,200.

Retirement developments: This area offers the best choice in Spain and there are now several retirement developments including:

- Azul Marbella (🖥 http://www.azulmarbella.com – Puerto Banús);

- Euroresidencias (🖥 http://www.euroresidencias.es – Sotogrande);

- Sanyres (🖥 http://www.sanyres.es – several developments);

- Sensara (🖥 http://www.sensara.com – Benalmádena);

- Sol Andalusi (🖥 http://www.solandalusi.com – Alhaurín de la Torre);

- Vitalis Park (🖥 http://www.vitalispark.com – Rincón de la Victoria);

- Vitania Resort (🖥 http://www.vitania.net – Mijas Costa).

Health facilities: Excellent. There are seven public and numerous private hospitals. All towns have public health centres, although services are overstretched in some areas. Some health centres and hospitals provide translation services run by volunteers. Regional health authority information is available from ☎ 902 505 060 and 🖥 http://www.juntadeandalucia.es/servicioandaluzdesalud.

Amenities: Excellent

Leisure activities: Generally an excellent choice. Expatriate clubs and societies are active everywhere. Cultural activities tend to be concentrated in Malaga.

Sports facilities: The region is a sports paradise, particularly if you're keen on golf (there are over 40 courses), tennis or water sports.

Language: Spanish. English is widely spoken almost everywhere, with the exception of inland areas and Malaga. Expatriate communities exist along most of the coast, particularly between Malaga and Estepona, where foreign residents often outnumber locals.

Foreigners departments: Benalmádena (☎ 952 561 231); Estepona (☎ 952 802 002), Fuengirola (☎ 952 589 357); Marbella (☎ 952 761 116); Mijas (☎ 952 485 900); Nerja (☎ 952 548 401); Torremolinos (☎ 952 374 231).

Useful websites:

🖥 http://www.costadelsol.com

🖥 http://www.visitacostadelsol.com (official tourist website)

🖥 http://www.webmalaga.com

Further reading: *Costa del Sol Lifeline* (see page 383).

Costa Dorada

Overview: One of Spain's longest stretches of coastline, the 'Golden Coast' runs from the river Ebro Delta (one of Europe's largest marine reserves) in the south to the busy town of Castelldefels, south of Barcelona. The Costa Dorada is mainly flat with miles of golden sands and is quiet out of season. Few foreign residents live here and it's generally of more interest to Spanish holidaymakers and property buyers.

Main resorts: The southern section of the coast from the river Ebro to the city of Tarragona (known as the Baix Ebre and Baix Camp) is one of Spain's least developed coastlines. There are several small towns including L'Ampolla and L'Ametlla de Mar, both with fishing ports and marinas, and good amenities; Miami Beach, the largest resort, has a good cultural scene in the summer, but is quiet otherwise; Cambrils is a large town with an excellent marina and year-round services; while Salou, one of Spain's top package-holiday destinations, has good amenities including the huge Port Aventura theme park. Tarragona is a mainly industrial city with impressive Roman ruins, including one of Europe's best preserved amphitheatres.

North of Tarragona, the Baix Penedès and Garraf areas are more developed and less attractive than the Baix Ebre and Baix Camp. Main towns here include Torredembarra, a small but lively town; Calafell and its resort, Segur de Calafell, with excellent beaches and popular with foreign residents; Vilanova I La Geltrú, the main services centre, has excellent amenities and a superb marina; Sitges, one of Spain's most attractive seaside towns, has good amenities and is popular with foreign residents and has a large gay community; and Castelldefels, a popular commuter town for Barcelona, offers excellent facilities and excellent beaches.

Advantages: Lack of development, proximity to Barcelona (one of Europe's most vibrant cities), good-value property and beautiful beaches.

Disadvantages: Poor communications in the south, lack of amenities and activities in some resorts outside the summer.

Population: 410,000

Expatriate population: Very small (around 1,300 Britons are officially resident here)

Climate: Pleasant year-round with warmer temperatures than the Costa Brava, but cooler than the resorts further south. Winters can be cold and damp, particularly in the south near the river Ebro.

- **Average annual hours of sunshine:** 2,509

- **Average annual days of rain:** 51

- **Average January temperature:** 8.9°C (48°F)

- **Average July temperature:** 23.7°C (74°F)

Getting there: Reus airport (information ☎ 977 779 832) has flights from several European destinations, including the UK. The airport is small but has good services.

Barcelona airport is a useful alternative, particularly for resorts in the north of the Costa Dorada. See page 41 for further information.

Public transport: Bus services are reasonable, but less frequent south of Tarragona. Resorts between Tarragona and Barcelona are well-connected with Barcelona by bus and a local train service. There's also a regional train service along the coast from Barcelona to Tortosa, which stops at most resorts.

Private transport: The area has excellent roads with the AP-7 toll-road running the length of the coast to Barcelona together with the A-7 (N-340), which provides access to all resorts. Roads, particularly those nearer Barcelona, tend to be crowded at weekends and during the summer.

Property prices: €1,651 per m². The property market remains stable in the area and prices rose by 8.8 per cent in 2005, one of the lowest increases on the Spanish *costas*, although previous annual gains were the highest in Spain. An average two-bedroom apartment costs from €140,000 and a small villa from €250,000.

Rental prices (per month): A two-bedroom apartment costs from €500 and a three-bedroom villa from €900.

Retirement developments: Private nursing homes are the only option apart from Euroresidencias (⌨ http://www.euroresidencias.es) who have a development in Tarragona.

Health facilities: Generally very good, although resorts in the south are some distance from the nearest public hospital at Tarragona. Regional health authority information is available from ☎ 934 824 220 and ⌨ http://www.gencat.es/ics. Private health treatment is available in the large towns.

Amenities: Good, although limited in some areas outside the summer.

Leisure activities: Generally good. Sitges and Cambrils have excellent year-round cultural calendars and Barcelona provides world-class culture. Expatriate society is limited, although there are sizeable foreign communities in Barcelona and Sitges.

Sports facilities: Good, particularly the provisions for water sports and the marinas in the area are excellent. Golf enthusiasts have a choice of six courses, mainly in the Baix Camp, including one of Europe's top courses at Bonmont Terres Noves.

Language: Spanish and Catalan. English is spoken in resort areas. Despite the huge influx of tourists in the summer, the Costa Dorada remains virtually unmarked by foreign influences and the area is essentially Spanish. The ability to speak Spanish (and Catalan) is essential.

Useful websites:

⌨ http://www.costadaurada.org

Barcelona, Madrid & Northern Spain

Barcelona

Overview: Barcelona is Spain's second-largest city and one of Europe's most vibrant cities with a flamboyant international cultural scene. Home to a magnificent range of architecture from the Gothic old quarter boasting several impressive medieval monuments to the ultra-modern Agbar Tower finished in 2005, via numerous fine examples of Modernism, Barcelona is increasingly popular with foreign retirees attracted by the city's excellent communications, amenities and services.

Popular residential areas: Born, in the old town and within easy reach of amenities; Eixample, north of the old quarter, is highly sought-after and its elegant apartments are some of the most expensive in the city; Barceloneta, one of the city's most up and coming areas, offers the best of the beach and the city; and Sarrià, to the north of the city centre, with terraced and detached houses and good public transport links.

Advantages: Plenty to do and see, excellent year-round cultural calendar and good communications.

Disadvantages: Pollution, traffic congestion, lack of parking and high property prices.

Population: 1.5m

Expatriate population: 260,000 (around 5,000 Britons live here).

Climate: Mild year-round although winters can be very wet.

- **Average annual hours of sunshine:** 2,524

- **Average annual days of rain:** 55

- **Average January temperature:** 8.9°C (48°F)

- **Average July temperature:** 23°C (73°F)

Getting there: Barcelona airport (information ☎ 932 983 838) is the country's second-busiest and offers an excellent choice of flights to many European destinations, including several UK airports, and domestic flights. Public transport to the city centre is good and taxis are reasonable.

Public transport: Generally excellent: The city metro is efficient, although many parts of the city aren't covered by the six lines. Local train routes serve the outlying districts including coastal resorts and bus services are efficient and cover most of the city. Transport information is available from ▣ http://www.tmb.net.

Private transport: Barcelona suffers from almost permanent traffic congestion and if possible, it's better (and quicker) to use public transport. Street parking is a nightmare and it's worth buying a parking space or renting a space in a garage. Access to the city is via dual-carriageway in all directions and roads are generally good.

Property prices: €2,366 per m². Home to the country's second most expensive housing, the Barcelona property market is currently experiencing less buoyancy than in previous years and prices rose by 8.8 per cent in 2005. An average two-bedroom apartment costs from €250,000 and a townhouse from €1m.

Rental prices (per month): A two-bedroom apartment costs from €750 and a three-bedroom townhouse from €1,000.

Retirement developments: Private nursing homes are generally the only option except for Euroresidencias (🖥 http://www.euroresidencias.es) with a development in the Les Corts area of the city and Casa Club (🖥 http://casaclubsc.com – in Catalan only) situated in Sant Cugat, north of the city.

Health facilities: Excellent. Barcelona has good public hospitals, including several specialist hospitals. Regional health authority information is available from ☎ 934 824 220 and 🖥 http://www.gencat.es/ics. Private health treatment is widely available in the city, home to three of Spain's top four private clinics.

Amenities: Excellent, although better in some districts than in others.

Leisure activities: An almost unlimited range is on offer from the cultural (museums, theatre, opera, etc.) to the social – Barcelona is a very cosmopolitan city.

Sports facilities: Excellent, including the 1992 Olympic facilities.

Language: Spanish and Catalan. English is spoken in tourist spots, but otherwise, the ability to speak Spanish (and Catalan) is essential.

Useful websites:

🖥 http://www.bcn.es

🖥 http://www.xbarcelona.com

Madrid

Overview: Spain's capital city offers fine architecture, from elegant palaces to avant garde office blocks, world-class museums including the 'Art Triangle' (the Prado, Reina Sofía and Thyssen Museums), a year-round cultural calendar, Spain's best shopping, and excellent services and amenities. Madrid is home to a large foreign population, although few foreigners choose to retire here.

Popular Residential Areas: Those within close proximity to the city centre include the Salamanca and San Jerónimo districts, close to the main museums and parks, and relatively quiet. Accommodation here is expensive and consists mainly of large period apartments; Chamartín, popular with foreign residents, has good amenities and connections to the city centre, while Lavapiés, one of Spain's most multi-cultural districts, offers a lively atmosphere and more affordable accommodation.

Districts in the suburbs popular with foreign residents include Tres Cantos, a pleasant modern town with good amenities and public transport links to the centre; La Moraleja, probably the country's most exclusive residential area and home to many rich and famous residents; Las Rozas and Majadahonda, with good amenities and mostly modern developments; and Aravaca and Moncloa, quiet districts within easy reach of the centre.

Advantages: Good communications and plenty to do and see

Disadvantages: Pollution, traffic congestion, high noise levels and expensive property.

Population: 3.1m

Expatriate population: 453,900 (around 3,800 Britons live here)

Climate: Continental climate with cold, dry winters and hot summers, when temperatures often exceed 30°C (86°F), although nights are usually cool.

- **Average annual hours of sunshine:** 2,761

- **Average annual days of rain:** 60

- **Average January temperature:** 5.7°C (42°F)

- **Average July temperature:** 25°C (77°F)

Getting there: Madrid airport (information ☎ 902 404 704) has recently been extensively modernised and a vast new terminal (T4) opened. Flights are available to many European and Central and South American destinations, but limited to other parts of the world. Facilities are excellent and public transport to the city centre is good.

Public transport: The public transport network is efficient and cheap, and covers most of the city and outlying districts. Madrid has an extensive metro service (13 lines, 🖳 http://www.metromadrid.es), numerous local train services operate from the city centre to the suburbs, and a bus network covers most areas (🖳 http://www.emtmadrid.es).

Private transport: Although Madrid has one of the best road networks in the country with countless dual-carriageways connecting the city with all corners of Spain, it also has the worst traffic congestion (spending hours in traffic jams is common) and parking is almost impossible.

Property prices: €2,785 per m². Madrid has Spain's most expensive property and some of the country's most frenzied building activity – prices rose by 10.5 per cent in 2005. An average two-bedroom apartment costs from €200,000 and a small townhouse from €400,000.

Rental prices (per month): A two-bedroom apartment costs from €750 and a three-bedroom villa from €1,250.

Retirement developments: Euroresidencias (🖳 http://www.euro residencias.es) and Sanyres (🖳 http://www.sanyres.es) have several developments in and around the capital.

Health facilities: As you would expect for a capital city, Madrid has excellent health facilities, although waiting lists are among the longest in Spain. There are numerous public hospitals, including several specialist centres. Regional health authority information is available from 🖳 http://www.madrid.org/sanidad/es. Private health facilities are also excellent with a wide choice of prestigious clinics.

Amenities: Excellent, although better in some districts than in others.

Leisure activities: Among the best in Spain, plenty going on year round.

Sports facilities: Excellent with most sports catered for. The city has around 20 golf courses within close proximity and three ski resorts are within easy reach.

Language: Spanish. Madrid is a cosmopolitan city, but in spite of the influx of thousands of immigrants, society remains traditionally Spanish and English is spoken only in tourist spots. The ability to speak Spanish is essential.

Useful websites:

🖳 http://www.madrid.org/turismo

Northern Spain

Overview: Northern Spain, also known as the Costa Verde ('Green Coast'), is a succession of spectacular mountain ranges, rocky coves that are home to small fishing ports, rolling hills and historic cities. Four regions line this part of Spain as it runs for miles along the Atlantic and Cantabrian coasts to the French border in the Pyrenees. In the far west is Galicia, Spain's greenest and wettest region,

1. Galicia
2. Asturias
3. Cantabria
4. Basque Country

with a strong Celtic influence and some of Europe's finest seafood, bordering Asturias with its stunning peaks, rural landscapes and small sandy coves. The Picos de Europa mountains, home to unique flora and fauna as well as spectacular walking and climbing, lie within both Asturias and the smaller region of Cantabria, further east. Cantabria has fine sandy beaches, green pastures and attractive stone villages. In the east is the Basque Country (País Vasco or Euskadi), a unique mixture of rural landscapes and industrial ports based around Bilbao, one of Spain's up and coming cities boasting the fine Guggenheim Museum.

In spite of its good communications, the Basque Country isn't popular with foreign property owners and few foreigners retire here. The rest of Northern Spain is still relatively unknown to foreign visitors, although in recent years there has been a marked increase in the number of foreign residents, including many retirees. This trend is expected to continue. Resorts in Northern Spain tend to be packed to bursting point in July and August, but are otherwise quiet.

Main resorts:

- **Asturias:** Popular seaside spots and busy fishing ports include Llanes, Luarca and Ribadesella. The main cities of Gijón and Oviedo are both attractive, lively centres with excellent amenities. In the Picos de Europa, Cangas de Onís and Arriondas are busy market towns within easy reach of the mountains.

- **The Basque Country:** The main cities all have excellent amenities (Vitoria has one of the highest standards of living in Spain) and San Sebastián is a particular gem with fine architecture and a beautiful beach. Property is expensive, as is the cost of living.

- **Cantabria:** Seaside resorts include Comillas, Laredo, Santoña and San Vicente de la Barquera, with reasonable year-round services. Santander, the capital, is an elegant seaside city with good amenities and communications (including a ferry service to the UK).

- **Galicia:** The most popular areas with foreign residents include the Miño Valley in the south (on the border with Portugal) with verdant hills, superb beaches and plenty of outdoor activities; Santiago de Compostela, one of Spain's most beautiful cities and a major pilgrimage centre, with excellent amenities and services; and Lugo, a small attractive city with a well-preserved medieval centre and good services.

Asturias and Cantabria also have dozens of attractive small villages and hamlets, but these are often difficult to get to and services and amenities are basic.

Advantages: Spectacular natural surroundings, generally good-value property and an unspoilt coastline.

Disadvantages: Less sun than the rest of Spain, poor communications in the west and little to do in many rural spots.

Climate: Coastal areas generally have a mild climate with wet and windy winters, and good summers, although sunshine isn't guaranteed here as it is in other parts of Spain. Inland temperatures are more extreme with cold winters in most places (snow is common) and humid summers – southern parts of inland Galicia can be stiflingly hot.

- **Asturias**

  - **Average annual hours of sunshine:** 1,702

  - **Average annual days of rain:** 131

  - **Average January temperature:** 9°C (48°F)

  - **Average July temperature:** 17.9°C (64°F)

- **Basque Country**

  - **Average annual hours of sunshine:** 1,584

  - **Average annual days of rain:** 128

  - **Average January temperature:** 9°C (48°F)

  - **Average July temperature:** 20°C (68°F)

- **Cantabria**

  - **Average annual hours of sunshine:** 1,638

  - **Average annual days of rain:** 128

  - **Average January temperature:** 9.5°C (50°F)

  - **Average July temperature:** 19.4°C (68°F)

- **Galicia**

  - **Average annual hours of sunshine:** 1,966

  - **Average annual days of rain:** 131

  - **Average January temperature:** 10.4°C (50°F)

  - **Average July temperature:** 18.7°C (65°F)

Getting there: Four airports serve the area: Bilbao airport (information ☎ 944 869 664) is the largest and has the best choice of flights including to several airports in the UK. Santander airport (information ☎ 942 202 100) is tiny with a limited range of flights. Asturias airport (information ☎ 985 127 500) is slightly larger, but again has few flights. Galicia's regional airport (information ☎ 981 547 501), located near Santiago de Compostela, is small with limited facilities and few international flights.

Public transport: The large towns and cities have good public transport network including a metro in Bilbao, but outside these areas services are less reliable and in many rural areas there's no public transport at all. Asturias has a good local train network connecting Avilés, Gijón and Oviedo. Private transport is essential in most parts of Northern Spain.

Private transport: Roads connecting the main cities are generally good and the Cantabrian motorway runs most of the way along the coast. The Basque Country has the best road network in Spain and journeys are generally fast, although roads can be congested. Roads in rural areas aren't always well maintained and those in mountain areas are often closed in winter.

Property: Northern Spain (with the exception of the Basque cities and Santander) has some of the country's cheapest property and real bargains can be found in rural areas. In complete contrast, Santander and San Sebastián have some of Spain's most expensive homes with prices for seafront apartments exceeding those paid for period apartments in central Madrid.

Property prices:

- **Asturias:** €1,506 per m². Despite increased foreign interest in the region, property prices remain reasonable and rose by 10 per cent in 2005.

- **Basque Country:** €2,585 per m², one of the highest in Spain. Foreign buyers show little interest in this part of Spain where the property market is buoyant and prices rose by 11 per cent in 2005. With the exception of the cities of San Sebastián and Vitoria (both home to some of the country's most expensive property), prices for a two-bedroom apartment are from €180,000 and from €160,000 for a small rural property.

- **Cantabria:** €1,730 per m². The property market is generally slow (prices rose by 6.4 per cent in 2005) and despite the region's high average price per square metre, there are plenty of cheap rural properties. An average two-bedroom apartment costs from €140,000 and a traditional (restored) rural property from €75,000.

- **Galicia:** €1,282 per m². Galicia has one of Spain's cheapest property markets and foreign interest has increased markedly over the last few years, reflected in the annual price rise of over 14 per cent in 2005. An average two-bedroom apartment costs from €120,000 and a small villa from €150,000.

Rental prices (per month): A two-bedroom apartment costs from €500 and a three-bedroom apartment from €750. Prices are much higher in Santander and Basque cities. Long-term rural rental accommodation is in short supply.

Retirement developments: Private nursing homes are the only option except in Santander where there's a Euroresidencias development (🖳 http://www.euroresidencias.es).

Health facilities: Generally very good throughout the area. Asturias has one of Spain's highest healthcare budgets and the region's aging population (one of the country's oldest) is well provided for. There are seven public hospitals and health centres in most population centres. Regional health authority information is available from ☎ 012 and 🖳 http://www.princast.es. The Basque Country generally has good health facilities with numerous state hospitals and health centres. Regional health information is available from 🖳 http://www.osanet.euskadi.net.

Cantabria has three public hospitals located in Laredo, Santander and Sierrallana. Regional health authority information is available from ☎ 942 202 770 and 🖳 http://www.scsalud.es. Galicia also provides good public healthcare (information is available from ☎ 981 542 737 and 🖳 http://www.sergas.es – GP appointments can be booked online). Private health treatment is available in the larger towns.

Amenities: Generally excellent in large towns and cities, limited elsewhere, particularly outside the summer.

Leisure activities: Most cities have a good choice of activities including year-round cultural calendars. Outside the main population centres, possibilities are limited. Northern Spain is essentially an outdoor destination.

Sports facilities: Walkers and climbers have endless opportunities here. Water sports facilities are also good and there are several golf courses.

Language: Spanish in Asturias and Cantabria. Spanish and Galician (*gallego*) in Galicia, where some people don't speak Spanish in rural areas. Spanish and Basque (*vasco* or *euskera*) in the Basque Country. English isn't widely spoken and the ability to speak Spanish is essential.

Useful websites:

- Asturias – 🖳 http://www.infoasturias.com

- Basque Country – 🖳 http://www.paisvascoturismo.net

- Cantabria – 🖳 http://www.turismo.cantabria.org

- Galicia – 🖳 http://www.turgalicia.es

5.

PROPERTY MATTERS

Once you've chosen your retirement spot, you'll need to find somewhere to live. Spain has a wealth of property options for all pockets, although your final choice may depend more on your personal circumstances and whether you plan to live permanently in Spain, than your finances.

 Experts advise renting for a period before buying a property in order to avoid making a costly and stressful mistake.

Property in Spain is generally cheaper than in most northern European countries and many retirees use their retirement as an opportunity to downsize. Your property in your home country can usually be sold for a higher price than a home in Spain and you can use the equity released as a financial safety net or to supplement your pension.

This chapter includes essential information on what to buy, a brief guide to the buying process and letting your Spanish property. Information is also provided about home security, utilities (electricity, gas and water – connections and general information), and heating and air-conditioning.

For comprehensive information about buying a property in Spain, see this book's best-selling sister publication, **Buying a Home in Spain** by David Hampshire, the only Spanish property book that's updated annually (see page 383).

WHAT SORT OF PROPERTY?

Spain offers a wealth of different properties, from small holiday apartments to huge country mansions set in acres of land, with just about everything in between. Each region has a typical type of property, for example a *cortijo* (large white-washed country house in Andalusia), a *masía* (a large stone country house in Cataluña) or a *pazo* (a typical country house) in Galicia. The purchase and restoration of Spanish country homes is becoming increasingly popular among foreigners, particularly those seeking to establish small hotels or bed and breakfast businesses (although this isn't exactly retirement!). However, the vast majority of foreign retirees buy on the *costas* or islands where property generally consists of apartments, townhouses and villas, most of which are purpose-built for the holiday-home market.

> **SURVIVAL TIP**
> When choosing a retirement property, bear in mind
> restoration, refurbishment and maintenance costs – do
> you want to spend large amounts of time and money on
> doing up a property and/or on its upkeep?

Below is a brief guide to the types of property available in Spain, including country properties.

Apartments

Apartments and flats (*apartamento* or *piso*) abound in Spain and the vast majority of Spaniards live in apartment blocks, particularly in large towns and cities. Resorts such as Benalmadena, Benidorm, Lloret del Mar, Magaluf and Torremolinos are inundated with apartment blocks purpose-built for the holiday market, although it's now difficult to find any stretch of popular coastline without a skyline of apartment blocks (and high-rise hotels). Construction of apartment blocks has continued unabated throughout Spain (as the numerous cranes dotting the horizon testify) since the late '60s, and there's remains a buoyant market.

The quality and size varies enormously, from tiny studio apartments crammed into multi-storey blocks with '70s-style bathroom fittings to spacious marble-floored, luxury apartments complete with all mod-cons. Some are dark and cramped and situated in small back streets, while others are spacious front-line beach or golf developments with views stretching as far as the eye can see. Prices range from €80,000 for a small one-bedroom apartment in a less popular resort (e.g. on the Costa del Azahar or Costa Cálida) to well over €1m on Marbella's golden mile. Bargain apartments are few and far between in popular areas and lower-priced properties usually require extensive modernisation and renovation. Under Spanish law, all owners of apartments (irrespective of their number or size) are members of the community of owners (*comunidad de propietarios* – see page 150) and as such must abide by the community's rules and regulations and pay community fees.

Advantages of apartments include low maintenance (once you've carried out any necessary work), good security – especially if the block with 24-hour security or a concierge (*portero*) – and the use of communal gardens and pool (and possibly other facilities such as tennis courts). Apartments situated in towns also have the added advantage of local facilities and amenities within walking distance. Disadvantages are noisy neighbours, poorly-maintained communities, crowded developments during holidays and possibly poor parking facilities if you don't have your own garage or parking space.

Townhouses

Townhouses (*casa adosada*) are generally rows of terraced houses, often in typical regional style set around communal gardens with a pool. Townhouse developments are increasingly popular around large towns and cities, particularly Madrid, where there are vast suburbs lined with row upon row of townhouses. In coastal resorts, townhouses are often built in a style known as the 'Mediterranean village' (*pueblo Mediterráneo*) and houses may be white-washed or, as is increasingly popular nowadays, painted in pastel shades. Townhouses are usually spacious with roomspace laid out over three or four floors, including a basement garage and storage, and a roof area with a roof terrace known as a *solarium*. Townhouses generally have little outside space or garden except for a small patch at the front and back, often paved as a patio. Construction tends to be recent and is generally of reasonable to good quality.

Townhouses usually form part of a community property (see below) and owners must abide by the community's rules and regulations and pay community fees.

Townhouses are generally located on the outskirts of resorts and towns or within urbanisations (see below), with prices ranging from €100,000 for a one-bedroom townhouse in a less popular area, e.g. Costa de la Luz, to over €750,000 for three bedrooms in a top quality development or resort. Advantages include low maintenance, plenty of living and storage space, use of communal gardens and pool without the upkeep, and community living with fewer neighbours than in an apartment. On the other hand, you may suffer from noisy neighbours, poorly-maintained communities, crowded developments during holidays, a lack of parking and exhaustion from climbing the endless flights of stairs!

Villas

In general, the Spanish don't live in detached houses (*casa, chalet* or *villa*) and in many large towns and cities it's difficult to find a large house unless it's a mansion or palace belonging to the local aristocracy. On the coast, however, detached houses abound and are generally owned by foreigners or wealthy Spaniards who use them as second homes. Some villas form part of a development and may share communal gardens and a pool, and are situated on small individual plots, while others are set in huge grounds. Villas built in the '60s and '70s tend to be single-storey and often need extensive renovation work, particularly if they've only been used as holiday homes and not properly maintained. Construction quality can be poor in older properties, although the quality is usually excellent in newer properties, which tend to have at least two storeys and be more spacious than older villas. Prices start at €200,000 for a small two-bedroom villa with a communal pool in a less popular area, although villas in many parts of the Costa del Sol, the northern part of the Costa Blanca, and Ibiza and Majorca cost at least €1m.

If a villa forms part of a community property (see below), owners must abide by the community's rules and regulations, and pay community fees.

Urbanisations

Urbanisations (*urbanizaciones*) are purpose-built estates or developments which may include apartments, townhouses and villas. They form an essential part of Spanish resort landscapes and cities, and most popular areas are packed with them. Some have been part of the holiday home market since the first sun-worshippers arrived in Spain in the '60s, although most are more recent. Some are small with a limited number of properties, while others are huge developments, almost towns in their own right, such as Sitio de Calahonda on the Costa del Sol or La Marina in the southern Costa Blanca.

The type of property available in urbanisations is varied and caters for different needs and price ranges, and many urbanisations contain a mixture of apartment blocks and individual villas. Facilities and amenities also vary hugely from extensive shopping facilities, transport systems and sports developments to little more than a local bar (which may only be open in summer). Some urbanisations have permanent resident populations while others become ghost towns outside the high season. Many urbanisations are populated mainly by foreigners and some tend to cater mainly for one nationality only, e.g. British or German, particularly on the Costa del Sol, Costa Blanca and the islands.

Advantages include general tranquillity, pleasant surroundings, good security (if the urbanisation has private security), and a ready-made foreign community often with a good social scene. Disadvantages may include few amenities and facilities, limited public spending (local councils collect rates and local taxes enthusiastically, but invest as little as possible in urbanisations) and a possibly claustrophobic expatriate atmosphere.

Most urbanisations are community properties (see below), where owners, who automatically form a community of owners, must abide by the community's rules and regulations and pay community fees. In some cases, a property may belong to a sub-community within the larger community of the urbanisation.

Country Properties

As property prices have risen on the coast and resort areas have become more crowded, foreigners are increasingly looking further inland to the Spanish countryside in their search for a home. Property here, known as *fincas* – a term loosely used to describe just about anything from a hut to a well-preserved farmhouse – is generally cheaper than resort property and widely available except in areas in the immediate vicinity of coastal resorts. *Fincas* range from a ruin set in a large area of land to cottages or large country homes, sometimes together with working farmland. Almost all *fincas* come with large plots of land and may include fruit trees, olive groves or meadows. Renovation is almost always necessary unless you pay a premium and buy a property that's already been modernised.

Advantages of country properties include cheaper prices, peace and quiet, low local taxes and the opportunity to live in the 'real' Spain. On the other hand, rural properties usually involve extensive maintenance as well as restoration work, utilities may be poor or non-existent, amenities and facilities are often some distance away and you don't have the advantage of a ready-made community. The good news is that Spanish village communities are generally among the friendliest and most welcoming in the world, although you will need to speak good Spanish to become part of it.

Retirement Developments

Retirement developments (or sheltered housing) are generally purpose-built communities for the over 55's and are still quite rare in Spain where some regions have none at all. However, increased interest from retirees (mostly foreigners), particularly on the Costa Blanca and Costa del Sol, means purpose-built retirement developments are gradually making an appearance on the Spanish property market. Most urbanisations are developed by foreign companies for foreigners, as the Spanish prefer to live among their family and friends in their 'twilight' years. Many sheltered housing developments attract older people, e.g. aged 65 plus, although they're increasingly popular with younger retirees, e.g. the over 55's.

Developments usually consist of one and two-bedroom apartments or a combination of apartments, townhouses and villas, and many provide restaurants giving residents the choice of self-catering or eating out. The quality of construction varies and older developments tend to be in need of refurbishment, although some of the more recently-built developments contain luxury fittings and furnishings.

Freehold property prices start at €100,000 for a one-bedroom apartment and €250,000 for a small detached villa. If you buy freehold, check the development's regulations regarding inheritance of the property – some developments only allow the property to be inherited by someone aged over 55. Leasehold options are also available such as leasehold for 99 years or a life-lease lasting the owner's lifetime. Leasehold options are considerably cheaper, e.g. €45,000 for a two-bedroom apartment. If you choose a leasehold option, find out who (if anyone) is permitted to inherit the property.

Properties usually have central heating, air-conditioning, fully-fitted kitchens and satellite TV. A wide range of communal facilities and services are provided, including medical and dental clinics (possibly with a resident doctor and dentist), nursing facilities, lounges, laundry, housekeeping, sauna, Jacuzzi, restaurant, bar, meal delivery, handyman, mini-supermarket and shops, post and banking facilities, guest apartments, free local transport, 24-hour security with closed-circuit television (CCTV), intercom service, personal emergency alarm system and a 24-hour multi-lingual reception. Sports and leisure services may include swimming pools, tennis courts, lawn bowling, gymnasium, video room, library and a social club.

The vast majority of retirement developments levy monthly service charges, e.g. between €150 and €500, which may include a number of weeks' (e.g. six) nursing care per illness, per year in a residents' nursing home. Charges usually include heating and air-conditioning, hot and cold water, satellite TV, and some or all the other services listed above. Bear in mind that the more facilities a development offers, the higher the service charges will be. It's probably only worthwhile paying high service charges if you feel you're going to benefit from most of the facilities.

Retirement developments are increasingly popular among foreign residents in Spain and many properties are sold within a short time of the project's release onto the market. The most popular retirement developments – or those in areas where there's little choice – have waiting lists for properties. Bear this in mind if you're planning to live in a purpose-built retirement development because you may have to commit yourself to a property purchase well in advance (e.g. three years) if you want to be sure of securing a property.

The main companies currently development retirement developments are:

- **Euroresidencias** (🖳 http://www.euroresidencias.es) – 12 retirement developments throughout Spain, with a further seven due to open before 2008, located in Alicante, Barcelona, Galicia, Madrid, Santander, Sotogrande, Tarragona and Valencia.

- **Kei Retirement** (🖳 http://www.kei-retirement.com) – developments are centred on the Costa Blanca with another in Turre, Almería.

- **Polaris World** (🖳 http://www.sainmo.com) – several developments in Murcia, based around the Mar Menor.

- **Sanyres** (🖳 http://www.sanyres.es) – Spain's largest builder of retirement developments with 'Hotel Residences' in several locations including the Costa Blanca, Costa del Sol and Madrid. Sanyres plans to add nearly 7,000 homes by 2007.

For retirement developments in specific areas see **Popular Retirement Hot Spots** on page 100. For information about nursing homes see page 221.

Community Properties

Properties in Spain with common elements (whether a building, amenities or land) shared with other properties are owned outright through a system of part-ownership, similar to owning a condominium in the US. In practice, almost all properties in Spain (with the exception of detached houses on individual plots in public streets or on rural land), are community properties whose owners not only own their homes, but also own a share of the common elements of a building or development, including foyers, hallways, passages, lifts, patios, gardens, roads, and leisure and sports facilities (such as swimming pools and tennis courts). When you buy a community property you automatically become a member of the community of owners, as is the case for some two-thirds of foreign property owners in Spain.

Owners of community properties must pay community fees (*gastos de comunidad*) for the upkeep of communal areas and for communal services. Charges are calculated according to each owner's share (*cuota de participación*) of the development or apartment building and **not** whether they're temporary or permanent residents. Shares are usually calculated according to the actual size of properties, e.g. the owners of ten properties of equal size usually each pay 10 per cent of community fees. The percentage to be paid is detailed in the property deed. Shares not only determine the share of fees to be paid, but also voting rights at general meetings.

Further information about community ownership can be found in **Buying a Home in Spain** by David Hampshire (see page 383) and in *The Community of Owners* published by the Foundation Institute of Foreign Property Owners (🖳 http://www.fipe.org).

COST OF PROPERTY

Since 1997, property prices have risen at a steady rate annually and over the last five years have soared throughout the country reaching an increase of 15.5 per cent in 2004 and 12.6 per cent in 2005. Rises were higher in many areas, e.g. Almería and Huelva (Costa de la Luz) 16 per cent, Castellón (Costa del Azahar) 18 per cent and Galicia 14 per cent, and in many areas prices have increased by over 50 per cent in the last six years. The most expensive provinces to buy a property are Madrid (average €2,785 per m^2), Barcelona (€2,366 per m^2), Malaga (€2,049 per m^2) and the Balearics (€2,026 per m^2). In complete contrast, prices in the provinces in the regions of Extremadura and Galicia average around €1,000 per m^2. The national average is €1,824 per m^2. (Source: Ministry of Housing 2005 report, 🖳 http://www.mviv.es.)

The property boom has brought with it a massive increase in construction (over a fifth of Spain's 22.5m homes have been built in the last ten years), as the skyline of cranes in many areas testifies. In resort areas, rising prices are fuelled by the seemingly endless demand for holiday homes, particularly from foreigners (especially British) and nearly one-third of homes in Spain are second or holiday homes.

Many market analysts (including the International Monetary Fund, *The Economist* and architects' associations in Spain) have warned that the current property price 'bubble' in Spain is unsustainable and that price growth will slow dramatically or even fall over the next few years, although most experts agree that the bubble will deflate rather than burst. Property price rises were lower in most areas in 2005 than the previous year and properties are now taking longer to sell. However, despite the price increases, property remains good value in most areas and is expected to remain so for the next few years at least.

Apart from obvious factors such as size, quality and land area, the most important consideration influencing the price of a home is its location. The closer a property is to a major city or a coastal resort, the more expensive it is; for example, an average quality two-bedroom apartment in a reasonable area costing €100,000 in a town costs two or three times as much in a major city or a fashionable coastal resort. Property is cheapest in rural areas, where a farmhouse with outbuildings and land may cost the same as a studio apartment in Madrid or Marbella, although prices in rural areas situated relatively near popular resorts have risen spectacularly in recent years. The quality of properties varies considerably in respect to materials, fixtures and fittings, and workmanship. Value for money also varies considerably and you should compare at least five to ten properties to get a good idea of their relative values. You usually pay a premium for a beachside or golf course 'front-line' property.

When property is advertised, the total living area in square metres (*metros cuadrados*), written as m², and the number of bedrooms (*dormitorios*) are usually stated. When comparing prices, compare the cost per square metre of the habitable or built (*construidos*) area, usually referred to as *metros útiles*, excluding patios, terraces and balconies, which should be compared separately. If you're in any doubt about the size of rooms you should measure them yourself, rather than rely on the measurements provided by the vendor or agent. A garage (*garaje*) is rarely provided with apartments or townhouses, although there may be a private parking space or a communal parking area. Some apartment blocks have underground garages, and lock-up garages can often be purchased separately for apartments and townhouses for €10,000 to €30,000 in resort areas. Villas usually have their own car port or garage.

SURVIVAL TIP
**Without a garage, parking can be a nightmare,
particularly in cities and in busy resort towns and
urbanisations in summer.**

For those seeking the sun and who can choose to retire anywhere in Spain, the cheapest properties are on the lesser known *costas*, such as the Costa de Almería, Costa Cálida and Costa del Azahar.

Prices on the most popular *costas*, the Costa Blanca and the Costa del Sol, have risen dramatically in the last few years and it's now almost impossible to find a bargain. The Costa del Sol has some of Spain's most expensive property, particularly along Marbella's 'golden mile' where you have to pay at least €1m for a fashionable address. Prices on the Costa Blanca start at €120,000 for a two-bedroom apartment and from €350,000 for a two-bedroom villa (on the southern stretch of the coast). Prices on the Costa del Sol are usually at least 25 to 50 per cent higher than the Costa Blanca, although they vary considerably depending on the area and town.

Prices are generally slightly lower on the less popular eastern Costa del Sol than at the western end, i.e. west of Malaga city.

Property in the Balearics is generally around 25 to 50 per cent more expensive than on the *costas* (with the exception of the Costa del Sol) and Ibiza and Majorca have some of Spain's most expensive property. Prices in the Canaries (which have year-round letting potential) are now less expensive than on the mainland, particularly on the smaller and less accessible islands, although island properties generally command a premium over their mainland counterparts due to stricter building controls, the higher cost of building land and the smaller market. Approximate prices on the *costas* are shown below:

Property	Price Range
Studio	€50,000 to €125,000+
1-bedroom apartment	€80,000 to €200,000+
2-bedroom apartment	€100,000 to €200,000+
3-bedroom apartment	€120,000 to €400,000+
2-bedroom townhouse	€150,000 to €250,000+
3-bedroom townhouse	€175,000 to €450,000+
2-bedroom detached villa	€200,000 to €350,000+
3-bedroom detached villa	€250,000 to €500,000+
4/5-bedroom detached villa	€300,000 to €1,000,000+

The more expensive your home, the more you must pay in property taxes, wealth tax and the deemed income tax on letting income (see **Chapter 8**), which are based on a property's fiscal or rateable value. Community fees for a community property (see above) also rise in direct relation to the value of a property.

Fees

A variety of fees are payable when you buy a property in Spain, which usually add a total of around 10 per cent to the purchase price, which is higher than in many other EU countries. Fees are slightly higher (e.g. plus 1 or 1.5 per cent) on new properties than on resale properties.

The fees payable when buying a property in Spain generally include the following:

- **Transfer Tax** (*Impuesto de Transmisiones Patrimoniales/ITP*) – levied on resale properties at 6 per cent in the Basque Country and Navarra, 6.5 per cent in the Canaries and 7 per cent in all other regions.

- **Value Added Tax** (*Impuesto sobre el Valor Añadido/IVA*) – levied only on new properties at 7 per cent (4.5 per cent in the Canaries).

- **Legal Document Tax** (*Impuesto sobre Actos Jurídicos Documentados/AJD*) – levied on new properties only (in addition to VAT) at 0.5 per cent in the Basque Country and Navarra, 0.75 per cent in the Canaries and 1 per cent in all other regions.

- **Land Tax** (*Impuesto Municipal sobre el Incremento del Valor de los Terrenos*, usually called *plus valía*) – a municipal tax levied on all properties based on the value of the land and the length of ownership. It's usually paid by the vendor, although in some areas it's common practice for the buyer to pay it.

- **Notary's Fees** – Fees for the notary (*notario*) who oversees the sale are based on a sliding scale and depend on the value of the property and the length of the title deeds. Expect to pay in the region of €350 to €1,000.

- **Legal Fees** (optional but strongly advised) – Legal fees are usually 1 to 2 per cent of the price.

- **Deed Registration Fee** – Fees for registering title deeds at the Land Registry range from €150 to €500.

- **Surveyor's Fees (optional)** – Fees range from €500 to €2,000, depending on the type of survey, any special requirements and the value of the property or land.

- **Selling Agent's Fees** – The selling agent's fee is usually between 5 and 10 per cent (but up to 35 per cent in rural areas) of the selling price, depending on the cost of the property and the type of contract, and is paid by the vendor. However, it's usually allowed for in the asking price, so in effect is paid by the buyer.

- **Utility Fees** – In new properties, these include electricity, gas and water connections, and the installation of meters. For resale properties, you must usually pay for new contracts, particularly water.

Running Costs

In addition to the fees associated with buying a property, you should also take into account the running costs. These include local property taxes (rates); annual wealth tax, income tax on deemed letting income (see page 254) and a fiscal representative or tax consultant's fees, if you're non-resident in Spain; rubbish tax; community fees for a community property (see page 150); garden and pool maintenance (for a private villa); building and contents insurance (see page 271); standing charges for utilities (electricity, gas, telephone, water); plus a caretaker's or management fees if you leave a home empty or let it. Annual running costs usually average around 2-4 per cent of the cost of a property.

SURVIVAL TIP
Think twice before buying a property with a large garden and pool. If you plan to maintain them yourself, bear in mind that it's time-consuming and hard work (gardens in most of Spain need year-round watering and pools need cleaning twice a week in the summer).

This may be fine while you remain fit and able, but less easy as you advance further into retirement. If you plan to employ someone to maintain your pool and/or garden, it can be expensive – expect to pay at least €100 a month for a gardener and at least €50 a month for pool maintenance.

THE PURCHASE PROCEDURE

The purchase procedure in Spain isn't especially complicated, but it's different from other countries and there are numerous pitfalls for the unwary.

First Steps

When you've found a property you may be required to sign a reservation contract and pay a small reservation fee, e.g. €3,000, which ensures that the property is taken off the market for a short time (say two weeks). Your lawyer should then start legal checks on the property and draft the private contract (*contrato privado de compraventa*). If you want the property surveyed you should arrange this before you sign the private contract. If you plan to buy with a mortgage you should make enquiries at your bank at this stage.

Once your lawyer has carried out the preliminary checks, both parties sign a private contract and the buyer pays a deposit (usually 10 per cent of the purchase price). The terms and conditions in a private contract vary and it's important to make sure you understand them and their implications, because once you have signed the contract it's binding.

You also need to apply for your foreigner's identification number (*Número de Identificación de Extranjero/NIE*), without which you cannot buy a property. See **Identification Number** on page 230 for details of the application procedure.

Completion

The time frame between signing a private contract and completion is usually between one and three months. When you're ready to complete the purchase, both parties sign the title deed (*escritura*) at a notary public's (*notario*) office and you pay the balance of the purchase price outstanding. Fees and taxes (see **Fees** above) are then paid on your behalf (usually by your lawyer) and the title deed is registered in your name at the local property registry office. Registration takes around a month and once this is complete your lawyer should provide you with official proof (*nota simple*) that the property is registered in your name.

Legal Advice

Don't be tempted to buy a property without the services of a registered lawyer. Numerous lawyers specialise in conveyancing in Spain and many in popular resort areas speak good English – ask around for recommendations. You may wish to check with the provincial Lawyers' Association (Colegio de Abogados – based in the provincial capital. See below for listings in the areas popular with foreign retirees) that the lawyer is registered and has professional insurance cover. Lawyers charge between 1 and 2 per cent of the property price plus 16 per cent VAT for conveyancing.

Lawyers' Associations

Province/Resort Area	Telephone Number & Website
Alicante/Costa Blanca	☎ 965 145 180 🖳 http://www.icali.es
Almería	☎ 950 237 533 🖳 http://www.icaalmeria.com
Asturias (Gijón)	☎ 985 346 304 🖳 http://www.netcom.es/icag
Balearics	☎ 971 714 225 🖳 http://www.icaib.org
Barcelona	☎ 934 960 880 🖳 http://www.icab.es
Cadiz/Costa de la Luz	☎ 956 287 611 🖳 http://www.cabocadiz.org
Cantabria	☎ 942 364 700 🖳 http://www.icacantabria.es
Castellón/Costa del Azahar	☎ 964 224 798 🖳 http://www.icacs.com
Girona/Costa Brava	☎ 972 210 208 🖳 http://www.icag.es
Huelva/Costa de la Luz	☎ 959 252 833 🖳 http://www.icahuelva.es
Las Palmas de Gran Canaria	☎ 928 310 200 🖳 http://www.colegiodeabogadosdelaspalmas.com
Madrid	☎ 917 889 380 🖳 http://www.icam.es
Malaga/ Costa del Sol	☎ 952 219 910 🖳 http://www.icamalaga.es
Murcia	☎ 968 900 100 🖳 http://www.icamur.es

Santa Cruz de Tenerife	☎ 922 205 075
	🖳 http://www.icatf.es
Tarragona/ Costa Dorada	☎ 977 240 650
	🖳 http://www.coladvtgn.es

For comprehensive information on the purchase procedure plus expert advice on how to avoid the pitfalls, see this book's sister publication **Buying a Home in Spain** by David Hampshire (see page 383).

LETTING YOUR PROPERTY

If you buy a property in Spain but decide not to retire there permanently, you may wish to consider letting your property while you're out of the country. Or you may choose to buy property to let in order to increase your monthly pension income. In popular resort areas, there's a good market for holiday lets (although it's becoming saturated in some areas, such as the Canaries and the Costa del Sol) and the income can be used towards maintenance of the property and running costs. Below is a brief guide to the main considerations.

For comprehensive information about letting your property and tips for successful marketing, see this book's sister publication **Earning Money From Your Spanish Home** by Anne Hall (see page 383).

Rules & Regulations

If you let a property in Spain, you're required by law to pay tax on your rental income in Spain and not in the country where the income is received (e.g. in the UK). Since July 1995, all legal short-term 'tourist' letting in the Canaries has been conducted by registered letting agencies, thus ensuring that income tax is paid on earnings. In other parts of Spain, the authorities have a problem getting foreign, non-resident owners to comply with these regulations and many simply turn a blind eye, although there are fines of up to €6,000 for offenders. However, several regional governments (e.g. Andalusia) have advanced plans to follow the example of the Canaries and it's expected there will be widespread clamp-downs on illegal letting. See also **Taxation of Property Income** on page 160.

If you provide bed and breakfast or something similar in a rural property, you must obtain a permit from the local tourist board and have the property inspected. If you're planning to buy a community property, you must check whether there are any rules that prohibit or restrict short-term letting. You may also be required to notify your insurance company.

Contracts

Most people who do holiday letting have a simple agreement form that includes a property description, the names of the clients, and the dates of arrival and departure. However, if you do regular letting you may wish to check with a lawyer that your agreement is legal and contains all the necessary safeguards. If you plan to let to non-English speaking clients, you must have a letting agreement in Spanish or other languages. If you use an agent, they provide a standard contract.

However, if you do longer lets, you must ensure that you or your agent uses the correct contract. In Spain, 'long-term' lets usually refer to lets of one year or more, for which contracts (*arriendos de vivienda*) are for a minimum of five years. The contract for short-term lets, usually of one year's duration or less, is called an *arriendo de temporada*. Contracts are available from tobacconists (*estancos*), but they don't apply to holiday letting.

Because of the dangers of a tenant refusing to leave after the rental period expires, some foreign landlords are wary of letting to Spaniards.

> **If you receive rent and accept a lessee without protest, you're deemed under Spanish law to have entered into a contractual relationship, even if there's no written contract.**

Rents

Rents vary hugely depending on the season, the region, and the size and quality of a property. An average apartment or townhouse sleeping four to six in an average area can be let for between €200 to €800 per week, depending on the season, location and quality. At the other extreme, a luxury villa in a popular area with a pool and accommodation for 8 to 12 can be let for €1,500 to €3,000 (or more) a week in the high season.

Most people who let year-round have low, medium and high season rates. The high season usually includes the months of July and August and possibly the first two weeks of September. Mid-season usually comprises June, late September and October, plus the Easter and Christmas/New Year periods, when rents are around 25 per cent lower than the high season. The rest of the year is classed as the low season, which may extend from October to May, when rates are usually up to 50 per cent lower than the high season. In winter, rents may drop to as low as €500 or €600 per month for a two-bedroom apartment on the *costas*.

Rates usually include linen, gas and electricity, although electricity and heating (e.g. gas bottles) are usually charged separately for long winter lets.

Taxation of Property Income

The tax on property income depends partly on your residence status.

Residents: Property income earned by residents is included in their annual income tax declaration and tax is payable at the standard income tax rate (see page 245). You're eligible for numerous deductions and should take professional advice to make sure that you claim everything you're entitled to.

Non-resident: Non-resident property owners are liable for tax at a flat rate of 25 per cent on property income and aren't entitled to any deductions.

Many foreign property owners don't register their property with the local authorities or declare property income to the Spanish tax authorities. The government is currently preparing legislation to clamp down on this practice and many regional governments plan to make rental accommodation impossible to let without registration. If you choose to let your property without registering it with the authorities, you won't be alone, but bear in mind that, if you're caught, fines start at €6,000 plus payment of estimated letting income for the previous five years. If you're non-resident in Spain, you may also be liable for fines in your home country for the non-declaration of foreign income.

Costs & Expenses

When letting your property, make sure you allow for the numerous costs and expenses that will inevitably reduce the profit you can expect to make. These may include: cleaning between and during lets; laundry of household linen; garden and pool maintenance; maintenance of appliances; replacement of damaged or soiled items; insurance; and utility bills (electricity bills can be high if your property has air-conditioning or electric heating). Some property owners find that costs and expenses account for as much as half the rental income.

Using an Agent

If you're letting a second home, the most important decision is whether to let it yourself or use a letting agent (or agents). If you don't have much spare time, then you're better off using an agent, who takes care of everything and saves you the time and expense of advertising and finding clients. Agents usually charge commission of between 20 and 40 per cent of the gross rental income, although some of this can be recouped through higher rents. If you want your property to appear in an agent's catalogue, you must usually contact him the summer before you wish to let it (the deadline for catalogues is usually September). Note that although self-catering holiday companies may fall over themselves to take on a luxury villa in Majorca or Ibiza, the top letting agents turn down many properties.

There are numerous self-catering holiday companies operating in Spain and many Spanish estate agents also act as agents for holiday and long-term lets.

 Take care when selecting an agent, as it isn't uncommon for them to go bust or simply disappear owing their clients thousands of euros.

If possible, make sure that your income is kept in an escrow account and paid regularly, or even better choose an agent with a bonding scheme who pays you the rent **before** the arrival of guests (some do). It's absolutely essential to employ a reliable and honest (preferably long-established) company. Anyone can set up a holiday letting agency and there are many 'cowboy' operators. Always ask a management company to substantiate rental income claims and occupancy rates by showing you examples of actual income received from other properties. Ask for the names of satisfied customers and contact them. Other things to ask a letting agent include:

- When the letting income is paid.

- What additional charges are made.

- Whether they provide detailed accounts of income and expenses (ask to see a sample). If they don't look elsewhere.

- Who they let to (e.g. what nationalities and whether they include families with young children and singles).

- How they market properties.

- Whether you're expected to contribute towards marketing costs.

- Whether you're free to let the property yourself and use it when you wish. (Many agents don't permit owners to use a property during the months of July and August.)

The larger companies market homes via newspapers, magazines, the internet, overseas agents and coloured brochures, and have representatives in a number of countries. Management contracts usually run for a year and should include arranging emergency repairs; routine maintenance of house and garden, including lawn cutting and pool cleaning; arranging cleaning and linen changes between lets; advising guests on the use of equipment (if necessary) and providing guests with information and assistance (24/7 in the case of emergencies).

Agents may also provide someone to meet and greet guests, hand over the keys and check that everything is in order. The actual services provided usually depend on whether a property is a budget apartment or a villa costing €1,500 or more per week. A letting agent's representative should also make periodic checks when a property is empty to ensure that it's secure and everything is in order. You may wish to check whether a property is actually let when the agent tells you it's empty, as it isn't unknown for some agents to let a property and pocket the rent (you can get a local friend or neighbour to check).

Doing Your Own Letting

Some owners prefer to let a property to family, friends, colleagues and acquaintances, which allows them more control – and **hopefully** the property will also be better looked after. In fact, the best way to get a high volume of lets is usually to do it yourself, although many owners use a letting agency in addition to doing their own marketing in their home country. You must decide whether you want to let to smokers or accept pets and young children – some people won't let to families with children under five due to the risk of bed-wetting. Some owners also prefer not to let to young, single groups. Note, however, that this will reduce your letting prospects.

HOME SECURITY

Security is important, particularly if your home will be left empty for long periods. Obtain advice from local security companies and neighbours.

No matter how good your security, a property is rarely impregnable, so you should never leave valuables in an unattended home unless they're kept in a safe.

When moving into a new home it's wise to replace the locks (or lock barrels), as you have no idea how many keys are in circulation for the existing locks. This is true even for new homes. In any case, it's advisable to change the external lock barrels regularly, e.g. annually, particularly if you let a home. If they aren't already in place, consider fitting high security (double cylinder or dead bolt) locks. Most modern apartments are fitted with an armoured door (*puerta blindada*) with individually numbered, high security locks with three sets of levers.

Doors should be steel reinforced, otherwise thieves will be able to force them open easily. In areas with a high risk of theft, your insurance company may insist on extra security measures such as two locks on external doors, internal locking shutters, and security bars or metal grilles (*rejas*) on windows and patio doors on ground and lower floors, e.g. the first and second floors of high and low-rise buildings. A policy may specify that all forms of protection on doors must be employed when a property is unoccupied and that all other forms (e.g. shutters) must also be used after 10pm and when a property is left empty for two or more days.

You may wish to have a security alarm fitted, which is a good way to deter thieves and may also reduce your insurance premium (see page 271). It should include all external doors and windows, internal infra-red security beams, and may also include a coded entry keypad (which can be frequently changed and is useful for clients if you let) and 24-hour monitoring (with some systems it's possible to monitor properties remotely via a computer from another country). With a monitored system, when a sensor (e.g. smoke or forced entry) detects an emergency or a panic button is pushed, a signal is sent automatically to a 24-hour monitoring station. The person on duty telephones to check whether it's a genuine alarm (a password must be given) and if he cannot contact you someone is sent to investigate. Some developments and urbanisations have security gates and are patrolled 24-hours a day by security guards, although they often have little influence on crime rates and may instil a false sense of security.

You can deter thieves by ensuring that your house is well lit at night and not conspicuously unoccupied. External security 'motion detector' lights (that switch on automatically when someone approaches); random timed switches for internal lights, radios and televisions; dummy security cameras and tapes that play barking dogs (etc.) triggered by a light or heat detector may all help deter burglars. In rural areas, it's common for owners to fit two or three locks on external doors, alarm systems, grilles on doors and windows, window locks, security shutters and a safe for valuables. Security grilles must be heavy duty, as the bars on cheap grilles can be prised apart with a car jack.

Many people also wrap a chain around their patio security grille and secure it with a padlock when a property is unoccupied (although it might not withstand bolt-cutters). You can fit UPVC (toughened clear plastic) security windows and doors, which can survive an attack with a sledge-hammer without damage, and external steel security blinds (which can be electrically operated), although these are expensive. A dog can be useful to deter intruders, although it should be kept inside where it cannot be given poisoned food. Irrespective of whether you actually have a dog, a warning sign showing an image of a fierce dog may act as a deterrent. You should have the front door of an apartment fitted with a spy-hole and chain so that you can check the identity of visitors before opening the door. **Remember, prevention is better than cure, as stolen possessions are rarely recovered.**

Another important aspect of home security is ensuring you have early warning of a fire, which is easily accomplished by installing smoke detectors. Battery-operated smoke detectors can be purchased for around €10 and should be tested periodically to ensure that the batteries aren't exhausted. You can also fit an electric-powered gas detector that activates an alarm when a gas leak is detected.

There are many specialist home security companies who will inspect your home and offer free advice on security, although you should always shop around and obtain at least two quotations before having any work done.

See also **Crime** on page 306 and **Household Insurance** on page 271.

UTILITIES

Immediately after buying or renting a property (unless utilities are included in the rent), you should arrange for the meter (if applicable) to be read, the contract (e.g. electricity, gas or water) to be registered in your name and the service switched on (e.g. mains gas). Make sure that all outstanding bills have been paid by the previous owner – you're only responsible for debts incurred from the day you buy or rent the property and aren't liable for any of the previous owner's outstanding debts, but utility companies sometimes cut off a supply because of a previous owner's debts. Unless you're certain all bills have been paid, it's advisable to provide your utility companies with a copy of your title deeds or rental contract so that they know when you took over ownership or tenancy of the property.

Registering a contract in your name usually entails a visit to the company's office, although you may be able to register online or by telephone. Note that in order to register for electricity via the internet or telephone you must give some identification (your name and your passport or identity card number), as well as the reference number for the electricity supply (usually found on the top left-hand corner of an electricity bill under *Contrato de Suministro No*).

If you visit the utility company's office, you must take some identification (passport or residence permit) and the contract and bills paid by the previous owner. **The registration procedure for water connection is sometimes via the local town hall.** If you've purchased a home in Spain, the estate agent may arrange for the utilities to be transferred to your name or accompany you to the offices (no charge should be made for this service).

If you're a non-resident owner, you should also give your foreign address in case there are any problems requiring your attention, such as a bank failing to pay the bills. You may need to pay a deposit.

Money saving tips for your utility bills can be found on page 80.

Electricity

Spain's main electricity companies include Grupo Endesa (the largest), Iberdrola, Union Fenosa and Hidrocantábrico. In January 2003, the energy market was completely deregulated and clients can, at least in theory, now choose which company provides their electricity. In practice, however, in many areas there's still only one company providing electricity. The following are the main electricity companies:

- **Endesa** (☎ 902 509 509, 🖳 http://www.endesaonline.com) – provides electricity under the following names: Fecsa in Catalonia; Gesa in the Balearics; Sevillana Endesa in Andalusia; and Unelco in the Canaries.

- **Gas Natural** (☎ 900 710 720, 🖳 http://www.gasnatural.com) – provides electricity in most of central Spain.

- **Hidrocantábrico** (☎ 902 860 860, 🖳 http://www.h-c.es) – provides electricity in Asturias and Madrid.

- **Iberdrola** (☎ 901 202 020, 🖳 http://www.iberdrola.com) – provides electricity in Asturias, the Basque country, Cantabria, Catalonia, Comunidad Valenciana (including the Costa Brava), Galicia and Madrid.

● **Unión Fenosa** (☎ 901 404 040, 🖳 http://www.unionfenosa.es) – provides electricity in central Spain, including Madrid.

Power Supply

The electricity supply in most of Spain is 220 volts AC with a frequency of 50 hertz (cycles). However, some areas still have a 110-volt supply and it's possible to find dual voltage 110 and 220-volt systems in the same house or even the same room! All new buildings have a 220-volt supply and the authorities have mounted a campaign to encourage homeowners with 110-volt systems to switch to 220 volts. Not all appliances, e.g. televisions made for 240 volts, will function with a power supply of 220 volts.

The power supply increases by increments of 1.1kW, e.g. 2.2kW, 3.3kW, 4.4kW, 5.5kW. The power supply rating is usually shown on your meter. If the power keeps tripping off when you attempt to use a number of high-power appliances simultaneously, e.g. an electric kettle and a heater, it means that the power rating (*potencia*) of your property is too low. This is a common problem. You will need to contact your electricity company and ask them to upgrade your power supply (it can also be downgraded if necessary).

In remote areas you must install a generator if you want electricity, as there's no mains electricity, although some people make do with gas and oil lamps. **In many urbanisations, water is provided by electric pump and, therefore, if your electricity supply is cut off, so is your water supply.** If you buy a rural property (*finca rústica*), there are usually public guarantees of services such as electricity (plus water, sewage, roads, telephone, etc.). However, you may be obliged to pay for the installation of electricity lines or transformers plus the connection to your property if the mains services don't run near your home.

Plugs, Fuses & Bulbs

Depending on the country you've come from, you will need new plugs (*enchufes*) and/or a lot of adapters. Plug adapters (*adaptador*) for most foreign electrical apparatus can be purchased in Spain, although it's wise to bring some with you, plus extension leads and multi-plug extensions that can be fitted with Spanish plugs. There's often a shortage of electric points in Spanish homes, with perhaps just one per room (including the kitchen), so multi-plug adapters may be essential. Most Spanish plugs have two round pins, sometimes with an earth built into the plug, although most sockets in older properties aren't fitted with earth contacts. Sockets in modern properties are usually earthed.

Small, low-wattage appliances such as lamps, small TVs and computers, don't require an earth. However, plugs with an earth must always be used for high-wattage appliances (e.g. fires, kettles). These plugs must be used with earthed sockets. Electrical appliances that are earthed have a three-core wire and must never be used with a two-pin plug without an earth socket. **Always make sure that a plug is correctly and securely wired, as bad wiring can be fatal.**

In modern properties, fuses (*fusibles*) are of the trip type. When there's a short circuit or the system has been overloaded, a circuit breaker is tripped and the power supply is cut. If your electricity fails, you should suspect a fuse, particularly if you've just switched on an electrical appliance.

Light bulbs (*bombillas*) in Spain are of the Edison type with a screw fitting. If you have lamps requiring bayonet bulbs you should bring some with you, as they cannot be easily purchased in Spain. You can, however, buy adapters to convert from bayonet to screw fitting (or vice versa). Bulbs for non-standard electrical appliances (i.e. appliances that aren't made for the Spanish market) such as refrigerators and sewing machines may not be available.

Connection

The cost of electricity connection (*acometida*) and the installation of a meter is usually between €100 to €300, although it varies considerably depending on the region, power supply and the type of meter installed.

Tariffs

Electricity in Spain is one of the cheapest in Europe, although prices have recently risen by 1 per cent and further rises are expected as electricity companies are forced to pay the cost of keeping to the limits of emission of gases under the Kyoto agreement. The actual charges depend on your local electricity company (the rates shown in the example below are those charged by Sevillana Endesa in Andalusia).

The tariff depends on your power rating, which for domestic users with a power rating of up to 15kW is 2.0 (above 15kW it's 3.0). This tariff is used to calculate your bimonthly standing charge. For example, if your power rating is 4.4kW this is multiplied by the tariff of 2.0 and then multiplied by the standing charge rate per kW (e.g. €1.53), i.e. 4.4 x 2.0 x €1.53, making a total of €13.64. The standing charge is payable irrespective of whether you use any electricity during the billing period. The actual consumption is charged per kW, e.g. €0.09 in Andalusia. VAT at 16 per cent is levied on charges.

Bills

Electricity is billed every two months, usually after meters have been read. However, companies are permitted to make an estimate of your consumption every second period without reading the meter. You should learn to read your electricity bill and check your consumption.

Paying your bills by direct debit (*domiciliación bancaria*) from a Spanish bank account is advisable for all homeowners and essential if you aren't a permanent resident. Bills should then be paid automatically on presentation to your bank, although some banks cannot be relied on 100 per cent. Both the electricity company and your bank should notify you when they've sent or paid a bill. Alternatively, you can pay bills at a post office, local banks (listed on the bill) or at the electricity company's office (in cash).

Electricity companies aren't permitted to cut your electricity supply without authorisation from the proper authorities, e.g. the Ministry of Industry and Energy, and without notifying the owner of a property. If you're late paying a bill, you should be sent a registered letter demanding payment and stating that the power will be cut on a certain date if you don't pay. If you disagree with a bill, you should write to the Servicio Territorial de Ministerio de Industria y Energía; if your complaint is founded your electricity company will be refused permission to cut your supply. If your supply is cut off, you must usually pay to have it reconnected (*reenganche*).

Gas

Mains gas is available only in major cities, although with the recent piping of gas from North Africa (Algeria and Libya) it may soon be more widely available. As with electricity, you're billed every two months and bills include VAT at 16 per cent. Like all utility bills, gas bills can be paid by direct debit from a Spanish bank account. In rural areas, bottled gas is used and costs less than half that of mains gas in most northern European countries. You can have a combined gas hot-water and heating system (providing background heat) installed, which is relatively inexpensive to install and cheap to run.

In most areas of Spain, gas bottles (*bombonas*) are delivered to homes by Repsol Butano, for which a contract is required. You must pay a deposit of around €25 and an exchange 12.5kg bottle costs around €12.50 (the price fluctuates frequently) when delivered to your home or less if purchased directly from a Butano depot. A contract is drawn up only after a safety inspection has been made of the property where the gas appliance is to be used. In some areas, you must exchange your bottles at a local supplier. A bottle used only for cooking lasts an average family around six to eight weeks. If a gas boiler is installed outside, e.g. on a balcony, it must be protected from the wind, otherwise you will continually be re-lighting the pilot light.

You must have your gas appliances serviced and inspected at least every five years. If you have a contract with Repsol Butano, they do this for you or it's done by your local authorised distributor. Some distributors try to sell you a package which includes third party insurance and free parts should they be required, although it isn't necessary to have this insurance and is a waste of money.

 Beware of 'bogus' gas company representatives calling unannounced to inspect gas appliances.

Most are usually legitimate companies, but their charges are extortionate and they will give you a large bill for changing tubing and regulators (which don't usually need changing), and demand payment in cash on the spot (e.g. €200). If you wish you can let them make an inspection and give you an estimate (*presupuesto*) for any work that needs doing, but don't let them do any work or pay any money before checking with your local Repsol Butano distributor. Incidentally, plastic tubes have an expiry date printed on them and you can buy them from a hardware store (*ferretería*) and change them yourself.

Water

Water, or rather the lack of it, is a major concern in Spain and the price paid for all those sunny days. Spain as a whole has sufficient water, but it isn't distributed evenly. There's (usually) surplus rainfall in the north-west and centre and a deficiency along most of the Mediterranean coast and in the Balearic and Canary islands. In the Canaries, there's a permanent water shortage and most drinking water is provided by desalination plants, while in the Balearics 20,000 wells are employed to pump water to the surface (there are also desalination plants in Majorca and Ibiza). Three large desalination plants are located in Almería, Marbella and Murcia.

Almost every year some part of southern Spain faces drought – in 2006, much of the south was critically short of water. Water shortages are exacerbated by poor infrastructure and wastage due to poor irrigation methods. There's also surprisingly little emphasis on water conservation, particularly considering the frequent droughts. For example, the Costa del Sol uses double the national average per person (500 litres a day), and people in towns and cities consume some 300 litres of water per person, per day, one of the highest figures in Europe. At the same time, hundreds of rural towns and villages have water on tap for just a few hours a day during the summer months and farmers regularly face ruin due to the lack of water for irrigation. However, domestic consumption has reduced in many regions with the sharp increase in water costs in recent years, and people have learnt to use less water during the prolonged drought.

Quality

Water is supposedly safe to drink in all urban areas, although it can be of poor quality (possibly brown or rust coloured), full of chemicals and taste awful. Many residents prefer to drink bottled water. In rural areas, water may be extracted from mountain springs and taste excellent, although the quality standards applied in cities are usually absent and it may be of poor quality. Water in rural areas may also be contaminated by fertilisers and nitrates used in farming, and by salt water in some coastal areas. If you're in any doubt about the quality of your water you should have it analysed. **Although boiling water kills any bacteria, it won't remove any toxic substances contained in it.** You can install filtering, cleansing and softening equipment to improve its quality or a water purification unit (costing around €1,300) to provide drinking water. **Note, however, that purification systems that operate on the reverse osmosis system waste three times as much water as they produce.** Obtain expert advice before installing a system, as not all equipment is effective.

Many areas have hard water containing high concentrations of calcium and magnesium. Water is very hard (*muy dura*) in the east, hard (*dura*) in the north and most of the south, and soft in the north-west (e.g. Galicia), and central and western regions. You can install a water softener that prevents the build-up of scale in water heaters and water pipes, which increases heating costs and damages electric heaters and other appliances. Costs vary considerably and can run into hundreds of euros for a sophisticated system, which also consumes large quantities of water for regeneration.

```
┌──────────────────────────────────────────────────────────────┐
│                         SURVIVAL TIP                           │
│   It's necessary to have a separate drinking water supply      │
│     if you have a water softener installed in your home.       │
└──────────────────────────────────────────────────────────────┘
```

Restrictions

During water shortages, local municipalities may restrict water consumption or cut off supplies altogether for days at a time. Restrictions can be severe and householders may be limited to as little as three cubic metres (m^3) per month, which is sufficient for around 10 baths or 20 showers. You can forget about watering the garden or washing your car unless you have a private water supply. If a water company needs to cut your supply, e.g. to carry out maintenance work on pipes and other installations, they usually notify you in advance (but don't be surprised if you have no warning!). In some areas, water shortages can create low water pressure, resulting in insufficient water to take a bath or shower.

Note that in many developments, water is provided by electric pump and therefore if your electricity is cut off, so is your water supply. In urbanisations, the tap to turn water on or off is usually located outside properties, so if your water goes off suddenly you should check that someone hasn't switched it off by mistake. In the hotter parts of Spain, where water shortages are common, water tankers deliver to homes. Some properties don't have a mains supply at all, but a storage tank (*depósito*) that's filled from a tanker. If you have a storage tank, water is pumped into it and you're charged by the litre plus a delivery charge.

Hot Water

Water heating in apartments may be provided by a central heating source for the whole building or apartments may have their own water heaters. If you install your own water heater, it should have a capacity of at least 75 litres. There are two main types of water heater: An electric water boiler with a capacity of 75 litres (sufficient for two people) costs from €130 to €250 and usually takes between 60 and 90 minutes to heat water to 40 degrees in winter. A gas flow-through water heater is more expensive to buy (from €150 to €275) and instal, but provides unlimited hot water. Solar energy can also be used to provide hot water (see page 174).

Costs

Water is a local matter in Spain and is usually controlled by local municipalities, many of which have their own wells. In some municipalities, water distribution is the responsibility of a private company. The cost of connection to the local water supply for a new home varies considerably from around €75 up to €500 (when a private company controls the distribution), or even €1,500 in an isolated area.

Consumption costs usually include a standing quarterly charge or a monthly charge (*cuota fija agua*), e.g. €10 a month, irrepective of consumption, a charge per cubic metre of water consumed (between €0.50 and €1 per m³ on the mainland and between €1.50 and €2.50 per m³ in the Canaries and some parts of the Balearics) plus VAT levied at 7 per cent. Water bills sometimes include a rental charge for the water meter and sewerage.

Bills

Bills are generally sent out quarterly. If you don't pay your water bill on time you should receive an 'enforced collection' (*recaudación ejecutiva*) letter demanding payment of your bill (plus a surcharge). If you don't pay your bill your water supply can be cut off. If your supply is cut, you must pay a reconnection fee, e.g. €40, plus any outstanding bills.

HEATING & AIR-CONDITIONING

Some form of heating (*calefacción*) is essential in winter in northern and central Spain and is useful in most other areas – with the exception of the Canaries where winter temperatures rarely fall below 15°C (59°F), winters can be chilly everywhere. If you're used to a warm home in winter, you will almost certainly miss central heating, even on the Costa Blanca and Costa del Sol. Central heating systems in Spain may be powered by oil, gas, electricity, solid fuel (usually wood) or even solar power. Oil-fired central heating isn't common due to the high cost of heating oil and the problems associated with storage and deliveries. In rural areas, many houses have open, wood-burning fireplaces and stoves, which may be combined with a central heating system. Whatever form of heating you use, it's important to have good insulation, without which up to 60 per cent of the heat generated is lost through the walls, windows and roof. Many homes, particularly older and cheaper properties, don't have good insulation and even with new homes, builders don't always adhere to current regulations.

In cities, apartment blocks may have a communal central heating system providing heating for all apartments, the cost of which is divided among the tenants. If you're a non-resident or absent for long periods, you should choose an apartment with a separate heating system, otherwise you will be contributing towards your neighbours' bills.

Heating

Electric

Electric heating isn't common, as it's too expensive and requires good insulation and a permanent system of ventilation. It's advisable to avoid totally electric apartments in regions with a cold winter, such as Madrid, as the bills can be astronomical. More economical options include a system of night-storage heaters operating on a night tariff with electric radiators (*radiador eléctrico*) incorporating the latest energy-saving advances. These radiators, available from DIY and department stores, are filled with a heat-retaining gel or liquid, which means that the radiator stays warm for longer. They are easy to install (requiring just two wall brackets and a socket) and are similar in appearance and size to conventional radiators. However, heating a property by electricity is never cheap and you should expect to pay between €50 and €125 a month during the coldest months, i.e. November to February.

An air-conditioning (*aire acondicionado*) system with a heat pump provides cooling in summer and reasonably economical heating in winter. However, air-conditioning systems can be noisy and the hot air produced is very dry and not recommended for people with allergies or asthma.

If you install electric central heating or air-conditioning, check that your power supply is high enough, as fires can be caused by over-loading the power circuit.

Ask an electrician to check or telephone your electricity company for advice.

Gas

Stand-alone gas heaters using standard gas bottles (*bombonas*) cost from €60 to €150 and are an economical way of providing heating in areas that experience mild winters (such as the Costa del Sol). Gas heaters must be used only in rooms with adequate ventilation, inspected and approved by Repsol Butano – it can be dangerous to have too large a difference between indoor and outdoor temperatures. Gas poisoning due to faulty ventilation ducts for gas heaters (e.g. in bathrooms) isn't uncommon in Spain. Gas heating also produces condensation and dampness in homes, therefore make sure you air rooms for at least 30 minutes a day.

It's possible to install a central heating system operating from standard gas bottles, which costs around €2,000 for a small home. The Spanish oil providers Cepsa and Repsol have good deals on gas central heating, including low-cost financing of the installation. Primus of Sweden is the leading foreign manufacturer. Mains gas central heating is popular in cities and is the cheapest to run.

Solar Energy

The use of solar energy to provide hot water and heating is still rare in Spain, where the amount of energy provided by the sun each year per square metre is equivalent to eleven gas bottles. New homes are usually fitted with a solar power system and the government has recently introduced legislation that will require all new homes to have solar power. A solar power system can be used to supply all your energy needs, although it's usually combined with an electric or gas heating system, as it cannot usually be relied upon for year round heating and hot water. Solar energy is a viable option in most of Spain, particularly on the Mediterranean coast and on the islands, and the authorities (regional and national governments) offer grants and interest-free finance to encourage homeowners to install solar-energy systems.

The main drawback is the high cost of installation, which varies considerably depending on the region and how much energy you require. A 400-litre hot-water system costs around €3,000 (grants and subsidies are available from regional governments and the EU) and must be installed by an expert. The advantages are no running costs; silent, maintenance-free operation; and no (or very small) electricity bills. A system should last 30 years (it's usually guaranteed for ten years) and can be upgraded to provide additional power in the future. It can also be used to heat a swimming pool. A solar power system can also provide electricity in a remote rural home, where the cost of extending mains electricity is prohibitive.

Air-conditioning

In some regions, summer temperatures can reach over 40°C (104°F) and although properties are built to withstand the heat, you may wish to install air-conditioning. Note, however, that there can be negative effects if you suffer from asthma or respiratory problems and it's easy to catch a chill from air-conditioning that's too cold. Air-conditioning units cost from around €600 (plus installation) for a 2,000 BTU (*frigorías*) unit, which is sufficient to cool an average size room. Some air-conditioners are noisy, so check the noise level before buying one. An air-conditioning system with a heat pump provides cooling in summer and economical heating in winter – a system with an outside compressor providing radiant heating and cooling costs around €1,200 per room. Many people fit ceiling fans for extra cooling in the summer (costing from around €65), which are standard fixtures in some new homes.

Humidifiers & De-humidifiers

Central heating and air-conditioning dry the air and may cause your family to develop coughs and other ailments. Those who find dry air unpleasant can install humidifiers (*humidificador*) which add moisture to the air. These range from simple water containers hung from radiators to electric or battery-operated devices. Humidifiers that don't generate steam should be disinfected occasionally with a special liquid available from chemists.

On the other hand, damp and humidity are common problems and it's worthwhile installing de-humidifiers (*deshumidificador*), especially in bedrooms, to prevent clothes and linen going mouldy. De-humidifiers are useful in homes on or near the coast where humidity levels in winter are high – many homeowners on the Costa del Sol own de-humidifiers and run them frequently!

6.

MOVING TO SPAIN

This chapter is concerned with the practicalities of moving yourself, your possessions (including your car) and your pet(s) to Spain. It also includes suggestions for finding local help, tips for settling in, and information about security and the connection of utilities.

SURVIVAL TIP
The whole process of moving to Spain and settling in is much easier if you rent a furnish property for a period (e.g. up to six months) before buying a home and making the move permanent.

MOVING HOUSE

Moving house ranks near the top of life's most stressful events and at first sight, moving to Spain will probably appear even more nerve racking than 'simply' moving to a new location in your home country. However, there's a lot you can do to ensure that your move and your arrival in Spain go as smoothly as possible. The secrets of success are allowing plenty of time to plan your move – if possible, start making at least six months in advance – and choosing a good removal company.

What to Take

Before you ask for quotes from removal companies (see **Quotes** below), decide how much you want (and need) to take with you. Moving anywhere provides an excellent opportunity to have a good clear-out and get rid of belongings that you've have been storing in cupboards or in the loft for years – there's little point paying to ship 'white elephants'. Selling, giving away or throwing out at least half your possessions also clears your mind and makes life simpler. Before making a list of what to ship, you might wish to consider the following:

- **The décor** – Coastal properties in Spain lend themselves to pale, modern furniture and fittings in order to reflect the Mediterranean light so your antique oak dining table will probably look totally out of place. On the other hand, if your new home is a rural farmhouse, your antiques will fit in perfectly.

- **The size** – Bear in mind that Spanish properties (with the exception of detached villas) are usually considerably smaller than those in northern European countries. This is particularly true of new apartments where a typical double bedroom measures 14m² and living-room space around 20m². Your current furniture may not fit into your new Spanish home or if it fits, it may overwhelm or clutter rooms. If you're down-sizing, it's better to take the basics only and start anew in Spain.

- **Storage space** – Most Spanish homes have poor storage provisions: bedrooms in apartments usually run to a small built-in wardrobe only and although some apartments come with purpose-built storage rooms (known as *trasteros*), these are rarely large (e.g. 2m by 3m); few houses have lofts; and many properties have an open car-port rather than a lock-up garage.

- **Household appliances** – There are many reasons for not shipping appliances to Spain including: the standard size of kitchen appliances (e.g. washing machines and dishwashers) in Spain is often different from those in other countries, including the UK; specifications are different, e.g. washing machines in Spain don't take in hot water (it's heated by the machine); some appliances, particularly televisions, may not work at all; all appliances need their plugs changing and voltage checking by an electrician; and spare parts and qualified servicemen may be unavailable in Spain. It's usually cheaper and less-time-consuming to buy new appliances in Spain rather than paying to have yours shipped.

Once you know exactly what you need to take to Spain, the next step is to choose a removal company.

Shipping Your Belongings

Choosing the Company

There are several ways to ship your belongings to Spain:

Removal companies: The best way to ensure a smooth start to your retirement in Spain is to put your move into the hands of the professionals. This is by no means the cheapest option, but it's certainly the easiest and one that will save you a lot of headaches. Many reputable removal companies specialise in moves to Spain and several have weekly routes to popular destinations, e.g. the Costa Blanca and the Costa del Sol.

Choose a company with experience in Spain which belongs to a removal association such as the International Federation of Furniture Removers (FIDI, 🖥 http://www.fidi.com), the Overseas Moving Network International (OMNI, 🖥 http://www.omnimoving.com), the British Association of Removers (UK only, 🖥 http://www.removers.org.uk) or the National Guild of Removers (UK only, 🖥 http://www.ngrs.co.uk). Members of removal associations must provide guarantees for clients and abide by a code of conduct.

Some removal companies have subsidiaries or affiliates in Spain, which is handy if you encounter problems or have to make an insurance claim. If you choose a Spanish company, make sure that it belongs to the Federación Española de Empresas de Mudanzas (FEDEM, 🖥 http://www.fedem.es) and has a Spanish business address, a registered licence number and a VAT (*IVA*) number.

SURVIVAL TIP
Pay for the best you can afford: paying for someone else to do the packing, customs clearing and driving means that you will enjoy an easier start to your new life.

'Man with a van': While some 'one man' operations are reliable and offer a cheap alternative to a registered removal company, others have been known to 'disappear' with their clients' worldly possessions on the way to Spain. A 'man with a van' is also unlikely to be able to provide insurance cover for your goods or storage facilities. However, if you have only a few items of furniture or personal possessions to ship that you cannot take yourself, it can be an economical solution.

DIY move: This may be the cheapest option, but unless you have a sense of adventure and a strong back, it's best to avoid a DIY removal. Moving to Spain is stressful enough without the added problems of struggling to move and pack everything in a hire van; driving for long hours (over a number of days) to Spain (and possibly getting lost or breaking down on the way); and finally unpacking and storing it all after you arrive. Also bear in mind that you will probably have to return the van to the country where you hired it and then return to Spain yourself.

Packing

Most removal companies provide complete packing services, which is by far the easiest option but also the most expensive. A cheaper alternative is to pack your belongings yourself and most removal companies provide a range of specialised packing materials, e.g. boxes, crates and wardrobe boxes. If you choose to pack things yourself, check the insurance policy as some companies refuse to insure goods they haven't packed themselves. If you do your own packing, don't over-pack boxes as squashed items can be broken or damaged and use wardrobe boxes for clothes to save yourself hours of ironing later on. Beware of packing aerosols and liquids due to the risk of explosion or spillage.

Regardless of who does the packing, you should make a room plan of your new home with rooms numbered or named and mark the corresponding number or name on furniture and boxes, so that the removal company (or you!) knows exactly where everything should go.

When packing keep your personal luggage in a separate place (preferably outside the house) so it isn't packed onto the lorry. It's also advisable to pack a small suitcase or bag containing first day 'essentials' such as tea bags (or whiskey!), kettle and first aid kit to take with you. It's advisable to take small valuable or sentimental items with you in person rather than risk them getting lost during a move. For larger valuable items (e.g. television, paintings and computers), it's advisable to make a videotape of them and make a note of their serial numbers in case you need to make an insurance claim. Make a complete inventory of everything (include the make and serial number of appliances) to be moved and give a copy to the removal company. Don't include anything illegal (e.g. guns, drugs or pornography) with your belongings, as customs checks can be rigorous and penalties severe.

Cost

Quotes: A reputable removal company should send a representative to provide a detailed quotation. Prices and services vary considerably between companies and it pays to obtain quotes from at least three. However, make sure you're comparing the same sort of service and that the company has given as accurate a quote as possible. Once you accept a quote, ensure you know exactly what you're paying for and what you will get for your money.

Price: When calculating the cost of your move, you need to consider shipping costs, the method of shipping and possibly import duty (see page 184). Shipping costs are usually calculated on the volume with a fixed rate per cubic foot or metre. (You can also send belongings by air freight, which is charged by weight and much more expensive than road/sea, but is also much quicker.) You should expect to pay from €5,000 to €10,000 to move the contents of a three to four-bedroom house by road/sea within western

Europe to Spain, e.g. from London to the Costa del Sol. Part loads (where you share the cost with others) are much cheaper and can result in savings of 50 per cent or more compared with a 'special' delivery.

Time Scale

The time scale for shipment of belongings depends on a number of factors, not least on how much you're prepared to pay. An average shipment within Europe to Spain takes from three to six weeks, although companies specialising in removals to Spain with weekly shipments can usually offer a quicker move. If delivery isn't urgent or you aren't taking much with you, your belongings can be shipped as a part load where the cost is shared with others, but you usually have to wait longer for them to arrive. Companies may offer an express service, although the cost may be prohibitive.

Insurance

Be sure to fully insure your belongings during removal with a well established insurance company. It isn't advisable to insure with a removal or shipping company that carries its own insurance, as they will usually fight every euro of a claim. Insurance premiums are usually 1 to 2 per cent of the declared value of your goods, depending on the type of cover chosen. Most insurance policies cover for 'all-risks' on a replacement value basis. Note, however, that china, glass and other breakables can usually be included in an 'all-risks' policy only when they're packed by the removal company. Insurance usually covers total loss or loss of a particular crate only, rather than individual items (unless they were packed by the shipping company).

If there are any breakages or damaged items, they must be noted and listed before you sign the delivery bill (although it's obviously impossible to check everything on delivery). If you need to make a claim, be sure to read the small print, as some companies require clients to make a claim within a few days, although seven is usual. **Always send a claim by registered post.** Some insurance companies apply an 'excess' of around 1 per cent of the total shipment value when assessing claims. This means that if your shipment is valued at €25,000 and you make a claim for less than €250, you won't receive anything.

> **SURVIVAL TIP**
> **Check and double-check the insurance cover. Is it**
> **sufficient? Read the small print carefully.**

Arrival

Give your shipping company detailed instructions on how to find your Spanish address from the nearest main road and a telephone number where you can be contacted. If you're moving to a rural property, make sure that access to the house is suitable (firm ground and wide enough) for a removal van or lorry. If you're moving into an apartment, large items of furniture may have to be taken in through an upstairs window or balcony. Some removal companies can provide this service at extra cost or you can arrange the hire of a 'removal ladder' (most Spanish removal companies have them).

SURVIVAL TIP
If you cannot be there yourself, it's essential to have someone on hand who can make decisions regarding where things are to be stored and to check that there's no damage to major items.

PAPERWORK

Immigration

On arrival, your first task is to negotiate immigration (*imigración*) and customs (*aduana*). Fortunately, this presents few problems for most people, particularly European Union (EU) nationals since the establishment of 'open' EU borders on 1st January 1993. Non-EEA (European Economic Area) or Swiss nationals coming to Spain for any purpose other than as a visitor usually require a visa (see page 30). Along with Austria, Belgium, Denmark, Finland, France, Germany, Greece, Iceland, Italy, Luxembourg, the Netherlands, Norway, Portugal and Sweden, Spain is a signatory to the Schengen agreement. Under the agreement, immigration checks and passport controls take place when you first arrive in a member country, after which you can travel freely between member countries without further checks.

When you arrive in Spain from a country that's a signatory to the Schengen agreement, there are usually no immigration checks or passport controls, which take place when you first arrive in a Schengen member country. Officially, Spanish immigration officials should check the passports of EU arrivals from non-Schengen countries (such as the UK and Ireland), although this doesn't usually happen except at airports. If you're a non-EU national and arrive in Spain by air or sea from outside the EU, you must go through immigration for non-EU citizens. Non-EU citizens are required to complete an immigration registration card, which are provided on aircraft, ships, trains and at land border crossings. If you have a single-entry visa it will be cancelled by the immigration official. Some people may wish to get a stamp in their passport as confirmation of their date of entry into Spain.

SURVIVAL TIP
If you require a visa to enter Spain and attempt to enter
without one, you will be refused entry.

If you're a non-EU national coming to Spain to retire, you may be asked to show documentary evidence. Immigration officials may also ask non-EU visitors to produce a return ticket and proof of accommodation, health insurance and financial resources, e.g. cash, travellers' cheques and credit cards. The onus is on visitors to show that they're genuine and that they don't intend to breach Spanish immigration laws. Immigration officials aren't required to prove that you will breach the immigration laws and can refuse you entry on the grounds of suspicion only.

Importing Your Belongings

Visitors

Visitors' belongings aren't subject to duty or VAT when they're visiting Spain for up to six months (182 days). This applies to the import of private cars, camping vehicles (including trailers or caravans), motorcycles, aircraft, boats and personal effects. Goods may be imported without formality, provided their nature and quantity doesn't imply any commercial aim. All means of transport and personal effects imported duty-free mustn't be sold or given away in Spain and must be exported when a visitor leaves. If you cross into Spain by road you may drive through the border post without stopping (unless requested to do so). However, any goods and pets that you're carrying mustn't be subject to any prohibitions or restrictions. Customs officials can still stop anyone for a spot check, e.g. to check for drugs or illegal immigrants.

If you arrive at a seaport by private boat, there are no particular customs formalities, although you must show the boat's registration papers on request. A vessel registered outside the EU may remain in Spain for a maximum of six months in any calendar year, after which it must be exported or imported (when duty and tax must be paid). However, you can ask the local customs authorities to seal (*precintar*) a foreign-registered boat while you're absent and unseal it when you wish to use it, thus allowing you to keep it in Spain year round (although you can use it for six months of the year only). Foreign-registered vehicles and boats mustn't be lent or rented to anyone while in Spain.

EU Retirees

Under the Single European Act (1993) the shipment of personal (household) effects to Spain from another EU country isn't subject to customs formalities. EU nationals planning to take up permanent or temporary residence in Spain are permitted to import their furniture and personal effects free of duty or taxes, provided they were purchased tax-paid within the EU or have been owned for at least six-months. A detailed inventory is advisable (although it's unlikely that anyone will check your belongings) and the shipping company should have a photocopy of the owner's passport legalised by a Spanish consulate. There are no restrictions on the import or export of banknotes or securities, although if you enter or leave Spain with €6,000 or more in cash or negotiable instruments (see page 183), you must make a declaration to Spanish customs.

If you require general information about Spanish customs regulations, or have specific questions, contact the Dirección General de Aduanas (☎ 917 289 608, 🖳 http://www.aeat.es, *Aduanas e I. Especiales*). Information about duty-free allowances can be found on page 188 and importing pets on page 190.

Non-EU Retirees

Non-EU nationals planning to take up permanent or temporary residence in Spain are permitted to import their furniture and personal effects free of duty or taxes, provided they've owned them for at least six months. An application form for primary (*cambio de residencia*) or secondary (*vivienda secundaria*) residence must be completed (available from Spanish consulates), plus a detailed inventory of the items to be imported showing their value in euros. All items to be imported should be included on the list (include the make and serial number of any electrical appliances), even if some are to be imported at a later date. These documents must be signed and presented to a Spanish consulate with the owner's passport. If the owner won't be present when the effects are cleared by customs, a photocopy of the principal pages of his passport are required, which must be legalised by the local Spanish embassy.

Primary residence: Non-EU nationals importing personal effects for a primary or permanent residence must present their residence permit (*residencia*) to the consulate, or if the permit hasn't yet been granted, evidence that an application has been made. Permanent residents must provide Spanish customs with a bank guarantee (of up to 60 per cent of the value of their belongings) until the residence permit is granted in the following 12 months. The deposit 'exempts' the holder from customs duties and is returned when a residence permit has been obtained.

> **SURVIVAL TIP**
> **You have one year in which to obtain a residence permit and request the return of your deposit. If you take longer than one year without obtaining an extension, you may lose your deposit!**

Secondary residence: Non-EU applicants importing personal effects for a secondary residence (*vivienda secundaria*) must present the title deed (*escritura*) of a property that they own in Spain or a rental contract (lease) for a minimum period of two years. They must provide a two-year bank guarantee (see above) issued by a bank in Spain to ensure that the goods will remain in the same dwelling, that the property won't be sub-let by the foreign owner or lessee, and that it will be reserved for his family's exclusive use. The deposit must be paid into a Spanish bank, which issues a certificate for the customs office stating that the funds have been received. The deposit is supposed to be returned after two years. When the two-year period has expired, you must obtain a certificate from your local town hall verifying that the goods are still in your possession. When customs receive the certificate they issue a document authorising your bank to release your funds.

An application must be made within three months of your entry into Spain and goods should be imported within one year of taking up residence. They may be imported in one or a number of consignments, although it's best to have one consignment only. If there's more than one consignment, subsequent consignments should be cleared through the same customs office. Items subject to special customs requirements such as electrical appliances, carpets and works of art should be packed last to facilitate customs inspection. Goods imported duty-free mustn't be sold in Spain within two years of their importation and if you leave Spain within two years, everything imported duty-free must be exported or duty paid.

If you use a shipping company to transport your belongings, they usually provide the necessary forms and take care of the paperwork. Always keep a copy of forms and communications with customs officials, both with Spanish customs officials and customs officials in your previous country of residence. **If the paperwork isn't in order, your belongings may end up incarcerated in a Spanish customs storage depot for a number of months.** If you personally import your belongings, you may need to employ a customs agent (*agente de aduanas*) at the point of entry to clear them. You should have an official record of the export of valuables from any country, in case you wish to re-import them later.

Because of the restrictions and the deposit payable by non-EU homebuyers in Spain, you may wish to consider buying a property that's already furnished or buy furniture and furnishings locally.

Prohibited & Restricted Goods

Certain goods are subject to special regulations and, in some cases, their import and export is prohibited or restricted. This particularly applies to the following goods:

- Animal products; plants (see below).

- Wild fauna and flora and products derived from them.

- Live animals.

- Medicines and medical products (except for prescribed drugs and medicines).

- Firearms and ammunition (see below).

- Certain goods and technologies with a dual civil/military purpose.

- Works of art and collectors' items.

If you're unsure whether any goods you're importing fall into the above categories, you should check with customs.

To import certain types of plants, you must obtain a health certificate. There's usually a limit on the number of plants that can be imported, although when they're included in your personal effects they aren't usually subject to any special controls.

If you're planning to import sports guns, you must obtain a certificate from a Spanish consulate abroad, which is issued on production of a valid firearms licence. The consular certificate must be presented to the customs authorities upon entry and can be used to exchange a foreign firearms licence for a Spanish licence when taking up residence.

Visitors arriving in Spain from 'exotic' regions, e.g. Africa, South America, and the Middle and Far East, may find themselves under close scrutiny from customs and security officials looking for illegal drugs.

Duty-free Goods

If you travel to Spain from another EU country you're entitled to import goods of an unlimited value provided they're for your personal use, plus cigarettes and alcohol as listed below. The 'official' list is intended only as a guideline, but if you import more than the amounts shown you should be prepared to prove that they are for your personal use only and not for resale. If you cannot, they can be confiscated by customs officials. Note that the guidelines are subject to change and you should check with an official source before importing large amounts of tobacco and alcohol.

- 800 cigarettes.

- 400 cigarillos.

- 20 cigars.

- 1kg tobacco.

- 90 litres wine (of which no more than 60 should be sparkling).

- 10 litres spirits.

- 20 litres fortified wine.

- 110 litres beer.

For each journey to a non-EU country, travellers aged 17 or over (unless otherwise stated) are entitled to import the following goods purchased duty-free:

- One litre of spirits (over 22 degrees proof) **or** two litres of fortified wine, sparkling wine or other liqueurs (under 22 degrees proof).

- Two litres of still table wine.

- 200 cigarettes **or** 100 cigarillos **or** 50 cigars **or** 250g of tobacco.

- 60cc/ml of perfume.

- 250cc/ml of toilet water.

- Other goods, including gifts and souvenirs to the value of €175 (€90 for under 15s).

Duty-free allowances apply on outward and return journeys, even if both are made on the same day, and the combined total (i.e. double the above limits) can be imported into your 'home' country. It's rarely worthwhile buying duty-free alcohol or tobacco when travelling to Spain (e.g. on ferries), as it's much cheaper in Spanish supermarkets and off-licences.

Importing Your Car

Anyone wishing to import a vehicle into Spain must be a permanent resident, own property in Spain or have a rental agreement for a minimum of one year and hold a Spanish driving licence. The regulations and paperwork regarding car importation are comparatively simple, but many people still find the red tape forbidding and employ a *gestor* to do the paperwork for them. It may be easier and cheaper to buy a car once you're settled in Spain.

 Anyone who illegally drives a vehicle on foreign plates can be fined up to €3,000 and the vehicle can be confiscated.

The exact paperwork required depends on whether the car you wish to import is new or second-hand and from the EU or outside the EU. Personal documentation for the importer includes proof of residence in Spain (residence card or personal identification from your country of origin plus a certificate from the local police in Spain stating that you live in the locality), proof of owning or renting a property (the rental contract must be for a minimum of one year) and your Spanish driving licence.

Documentation required for the vehicle includes the technical inspection certificate; the completed form for vehicle registration (*Certificado Unico para la Matrícula de Vehículos*) available from your local provincial traffic department; the invoice for the purchase of the car if you bought it within the last six months; proof of payment of road tax (*impuesto municipal sobre vehículos de tracción mecánica*/IVTM); and proof of payment of the appropriate taxes. Cars imported from outside the EU may also need to undergo a homologation (*homologación*) check to ensure that it conforms to Spanish/EH specifications. A vehicle imported tax and duty-free into Spain mustn't be sold, rented or transferred within one year of its registration.

Details for the exact paperwork and documentation required can be found in our sister publication **Living and Working in Spain** by David Hampshire (see page 383) and on the Department of Traffic's website (⌨ http://www.dgt.es, *Vehículos* – in Spanish only), where you can also download forms.

Importing Your Pet

If you plan to take a pet (*animal de compañía* or *mascota*) to Spain, it's important to check the latest regulations. Ensure that you have the correct papers, not only for Spain, but for all the countries you will pass through on the way. Particular consideration must be given before exporting a pet from a country with strict quarantine regulations, such as the UK. If you need to return prematurely with a pet to a country with strict quarantine laws, even after a few hours or days in Spain, your pet must usually go into quarantine for a period if it doesn't have a pet 'passport' (see also **British Regulations** below).

If you're transporting a pet by ship or ferry, you should notify the ferry company. Some companies insist that pets are left in vehicles (if applicable), while others allow pets to be kept in cabins. If your pet is of nervous disposition or unused to travelling, it's best to tranquillise it on a long sea crossing. A pet can also be shipped to Spain by air.

Spanish Regulations

A maximum of five pets may accompany a traveller to Spain. **All dogs, cats and ferrets must have a microchip or registration number tattooed in an ear before they enter Spain.** A rabies vaccination is usually compulsory, although this **doesn't** apply to accompanied pets (including dogs and cats) coming directly from the UK. However, if a rabies vaccination is given, it must be administered not less than one month or more than one year before export. A rabies vaccination is necessary if pets are transported by road from the UK to Spain via France. Pets over three months old from countries other than the UK must have been vaccinated against rabies not less than one month and not more than one year before being imported. If a pet has no rabies certificate it can be quarantined for 20 days. Pets under three months old cannot be imported into Spain.

An official certificate (*Certificado de Origen y Sanidad*) is required, which must be completed and signed by a vet. The certificate includes the owner's details, a description of the pet, the microchip number (and where and when it was inserted) and the date of the rabies vaccination. The certificate is written in Spanish and English and is valid for four months after it has been signed. The certificate can be obtained from Spanish consulates abroad and downloaded from the following website: ⌨ http://www.mapausa.org. Some animals require a special import permit from the Spanish Ministry of Agriculture and pets from some countries are subject to customs duty.

British Regulations

The Pet Travel Scheme (PETS – now under the auspices of the EU pet passport scheme) replaces quarantine for qualifying cats and dogs. Under the scheme, pets must be micro-chipped (they have a microchip inserted in their neck), vaccinated against rabies, undergo a blood test and be issued with a health certificate (passport). **Note that the PETS certificate/EU pet passport sometimes isn't issued until six months AFTER the above have been carried out!** In the UK, EU pet passports are issued by Local Veterinary Inspectors (LVI) only, while in other EU countries they are issued by all registered vets.

The scheme is restricted to animals imported from rabies-free countries and countries where rabies is under control which includes 22 European countries plus Bahrain, Canada and the US. However, the current quarantine law will remain in place for pets coming from Eastern Europe, Africa (including the Spanish enclaves of Ceuta and Melilla), Asia and South America. To qualify, pets must travel by sea via any major British ferry port, by train via the Channel Tunnel or via Bristol, Doncaster, London Gatwick, London Heathrow or Manchester airports. Only certain carriers are licensed to carry animals and these are listed on the Department for Environment, Food and Rural Affairs (DEFRA) website (⌨ www.defra.gov.uk/animalh/quarantine/index.htm). Additional information is available from DEFRA (☎ 0870-241 1710, ✉ helpline@defra.gsi.gov.uk).

Registration costs around £200/€300 (for a microchip, rabies vaccination and blood test), plus £60/€90 a year for annual booster vaccinations and around £20/€30 for a border check. Shop around and compare fees from a number of veterinary surgeons.

British pet owners must complete an Application for a Ministry Export Certificate for dogs, cats and rabies susceptible animals (form EXA1), available from DEFRA at the above address. DEFRA contacts the vet you've named on the form who then performs a health inspection, after which you receive an export health certificate which must be issued no more than 30 days before your entry into Spain with your pet.

Registering a Dog

Dog owners are required to register their dogs and have them tattooed with their registration number in an ear or have a microchip inserted in their neck (a painless process, apart from the bill). Registration costs around €15 to €30 and there are fines for owners who don't have their dogs registered. If your dog already has a microchip from your home country, go to your nearest vet in Spain and ask for your contact details to be changed on the microchip information. Irrespective of whether your dog is micro-chipped, it's advisable to have it fitted with a collar and tag with your name and telephone number on it and the magic word 'reward' (*recompensa*).

ARRIVAL

Embassy Registration

Nationals of some countries are advised to register with their local embassy or consulate after taking up residence. Registration isn't usually compulsory, although most embassies like to keep a record of their country's citizens resident in Spain and consulates play an important role in emergencies.

US nationals can register with the US embassy in Spain online before they leave the US (🖳 https://travelregistration.state.gov/ibrs). For a list of foreign embassies and British consulates in Spain, see **Appendix A**.

Local Council Registration

Registering with your local council (a process known as *empadronamiento* and similar to registering on the electoral roll in the UK), isn't compulsory, but provides the following:

● Registered residents are included on the electoral roll, allowing EU nationals to vote in local elections.

© Hugues Argence (www.shutterstock.com)

© Peter Elvidge (www.shutterstock.com)

© Freeflyer (www.bigstockphoto.com)

© Korovljevic Djordje (www.shutterstock.com)

© Jonathan Noden-Wilkinson (www.shutterstock.com)

© Alex James Bramwell (www.shutterstock.com)

© Jose Antonio Sanchez (www.shutterstock.com)

© Albo (www.shutterstock.com)

© Carolina (www.shutterstock.com)

© Hugues Argence (www.shutterstock.com)

© Hugues Argence (www.shutterstock.com)

© Hugues Argence (www.shutterstock.com)

▶

© Dainis Derics (www.shutterstock.com)

▼ © Duncan Walker (www.istockphoto.com)

▼ © Frank Ungrad (www.shutterstock.com)

© Alejandro Lapuerta Mediavilla (www.shutterstock.com)

© Nick Stubbs (www.shutterstock.com)

© Duncan Walker (www.istockphoto.com)

© Felixfotografia.es (www.shutterstock.com)

© www.shutterstock.com

- Some local councils (e.g. Benalmádena and Fuengirola on the Costa del Sol) provide discounts on annual property rates for registered residents. This is often a substantial reduction (e.g. 30 per cent) on the normal rate.

- Certain municipal activities, e.g. evening classes and day-trips, are only available to registered residents. Other activities and facilities, e.g. sports centres, are subsidised for registered residents who also have priority on waiting lists for activities.

- Being registered with your local council also provides proof of residence in the area if you don't have a residence card or it's out of date.

The Council also benefits from increased public funding: local councils receive public funding (from €60 per person) from central and regional governments towards provision of certain public services such as police services, health centres and local transport. If residents don't register with their local council, they aren't included in the local population figures and therefore the funding paid to the local council is less than it should be. As a consequence, local services are under-funded and over-stretched, and additional services (such as extra police) aren't provided. Councils in many coastal areas claim that, if all foreign residents were registered, provisions and facilities would improve markedly.

The Registration Process

Registration is straightforward whereby you simply visit your nearest council office, show some form of identification (passport, ID card or residence permit) and proof that you're living in the area (e.g. title deeds, rental contract or a utility bill in your name). Most councils will register you on the spot and give you a certificate of registration (*certificado de empadronamiento*) that's valid for three months.

Registering is a different process from applying for a residence permit and doesn't necessarily make you liable for Spanish taxes, although if you're resident you may have to pay income tax and all property owners are liable for property taxes.

Finding Help

One of the biggest difficulties facing new arrivals is how and where to obtain help with day-to-day problems (e.g. insurance, utilities, etc.). This book and many other publications from Survival Books (see page 383) were written in response to this need. However, in addition to the comprehensive information provided in these books, you also need detailed **local** information. How successful you are at finding local help depends on the town or area where you live (e.g. residents of resort areas wirh many foreign residents are far better served than those in rural areas), your nationality, Spanish language proficiency and your sex (women may be better catered for than men through women's clubs). For detailed information about the Costa del Sol and the Costa Blanca regions you may wish to buy a copy of our sister publications, *Costa del Sol Lifeline* and *Costa Blanca Lifeline* (see page 383).

There's an abundance of information available in Spanish, but little in English and other foreign languages. Another problem is that much of the information available isn't intended for foreigners and their particular needs. You may find that your friends and colleagues can help as they can often offer advice based on their own experiences. **But take care!** Although they mean well, you're likely to receive as much false and conflicting information as accurate (it may not necessarily be wrong, but often won't apply to your situation).

Your local town hall (*ayuntamiento*) may be a good source of information, but you must usually be able to speak Spanish to benefit and may still be sent on a wild goose chase from department to department. However, some town halls in areas where there are many foreign residents have a foreigners' department (*departamento de extranjeros*) where staff speak English and other languages such as Danish, Dutch, Finnish, French, German and Swedish (an advantage of living somewhere where there are many other foreigners). Apart from assisting with routine matters, a foreigners' department can be helpful when applying for a residence permit, social security membership or a Spanish driving licence (and other formal applications), and they may save you the expense of employing a *gestor* (see page 311).

A wealth of useful information is available in major cities and resort towns, where foreigners are well-served by English-speaking clubs and expatriate organisations. Contacts can also be found through many expatriate publications (see **Appendix B**). Most consulates provide their nationals with local information, which may include details of lawyers, translators, doctors, dentists, schools, and social and expatriate organisations.

You may wish to buy a copy of *Buying a Home in Spain* if you're planning to buy property and/or *Living and Working in Spain*, both written by David Hampshire (see page 383), which contain a wealth of essential information about everyday life in Spain.

SETTLING IN

Once you've recovered from unpacking boxes (or feel it's time for a break!), your first step should be to find your nearest amenities such as a supermarket, bank (with an ATM) and a good restaurant. One of your priorities should also be to find a doctor (English-speaking if necessary) and a hospital with a casualty department (make sure you know how to get there and, if necessary, make a dummy run). Make a list of local emergency numbers (see page 203) and keep them next to the phone.

Settling into a new environment can be more difficult for retirees who don't have the advantage of a ready-made social network that families and employees find in the school playground and the workplace. When you first arrive in Spain you will need to make an effort to be friendly and go out of your way to be sociable to people. Introduce yourself to your neighbours as soon as possible and make friends with them by inviting them round for a drink or tea/coffee. They will be the ones you will greet each morning and who will be on hand in an emergency.

Check out the local social clubs and societies (town halls and local newspapers are good sources of information) and join a few at the first opportunity. You may also wish to consider becoming a member of a local sports club; tennis leagues and golf courses (especially the club house!) are ideal for meeting people and keeping fit at the same time. See **Chapter 10** for further information about leisure and sporting options.

After the initial excitement of moving to Spain and investigating your new neighbourhood dies down, the most difficult part of settling in begins. If you've retired to Spain on your own, it can be difficult to meet people, but you need to make an effort. Expatriates who become recluses aren't uncommon in Spain, therefore you need to avoid the easy option of staying at home watching TV and becoming lonely. Even if you just go out for a coffee, you will at least speak to someone. If you've retired with a partner, settling in is much easier as the stress is shared and you have someone to talk to (or shout at!), but make sure you both get out and do things. If possible, it's a good idea to have at least one individual activity a week so that you have 'time out' from your partner and new things to chat about.

SURVIVAL TIP
Accept any social invitations that come your way (you
can be choosy later) and don't forget to reciprocate.

If you move to an area that's popular with other expatriates from your home country the lack of language barriers will make socialising much easier. Many resort areas have a well-established network of clubs and making yourself at home is often straight forward. However, beware of becoming too dependent on expatriate society, which can be unstable (expatriates tend to come and go) and claustrophobic, particularly in small communities where little goes on and everyone knows everything about everyone else. Try to extend your contacts further afield and also make an effort to meet the locals. The Spanish are naturally gregarious and many will go out of their way to help and offer advice, even if you speak only rudimentary Spanish. Getting to know them will also add variety and interest to your social life and open new doors.

Meanwhile, don't forget to enjoy yourself – after all, this is supposed to be your retirement! Aim to try out a new restaurant each week and be adventurous in where you go and what you do. Take advantage of local tourist sites and attractions and visit them all. And every so often treat yourself to a mini-break away and go somewhere completely different – Spain offers a wealth of possibilities from city-breaks to rural retreats, from hiking in the desert to skiing. If you live within easy reach of an airport, visiting cities abroad is also a possibility – Amsterdam, Paris, Rome and Marrakech are just a few destinations within two hours flying time of most Spanish cities. See **Travelling Around Spain** on page 298 and **Travelling Further Afield** on page 301 for further information and **Culture Shock** on page 307.

The following tips may help you to settle into your new life:

- Keep your expectations realistic – settling in can take months.

- Expect a flurry of contrasting emotions – feeling euphoric one minute and down the next is normal and all part of the psychology of moving abroad.

- Think positively and accept all aspects of your new life at face value. Make the most of the good points of retiring in Spain and try not to dwell on the negative ones. Remember: it wasn't perfect where you lived before either otherwise you would still be there!

- Listen to your instincts and don't trust strangers too much – when you arrive somewhere new you're at your most vulnerable.

- Don't believe everything your fellow expatriates tell you. Expatriate myths (inheritance and taxes are the most common) circulate freely in Spain and many people believe them. Always consult an expert if in doubt.

- Wherever you retire to in Spain, whether it's to Benidorm or Barcelona or the deepest Galician countryside, make your life there a **new** life, not just a continuation of the one you led in your home country. Try to enjoy the best of both worlds rather than limiting yourself to an expatriate bubble.

7.

HEALTH MATTERS

One of the most important aspects of retiring in Spain is your health, both maintaining good health and the provision of healthcare. The quality of healthcare and healthcare facilities in Spain is generally very good (the best are world-class) and praised by foreign residents. Medical staff are highly trained and major hospitals are equipped with the latest high-tech equipment. English-speaking professionals are widely available in resort areas and major cities, and many health centres and hospitals in popular retirement areas provide translation services provided by volunteers. The state and private systems operate alongside each other and complement one another.

This chapter examines many of the important health issues for anyone retiring in Spain including preparations before leaving home, health issues in Spain, the state and private health systems including insurance cover, information about medical centres and professionals, social services, resources for the disabled, useful associations and dying in Spain.

For information on healthcare provisions in specific areas and regional health authorities, see **Popular Retirement Hot Spots** on page 100. **Emergency numbers and phrases can be found on page 203.**

SURVIVAL TIP
Note that the Spanish health service is becoming alarmed by the number of foreign retirees in certain regions, particularly the Costa Blanca, who are a huge burden on the local health service. Many people don't register as residents and rely on the EHIC (see below) to obtain medical treatment. This is a risky business and you may find yourself being denied treatment if you aren't registered with Spanish social security.

BEFORE YOU GO

Pre-departure Health Checks

Before leaving for Spain it's wise to have a health check (medical or screening, eyes, teeth, etc.), particularly if you have a record of poor health or are elderly. If you suffer from an existing medical condition ask your doctor to prepare a written report for you to take to Spain and, if possible, have it translated into Spanish. As soon as you've registered with a doctor in Spain, you should give him a copy of the report for your new medical records. If you have an unusual blood group or suffer from allergies to medicine, prepare a note of these and have it translated into Spanish.

Unlike many other European countries, dental treatment in Spain isn't provided under the state health system (unless it's an emergency extraction) and private dental treatment is expensive. It's therefore advisable to have a full dental check-up before you arrive and sort out any dental problems, e.g. crowns, dentures and fillings. The state health system also provides no subsidies for spectacles or contact lenses, therefore it may be cheaper to have an eye test and buy a new pair before you leave for Spain. This also applies to hearing aids.

Drugs & Medicines

If you're already taking regular medication, bear in mind that the brand names of drugs and medicines vary from country to country, and you should ask your doctor for the generic name. If you wish to match medication prescribed abroad, you need a current prescription with the medication's trade name, the manufacturer's name, the chemical name and the dosage. Most drugs have an equivalent in other countries, although particular brands may be difficult or impossible to obtain.

It's possible to have medication sent from abroad, when no import duty or VAT is usually payable. British retirees living on the Costa del Sol also have the option of buying drugs and medicine in Gibraltar where there are many chemists selling British products.

Spanish chemists provide a huge range of drugs, but you might prefer to bring favourite over-the-counter remedies for flu, headaches and diarrhoea (etc.) with you – painkillers tend to be more expensive in Spain than some other countries, e.g. the UK. Some creams and lotions, particularly sunscreen, are also more expensive so it's worth taking a supply.

See also **Prescription Drugs** on page 218.

Health Insurance

Before you leave for Spain, one of the most important things you must do is ensure that you have adequate health insurance cover.

EEA-Retirees

Your first step should be to obtain a European Health Insurance Card (EHIC), which has now replaced the old E-111 and E-128 forms throughout the EEA. The EHIC is available from social security offices in your home country or online (e.g. in the UK 💻 http://www.ehic.org.uk and in Ireland 💻 http://www.ehic.ie) and is valid for three to five years depending on the issuing country.

The EHIC entitles you to free or subsidised emergency treatment in Spain, but doesn't cover routine treatment, healthcare through the private system or repatriation. The EHIC is, however, useful when you first arrive in Spain if you need emergency treatment before you've obtained your Spanish social security card or taken out private insurance. If you're entitled to cover under the Spanish state health system you must obtain form E-121 or E-106 (see page 209) from the social security authorities in your home country.

If you plan to take out private health insurance with a non-Spanish company, it may pay to do this before you leave for Spain. If you already have a private policy, make sure that it covers you for treatment in Spain – you may need to change your policy or insurance company.

The EHIC provides for emergency treatment only and is intended for visitors. In order to receive routine medical treatment you need to be a resident and be registered with Spanish social security and have a Spanish healthcard.

Non-EEA Retirees

Spain has few reciprocal health agreements with non-EEA countries so it's essential to take out private health insurance covering at least emergency treatment before you leave. This can be a travel insurance policy, which will cover you until you become a resident or take out private health insurance in Spain. Non-EEA retirees aren't generally entitled to healthcare under the state health system and should take out comprehensive private health insurance.

SURVIVAL TIP
Don't leave for Spain without making sure you have state and/or private insurance cover for every health eventuality, otherwise treatment could cost you thousands of euros.

EMERGENCIES

The emergency medical services (*urgencias*) in Spain are excellent. Keep a record of the telephone numbers of your doctor, local hospitals and clinics, ambulance (*ambulancia*) service, first aid, poison control, dentist and other emergency services (fire, police) next to your telephone (see Emergency Numbers below). Whoever you call, give the age of the patient and, if possible, specify the type of emergency so that the ambulance can bring a doctor if necessary. In a life-threatening emergency such as a heart attack or a serious accident, you should call for an ambulance and mention the nature of the emergency (see **Useful Emergency Words & Phrases** below).

If you're physically able you can go to a hospital emergency or casualty department (*urgencias*) or a 24-hour state health clinic (*ambulatorio* or *casa de socorro*). The telephone numbers of first aid stations are listed at the front of telephone directories and many are equipped with ambulances. Check in advance which local hospitals are equipped to deal with emergencies and the quickest route from your home. This information may be of vital importance in the event of an emergency, when a delay may mean the difference between life and death. In an emergency, a hospital must treat you, irrespective of your ability to pay. Most chemists post a list of local clinics and hospitals where emergency medical treatment is available. Note that if you're initially treated at a state medical centre (*centro de salud*) or out-patient clinic (*ambulatorio*) you will usually be referred to a state hospital for treatment (which you may not want if you have private health insurance).

Emergency Numbers

Number	Service
☎ 112	All-purpose emergency number (if you dial this number you' will be connected to the emergency service you require).
☎ 061	Ambulance (*ambulancia*)
☎ 062	Civil Guard (*guardia civil*)
☎ 080	Fire Service (*bomberos*)
☎ 091	National Police (*policía nacional*)

☎ 092   Local Police (*policía local*)

☎ 900 202 202   Maritime rescue (*salvamento marítimo*)

☎ 915 620 420   Poison Information Service (*información toxicológica*)

Emergency numbers are listed at the front of all telephone directories and should be kept next to your phone. If you're unsure who to call, ask operator information (☎ 11818) or call your local police station, who will tell you who to contact or contact the appropriate service for you. There are also 24-hour private medical centres (*centros médicos*) in resort areas with ambulance and emergency services.

Useful Emergency Words & Phrases

- accident – *accidente*

- allergic reaction – *reacción alérgica*

- bleeding – *sangrando*

- emergency – *emergencia/urgencia*

- heart attack – *infarto* or *paro cardiaco*

- I need an ambulance – *necesito una ambulancia*

- I need a doctor – *necesito un médico*

- no pulse – *sin pulso*

- not breathing – *no respira*

- overdose – *sobredosis*

- stroke – *parálisis cerebral*

- unconscious – *inconsciente*

- urgent – *urgente*

- wounded – *herido*

If you suffer from a particular medical condition, make sure you (and your partner) know what it's called in Spanish. For more useful medical phrases in Spanish see *Liz Parry's Spanish Phrase Book* (Santana).

KEEPING HEALTHY IN SPAIN

Keeping healthy in Spain shouldn't be difficult because there are so many factors in your favour: a warm, sunny climate throughout most of the country from April to October, mild winters along much of the coastline and two of the best microclimates in the world found on the Costa Blanca and in the south of Tenerife; one of the world's healthiest diets (Mediterranean), with its emphasis on olive oil, fresh fruit and vegetables, and fish rather than meat; a more relaxed approach to life meaning stress levels are lower; a predominantly outdoor life with more exercise and fresh air; and a generally unpolluted atmosphere (with the exception of the major cities).

Most foreigners living in Spain boast that they're healthier and fitter than they were in their home country, claiming they have fewer colds and generally feel better. Retirees frequently find their arthritis or rheumatism improves dramatically after moving to Spain and many feel that the process of 'growing old' slows down in Spain's warm and sunny climate. However, although Spain is one of the healthiest places to live, it isn't without its health risks, some of which are outlined below.

Alcohol

Although not a problem that's unique to Spain, alcohol is cheap and readily available in Spain and a daily glass (or two) is part and parcel of Spanish life. Bars and cafés serve alcohol all day and measures, especially for spirits, are usually much more generous than those served in northern European countries. Alcoholism exists among Spaniards, but it's far more prevalent among foreigners, particularly retirees who have little to do, but lie in the sun and drink alcohol all day. If you find yourself drinking more than is good for you (the recommended maximum weekly consumption for a man is 21 units and 14 units for a woman), try to limit your alcohol intake.

Alcoholics Anonymous (AA) have English-speaking groups in many parts of Spain including Barcelona, the Balearics (Ibiza and Majorca), the Canaries, Madrid and on the Costa Blanca and Costa del Sol. Details of meeting times and places can be found in the expatriate press and on the AA Europe website (🖳 http://www.aa-europe.net/countries – Spain).

Allergies

Sufferers from hay fever and asthma usually find their symptoms considerably worse in Spain, especially in spring when the countryside literally explodes into flower. If you suffer from hay-fever, you should avoid walking in the countryside during late April and May. Other common pollen allergies include:

- **Olive blossom pollen** – a surprisingly common allergy and a particular problem in central Spain and most of inland Andalusia during May and June;

- **Cypress tree pollen** – cypress trees (*cipreses*) are found on most of the Mediterranean coast and pollinate during early spring;

- **Plane tree pollen** – plane trees (*plátanos*) are found in most Spanish towns and cities, and their yellow pollen fills the air in April.

Anti-histamine tablets, eye-drops and inhalers are available over the counter in chemists, but be aware that many cause drowsiness. If your allergy is particularly bad, effective treatment (including vaccines) is available from the state and private health systems. Bear in mind, however, that treatment is usually long-term (around three years) and requires a daily dose of drops or monthly injection.

Daily pollen levels and alerts are published in local newspapers, shown on television weather forecasts and can be found on 🖳 http://www.uco.es/investiga/grupos/rea/mapactsema.htm.

Excessive Heat

Temperatures in mainland Spain (with the exception of the north coast) usually rise to over 30°C (86°F) throughout the months of July and August when midday temperatures can reach 40°C (104°F). Older people are particularly vulnerable to heat exhaustion and each year a number of elderly people die from the adverse effects of heat. During the hottest months keep out of the sun, drink plenty of fluids (not just water: make sure fluids include salt – *gazpacho* is widely considered to be the ideal mineral and vitamin replenishing drink) and avoid over-exertion. Take a leaf out of the Spaniards' book and enjoy a daily siesta along with the rest of the country in the hottest part of the afternoon.

Pollution

Although Spain generally boasts some of Europe's cleanest air, in some cities pollution levels regularly exceed the EU recommended limits. A report published in early 2006 by the environmental group, Ecologistas en Acción, found excessive levels of nitrogen dioxide in Barcelona, Madrid, Malaga and Valencia, as well as numerous other smaller cities such as Granada. Winter is a particularly bad time when fumes from cars and the lack of rain result in thick smog settling over cities, which is a common occurrence in Madrid. The report also estimated that some 16,000 deaths a year are caused by pollution. If you suffer from a respiratory problem such as asthma, it's advisable to give city living a miss!

Smoking

Tobacco is cheap in Spain where cigarettes cost up to two-thirds less than they do in some other European countries and (perhaps because of this) the Spaniards are big smokers (second only to Greece in the number of smokers per capita in western Europe). Many expatriates smoke more in Spain than they did in their home country and many ex-smokers start smoking again. Not surprisingly, smoking-related ailments and deaths are a serious problem and smoking is the leading cause of death among adults, directly responsible for some 56,000 deaths a year.

Anti-smoking legislation (introduced in 2006) prohibits smoking in most public areas, including the workplace, shops, and bars and restaurants larger than 100m². However, it's still permitted in bars and restaurants smaller than 100m², which, in practice, is most of them!

For those with the will-power, the state health service provides support for smokers wishing to kick the habit and over-the-counter remedies such as nicotine patches and tablets are available from chemists. Some areas also have support groups – ask at your local health centre for details of one near you. Bear in mind that the older you are, the more your health will suffer from smoking and that there are thousands of reasons for giving it up and not one for continuing to smoke!

Sunburn

Although the sun's warming rays have many beneficial effects, too much sun is highly damaging and can cause dry skin, wrinkles and skin cancer – the beetroot-red face so favoured by many expatriates isn't only unbecoming, but also potentially fatal. Fair-skinned northern Europeans burn very easily in the Spanish sun, so heed the Australian slogan in the battle against skin cancer: 'Slip, Slop, Slap' – slip on a shirt, slop on sunscreen and slap on a hat. Ensure that your sunscreen's protection factor is at least 20+ (at least

30+ for fair-skinned people) and at least double that for your face and other delicate areas. Keep out of the sun from 1 to 5pm in the hottest months and beware of a higher concentration of damaging UV rays in early spring and autumn when the ozone layer is at its thinnest. UV levels are published daily in local newspapers and on the internet (e.g. 💻 http://www.inm.es – *Predicciones/Rad. UV*).

HEALTHCARE PROVISIONS IN SPAIN

State Health System

The state health system is generally good and huge advances have been made over the last 20 years. Health centres are widely available and most large towns have at least one state hospital. Waiting lists to see specialists and for non-urgent operations have been considerably reduced in most areas, although waiting lists for surgery are still long in some regions. Spain's annual spending on health is below the EU average, although in 2006 the government vastly increased the health budget. While primary and specialist treatment is excellent, hospital nursing care and post-hospital assistance are below what northern Europeans and North Americans take for granted, and spending on preventive medicine is low. However, on balance, most foreign residents speak highly of the Spanish state health system.

There's no central state health system in Spain and each region operates its own state health system, which means there are sometimes marked differences between the quality and variety of healthcare facilities available in each region, e.g. making appointments via the internet is only available in some areas. However, patients can choose any specialist, surgeon or hospital in Spain and if you have an ailment for which treatment isn't covered in your region, you're usually referred to another region. Patients are also entitled to a second medical opinion, an increasingly common request in the state health system.

Getting Covered

The state health systems provide free or low cost healthcare to those who contribute to Spanish social security (*seguridad social*), plus their families and retirees who receive a state pension (including those from other EEA countries). Non-EEA retirees don't generally qualify for free healthcare unless they make monthly contributions to social security, which may be more expensive than taking out private health insurance. EEA retirees wishing to obtain healthcare cover under the state system need one of the following:

Form E-121: This form proves you're in receipt of a state pension or invalidity benefit in your home country.

Form E-106: This form entitles you to state health cover for a limited period after your arrival in Spain, provided you've made regular social security contributions in another EU country for two full years before coming to Spain. Cover under this form is usually limited to a few months, after which time you must take out a private health insurance policy or contribute to Spanish social security.

The above forms are obtainable from the social security authorities in your home country, for example the Department of Work and Pensions in the UK (☎ 0845-606 0265, UK only, or +44-191-218 7777, ⌨ http://www.dwp. gov.uk) and Pension Services Office in Ireland (☎ 1890-500 500, ⌨ http:// www.welfare.ie).

Registering: You must take your form to the local provincial office of the Instituto Nacional de la Seguridad Social/INSS (contact details are listed in the white and *Yellow Pages* and on the INSS website, ⌨ http:// www.seg-social.es) together with personal identification (passport or residence permit). You will be registered as a member of the social security, be given a receipt of your registration and will receive an electronic social security card (*tarjeta*) by post shortly afterwards which includes your name and your social security number. You should also receive a list of local medical practitioners and hospitals, and general information about services and charges.

You should then visit your nearest health centre to register with a general doctor (*médico de cabecera*) of your choice (ask other local residents for recommendations) where your personal and contact details will be recorded.

SURVIVAL TIP

You must take your card whenever you visit a doctor or go to hospital. If you make an appointment by phone or internet, you must quote your social security number.

Entitlements: Most aspects of healthcare (e.g. primary and specialist treatment, hospitalisation, laboratory services and transportation) and prescriptions are free to pensioners with the exception of some appliances (e.g. wheelchairs and crutches) and non-emergency dental care. Unlike some European countries, 'alternative' treatments such as chiropractic and acupuncture aren't available under state health system.

Private Health

Private healthcare is generally good and several private clinics in Spain are rated among the best in the world. Advantages of private health insurance include a wider choice of medical practitioners and hospitals, a higher likelihood of seeing an English-speaking professional, no (or short) waiting lists and more privacy in hospitals (private hospitals have single rooms whereas state hospitals have double rooms). On the other hand, policies can be expensive, private clinics don't always have adequate facilities (in which case you're referred to a state hospital) and cover isn't always available for the over-65s. Private insurance is a popular option among foreign retirees who can afford it and if you aren't covered by Spanish social security (see above), it's essential to have private health insurance unless you have a very large bank balance. Proof of a private health insurance policy is necessary for some visa and residence permit applications.

Obtaining Insurance

Both Spanish and foreign companies offer private health insurance policies covering Spain, although the extent of cover, limitations, restrictions, premiums and choice of doctors, specialists and hospitals varies considerably. Note that some foreign insurance companies don't provide sufficient cover to satisfy Spanish visa and permit regulations and therefore you must check the minimum cover necessary with a Spanish consulate in your home country before taking out a policy.

When comparing the cost of Spanish health insurance with a foreign policy, you should compare the benefits carefully and take particular note of exactly what's included and excluded. All policies include limitations and restrictions, e.g. injuries as a result of participation in certain high-risk sports aren't usually covered. Many Spanish companies limit the costs for a particular specialist or treatment in a calendar year, in addition to having a total overall annual limit for all treatment. Some companies include restrictive clauses, e.g. they may exclude dialysis treatment or may pay for only a limited number of days a year in hospital, e.g. 20 to 60. Steer well clear of policies with severe restrictions (such as a maximum 20-day hospitalisation period) and **always** check the small print.

Certain services aren't provided during the first six months cover, e.g. medical check-ups and dental care, and some services may be included only for an extra premium and an excess payment. Most policies don't cover illnesses contracted within a certain period of taking out a policy or pre-existing illnesses for a period, e.g. one or two years (irrespective of whether you were aware of the illness or not). Many policies have clauses allowing annual increases that bear no relation to inflation or increases in the cost of living.

Spanish Companies: The largest Spanish health insurance companies are:

● Adeslas (☎ 902 200 200, 🖳 http://www.adeslas.es) – nationwide;

● Asisa (☎ 901 101 010, 🖳 http://www.asisa.es) – nationwide;

● Sanitas (☎ 902 102 400, 🖳 http://www.sanitas.es) – nationwide;

● Vital Seguros (☎ 936 020 602, 🖳 http://www.vitalseguro.com) – Catalonia only.

There are also numerous smaller companies that operate locally or regionally, although non-national policies include participating hospitals throughout Spain for emergency cases.

Spanish insurance companies provide you with a membership card together with a list of contracted doctors, specialists and hospitals in their area which accept the company's cards. Some insurance companies also operate their own clinics.

SURVIVAL TIP
Note that if you're taken to a hospital in an emergency that isn't on your insurance company's list, you won't be covered under your policy.

Most companies offer a choice of plans, e.g. contracted doctors, specialists and other out-patient treatment; and all out-patient consultations and treatment plus hospitalisation and surgery. If you don't speak fluent Spanish, check that the insurance company offer English-speaking practitioners and hospital staff (not all do).

Annual premiums vary and most increase significantly when you're 60 or over, for example, the Adeslas 'Completa' policy option costs €70 a month for a man aged between 55 and 59 and €110 per month for men aged 60 to 64.

Policies for women aged 50 to 60 are more expensive than those for men of the same age, but cheaper for the over 60s. Discounts are offered if you pay every three or six months or annually (in advance) rather then monthly.

Spanish insurance companies can (and will) cancel a policy at the end of the insurance period if you have a serious illness with endless high expenses and some companies automatically cancel a policy when you reach the age of 65.

You should avoid such a company at all costs, as to take out a new policy at the age of 65 at a reasonable premium is difficult or impossible. Some companies won't accept new clients aged over 60 while others accept new clients up to the age of 75, e.g. Sanitas has a policy for the over 65s (*Oro Reembolso*).

It's important to note that Spanish health insurance policies are designed for those living permanently in Spain and most provide only emergency cover abroad. Emergency medical cover abroad is paid up to a limited amount only, e.g. €2,500 or €5,000, which is very little if you need to be hospitalised (international travel policies typically include medical expenses equal to €300,000 or more). Spanish policies, not surprisingly, don't include repatriation to another country. The consensus among expatriates is that although Spanish health insurance may sometimes be cheaper, it doesn't provide wide cover and isn't good value for money compared with some foreign health insurance schemes.

Foreign Companies: There are a number of foreign health insurance companies with agents or offices in Spain, including:

- AXA PPP Healthcare (🖳 http://www.axappphealthcare.com);

- BUPA Spain (🖳 http://www.bupaspain.com) with representatives in the Balearics (☎ 971 720 807), Costa Blanca (☎ 965 719 030), Costa del Sol (☎ 952 491 115) and Madrid (☎ 609 522 300);

- Exeter Friendly Society (🖳 http://www.exeterfriendly.co.uk);

- International Health Insurance (Denmark – 🖳 http://www.ihi.com).

These companies offer special policies for expatriates and usually include repatriation to your home country and international cover (although cover may be restricted in high costs regions such as North America). The main advantages of a foreign health insurance policy are that treatment is unrestricted and you can usually choose any doctor, specialist, clinic or hospital in Spain, and generally also in other countries.

Most foreign policies include repatriation (although it may be optional), which may be an important consideration if you need treatment which is unavailable in Spain, but available in your home (or another) country. Repatriation may also pay for repatriation of your body for burial in your home country. Some companies offer policies for different areas, e.g. Europe, worldwide excluding North America and worldwide including North America. A policy may offer full cover anywhere within Europe and limited cover in North America and certain other countries (e.g. Japan). Some policies offer the same cover worldwide for a fixed premium, which may be an important consideration for globetrotters. Note that an international policy allows you to choose to have non-urgent medical treatment in another country. Most companies offer different levels of cover, for example, AXA PPP Healthcare offer standard, comprehensive and prestige levels of cover.

There's always an annual limit on total annual medical costs (which should be at least €350,000 to €400,000) and some companies also limit costs for specific treatment or costs such as specialist's fees, surgery and hospital accommodation. Some policies include permanent disability cover, e.g. €150,000, for those in full-time employment. A medical isn't usually required for most health policies, although pre-existing health problems are excluded for a period, e.g. one or two years. Claims are usually settled in major currencies and large claims are usually settled directly by insurance companies (although your choice of hospitals may be limited).

> **SURVIVAL TIP**
> **Always check whether a company pays large medical bills directly.**

If you're required to pay bills and claim reimbursement from the insurance company, it may take you several months to receive your money (some companies are slow to pay). It isn't usually necessary to have bills translated into English or another language, although you should check a company's policy. Most companies provide 24-hour emergency telephone assistance.

The cost of international health insurance varies considerably depending on your age and the extent of cover. Premiums can sometimes be paid monthly, quarterly or annually, although some companies insist on payment annually in advance. Annual premiums vary from around €1,000 to over €4,500 for the most comprehensive cover, e.g. Exeter Friendly's Interplan

Euro (basic level) costs €856 a year for a man aged 60, €1,070 a year for a man aged 65 and €1,369 a year for a man aged 70.. Some companies have an excess of around €100 per claim (or €150 for dental treatment) and it may be possible to choose an increased voluntary excess of €300 to €1,000 and receive a discount (e.g. 10 or 20 per cent). The maximum annual cover is usually up to around €350,000 to €400,000 per person, per year, and may include permanent total disability cover up to €150,000. Payment may be accepted by Visa or Access. Policies usually include repatriation and limited worldwide cover, including North America.

If you have existing private health insurance in another country, you may be able to extend it to include Spain. If you already have a private health insurance policy, you may find you can save a substantial amount by switching to another company without losing any benefits (you may even gain some). To compare policies, it's best to contact an independent insurance broker who offers policies from a number of companies. If your stay in Spain is short, you may be covered by a reciprocal agreement between your home country and Spain.

SURVIVAL TIP
Make sure you're fully covered by health insurance in
Spain before you receive a large bill.

It's foolhardy for anyone living in Spain (or even visiting) not to have comprehensive health insurance. If you or members of your family aren't adequately insured, you could face some very high medical bills. When leaving Spain, you should ensure that you have continuous health insurance. If you're planning to change your health insurance company, you should ensure that no important benefits are lost.

Medical Centres

Health Centres

State health centres (*centros de salud* or *ambulatorios*) are found throughout Spain and all but the smallest villages have some sort of health centre. In large towns and cities there are usually several centres providing primary care (general doctors' surgeries, routine check-ups and services such as dressing changes, injections etc), x-ray facilities and emergency departments. Larger health centres are open 24-hours a day. In rural areas, a health centre may open for a few hours a day or only on certain days of the week.

Doctors' surgeries usually take place once daily (e.g. 8 to 11am or 3 to 6pm) and it's usually necessary to make an appointment (*cita previa*). This can be done in person, by phone or internet (in some regions only – see **Popular Retirement Hot Spots** on page 100) and appointments can usually be made within 24 or 72 hours. In an emergency you can visit an emergency clinic.

Hospitals & Clinics

Hospitals (*hospitales*) and clinics (*clínicas*) are found in most large towns and all cities, and most are modern establishments with highly trained staff and state of the art, high-tech equipment. Rural areas are less well-served and you may need to travel some distance to the nearest hospital.

State hospitals (*hospitales públicos* or *hospitales de la seguridad social*) have an emergency department (*urgencias*) and usually provide a range of specialist fields of medicine including outpatient departments (*consultas externas*). Some health districts have day-hospitals (*hospital de día*) for outpatient appointments and minor surgery only. Emergency departments in state hospitals tend to be swamped with patients and unless you have a life-threatening emergency, you should expect to be there for several hours. Note that most health centres provide emergency services (opening hours may be limited, e.g. 8am to 8pm) and it's often quicker to be seen here rather at a hospital. A list of local hospitals treating social security patients is available from your social security office.

Private clinics (*clínicas privadas*) tend to specialise in in-patient care in particular fields of medicine rather than being full-service hospitals, and not all private hospitals have emergency departments.

You must present your social security card or evidence of your health insurance or the ability to pay whenever you visit a hospital (except in emergencies, when you or your family can present proof of insurance afterwards). If you have no cover or your private insurance company doesn't have an arrangement with the hospital to pay bills direct, you must pay the bill yourself (credit cards are usually accepted).

 You should be aware that medical staff at some health centres and hospitals may refuse to treat patients who don't speak Spanish or who don't have an interpreter.

Hospices

Specialised hospices (*hospicio*) for terminally-ill patients are a relatively new concept in Spain and those that exist are part of a hospital, meaning patients never get away from a hospital environment. Palliative treatment and support for patients and their families lag behind the best practices in other western countries, although facilities in some areas, e.g. Barcelona, are more than adequate. There's currently only one independent in-patient hospice in Spain, situated on the Costa del Sol and run by Cudeca, an award-winning charity established by British expatriates (☎ 952 564 910, 🖳 http://www.cudeca.org). Two charities on the Costa Blanca are currently in the process of building a hospice – Sweet Charity Hospice (🖳 http://www.sweetcharityhospice.org) and the Costa Blanca Hospice Association (🖳 http://www.caringspain.com). All three of the above associations also provide advice and support for cancer sufferers and their families.

Medical Professionals

Doctors

The standard of medical training in Spain is high and there are excellent doctors throughout the country. English-speaking doctors can be found in most popular resort areas and on the islands, but elsewhere in Spain, particularly in rural areas, there are few. Don't count on your doctor being able to understand English – if your Spanish is poor, you may need to take a translator along with you. American, British, German and Scandinavian doctors also practise in Spain, although usually only in areas that are popular with foreign residents. Many embassies and consulates in Spain maintain a list of English-speaking doctors and specialists in their area, and your employer, colleagues, friends or neighbours may be able to recommend someone. Tourist offices may also keep a list of English-speaking doctors and the names and telephone numbers of English-speaking doctors and dentists are often listed in local English-language newspapers and magazines.

All doctors practising in Spain must be registered with the doctors' association (*Colegio de Médicos*) in the province where the practice is located. Doctors in the state sector are automatically registered by the authorities, but this isn't the case with the private sector, therefore you may wish to check a private doctor's credentials before becoming a patient. Doctors are permitted to advertise their services and some advertise in the expatriate press. General practitioners (GPs) or family doctors are listed in *Yellow Pages* under *Médicos* and specialists under their speciality such as heart specialists (*Médicos Cardiología*).

Dentists

Dentists (*dentistas*) are generally good throughout Spain, although outside resort areas it can be difficult to find a dentist who speaks good English (although *aaargh*! Is the same in any language). English-speaking Spanish dentists and foreign dentists (particularly British and Scandinavian) practise in most resort areas. Ask around for recommendations.

Dental treatment is generally expensive in Spain (the state health service only covers emergency extractions), so compare fees and services carefully. Some private health insurance policies cover dental treatment and some dental practices operate a membership scheme (e.g. €150 a year for two check-ups, consultations and discounts on treatment). The cost of treatment varies widely, but as a rough guide you can expect to pay from €50 for an extraction and from €40 to €100 for a filling. Before committing yourself to a large bill, it's advisable to obtain a written quotation for expensive treatment. Note that not all dentists provide all services, e.g. most dentists will fill a tooth, but they may not do extractions, which means that you may have to go to another dentist. Check in advance.

Opticians

You don't need to register with an optician (*óptico*) in Spain; simply make an appointment with the optician of your choice. Ask for recommendations and compare prices and services carefully as costs vary hugely. Opticians are listed in the *Yellow Pages* under *Óptica* and private specialist eye doctors (ophthalmologists) under *Médicos Oftalmología*. The state health service covers eye problems requiring treatment by an ophthalmologist and eye tests are usually free at any opticians. Retirees may be entitled to subsidised spectacles, but, as in many countries, the choice of frames is limited. Competition between opticians is fierce and it's worth shopping around for offers and discounts.

Drugs & Medicines

Drugs (*medicinas*) and medicines (*medicamentos*) prescribed by a doctor are obtained from a chemist (*farmacia*) denoted by the sign of a green cross.

Most chemists are open from 9.30am to 1.30pm and from 4.30 to 8pm from Mondays to Saturdays. Outside normal opening hours, a notice is posted in windows giving the address of the nearest duty chemist (*farmacia de guardia*) open after 8pm (a weekly roster may be displayed). There are 24-hour duty chemists in all towns (usually indicated by a red light), although there may also be duty daytime (e.g. from 9.30am until 10pm) and night time chemists (e.g. from 10pm until 9.30am the following day). Legislation permits unlimited opening hours for chemists.

Pharmacists in Spain are highly trained and provide free medical advice for minor ailments, although you must usually speak Spanish. They're often able to sell you the proper remedy without recourse to a doctor and will also recommend a local doctor, specialist, nurse or dentist where necessary. They can supply a wide range of medicines over the counter without a prescription. Chemists also stock baby food and essentials and a limited range of cosmetics, diet foods and toiletries (although these items are almost always more expensive than the equivalent in a supermarket), but don't sell non-medical wares that you find in chemists in other countries, e.g. Boots in the UK.

Prescription Drugs

Retirees who are pensioners and who qualify for healthcare under the state health system (see page 208) pay nothing for prescribed medicines and drugs. Non-pensioners who qualify for healthcare under the state health system are entitled to a 60 per cent discount on prescribed medicines and drugs, and therefore pay 40 per cent of the price. This is expensive if you have a chronic condition, e.g. diabetes, requiring constant medication. No other discounts are available on drugs and medicines prescribed by doctors under the state healthcare system.

Many private health insurance schemes also reimburse members for drugs and medicines. Note that there's no refund for some prescribed medicines or for medicines purchased without a doctor's prescription.

SOCIAL SERVICES

Spanish culture considers it to be a family's moral duty to care for the elderly and it's still common for a grandparent unable to look after themselves to move in with his son or daughter's family (25 per cent of Spain's old people live alone compared to 40 per cent in France). As well as a cultural matter, moving in with your family is also practical as the Spanish state provides very little social provision for the over 65s, who comprise over 17 per cent of the population, a percentage that's increasing by nearly 4 per cent annually (Spain has the fifth-oldest population in the EU).

Despite the fact that the over 65s account for nearly 80 per cent of the country's pharmaceutical bill and occupy half the hospital beds and health centre appointments, nursing home places are available for a mere 4 per cent and only one in four state hospitals has a specialised geriatric unit. Spain's social services for the elderly are clearly inadequate and lag far behind those in other EU countries. However, the situation is gradually improving and is one of the government's priorities and most councils now provide social services for the elderly in their municipality, although the quality and scope varies widely. Note that in order to qualify for council social services, you must be registered with your local council, a process known as *empadronamiento* (see page 192).

What's Available

Nationally

Within the Spanish system of regional autonomy, social services are provided at regional, provincial and local level, rather than national. However, the National Institute for the Elderly and Social Services (Instituto de Mayores y Servicios Sociales/ IMSERSO) acts as an umbrella association and is a useful source of information for social services nationwide. The only services for the over 65s provided by the IMSERSO itself are (excellent value) subsidised holidays within Spain and spa treatments at some of Spain's many spa resorts (*balnearios*). As you would expect, demand for the holidays and spa treatments usually exceeds supply! Information about these (and IMSERSO generally) is available from provincial social security offices or from the Institute's website (🖳 http://www.imsersomayores.csic.es – some information is in English).

Dependency Law: In April 2006, the government approved the Dependency Law (*Ley de Dependencia*) whose principal objective is to provide better services and funds for the elderly and disabled in Spain and their carers. It's calculated that around 1.5m people will benefit financially and socially from the law, which comes into effect in 2007.

Regionally

Social services provided by regional governments generally include residential services and day centres (see below); support for carers of the aged and/or disabled; financial assistance in the form of grants, loans and pension supplements; subsidised holidays; and education opportunities such as day classes (most regions provide IT classes). Some regions provide further benefits, such as Andalusia, where the over 65's can take advantage of free legal advice, a 50 per cent discount on bus journeys in the region, and discounts on glasses and hearing aids.

If you wish to benefit from regional social services, you must be aged over 65 and resident in the region. Financial assistance is generally only given to pensioners whose monthly income is below the national minimum wage (€540.90).

Further information about the social services available in individual regions is available from the regional government website:

- **Andalusia** – 💻 http://www.juntadeandalucia.es/igualdadybienestarsocial for the Costa de Almería, the Costa de la Luz and the Costa del Sol;

- **Balearics** – 💻 http://www.caib.es (go to 'Dirección General de Servicios Sociales');

- **Canaries** – 💻 http://www.gobcan.es (go to 'Empleo y Asuntos Sociales');

- **Catalonia** – 💻 http://www.gencat.net (go to 'Benestar i Familia' – in Catalan only) for Barcelona, the Costa Brava and the Costa Dorada;

- **Murcia** – 💻 http://www.carm.es (go to 'Consejería de Trabajo y Política Social') for the Costa Cálida;

- **Valencia** – 💻 http://www.gva.es (go to 'Conselleria de Bienestar Social') for the Costa Blanca and the Costa del Azahar.

Telephone helpline: Andalusia and Valencia are the only regions to provide a free telephone helpline specifically for the elderly. Lines are open 24-hours a day, 365 days a year and telephonists provide advice, counselling, medical assistance and a 'friendly ear'.

- **Andalusia** – ☎ 900 858 381

- **Comunidad Valenciana** – ☎ 900 100 011

Provincially/Locally

The main social services for the elderly are provided by local council or provincial bodies (*diputación*) and vary considerably and may include:

- **Help at home** (*servicio de atención a domicilio*) – this includes visits by a nurse (for medical attention and personal hygiene), home help (for domestic chores such as cleaning and cooking) and 24-hour emergency help (*servicio de teleasistencia*) consisting of a portable call button you press if you need help (this is usually available only to people living alone).

- **Day centres and clubs** (*servicio de atención diurna*) – these consist of social clubs providing a meeting place and activities, and day centres (*centros de día*) offering care and meals, but not accommodation.

- **Residential services** (*servicios residenciales*) – there are three kinds of nursing homes for the elderly in Spain; homes for those able to look after themselves, residences for invalids or the chronically ill and mixed residences. There's a chronic shortage of nursing homes in Spain where places are available for a mere 4 per cent of the over 65s. State-run homes are the cheapest (costing from around €500 a month – subsidised for those on low incomes), but these are few and far between. There are far more privately-run homes (some homes are jointly run by the state and a private company) and average costs here are €1,500 a month for an individual room with private bathroom. Prices are around 10 per cent higher in Barcelona and 20 per cent higher in Madrid.

  Private nursing homes vary in terms of facilities and services, although all must fulfil strict minimum criteria and standards. Before committing yourself, look around and compare facilities, levels of care and privacy, staff qualifications and extra services. You should also check that a home is registered with the local and regional authorities. See also **Retirement Complexes** on page 148.

The website *Inforesidencias* (⌨ http://www.inforesidencias.com – Spanish only) provides a useful search tool for vacancies in nursing homes as well as a listing (by province) of homes together with their fees and the services offered. This site also provides a wealth of advice on how to choose a nursing home and a useful checklist of services.

If you wish to apply for any of the above services, you must apply at your local council with the correct documentation, usually consisting of a residence permit, tax return, certificate of registration with the council (*certificado de empadronamiento* – see page 192) and a medical report.

DISABLED FACILITIES & RESOURCES

According to a national survey in 2004, almost 9 per cent of the Spanish population suffers from some sort of disability. The same survey also investigated Spain's disabled facilities and resources, and highlighted the country's extremely poor provision for its disabled population. The survey showed a general lack of consideration among the population towards the disabled and an almost total lack of facilities. All the public buildings included in the survey had physical barriers (e.g. steps instead of ramps and lack of handrails) and the majority of public transport facilities were inaccessible for disabled passengers. Few telephones were adapted for the hard of hearing or partially sighted and there were no specially-adapted mobile telephones.

In the light of these depressing results, the government has introduced the National Plan for Accessibility whose (ambitious) objective is to make Spain 'disabled-friendly' by 2010. Some results can already be seen – there are more disabled parking spaces in towns and car parks; many underground train stations have lifts for wheelchairs; ramps have been installed on kerbs and road crossings; and all new buildings must be accessible for wheelchairs. The city of Malaga received the national 'prize for accessibility' in 2006 for its outstanding improvements on disabled access in the city.

The following facilities are available for the disabled:

- **Grants & Subsidies** – Some regions and local councils offer grants to individuals or communities of owners towards the adaptation of facilities for the disabled, e.g. for the conversion of steps into a ramp.

- **Parking Display Card** – These cards, available from your local council, allow the disabled to park in designated spaces in car parks and town centres. The card should be displayed behind your windscreen. Parking spaces for the disabled are often occupied by other cars – if this is the case, phone the local police and ask for the car to be removed. You might not have time to wait for it to be towed away so that you can use the space, but at least you will have the satisfaction of knowing the driver has to pay a fine to get his car back!

- **Tax Deductions** – Depending on your degree of disability, you may be entitled to a reduction on your annual income tax bill, e.g. €2,000 for a disability of between 33 and 65 per cent.

The Spanish are gradually becoming more aware of the needs of the disabled, but it's still common to find cars parked on pavements or across the ramp to a zebra crossing. Spain still has a long way to go compared to many other EU countries.

The Spanish Association of the Blind (Organización Nacional de Ciegos Españoles/ONCE) provides advice and support for the disabled and their families, and has branches in most large towns and cities (🖳 http://www.once.es).

USEFUL ASSOCIATIONS

Counselling

Counselling and help for special health and social problems isn't as widely available in Spain as in some other countries, although this is gradually changing and self-help groups and associations have sprung up throughout Spain in the last few years. As a result, support is available for many common chronic illnesses and health problems. In areas popular with expatriates, there may be English-language support groups, but you shouldn't count on this. Voluntary groups are also common in expatriate communities, particularly organisations helping the elderly and infirm. All services are strictly confidential.

In the first instance, you should contact your family doctor or the social services department (*departamento de servicios sociales*) in your local council, who can usually provide advice and put you in touch with the appropriate organisation or professional counsellor.

For listings, look in the white pages under '*ONGs*' or '*Asociaciones de ayuda*'. Below is a list of the largest associations in Spain.

Chronic Illnesses

- **AIDS** – (☎ 900 850 000);

- **Alzheimers** – Fundación Alzheimer España (☎ 913 431 165, 🖳 http://www.alzheimer.rediris.es);

- **Cancer** – Asociación Española contra el Cáncer, support groups in most large towns and cities (☎ 900 100 036, 🖳 http://www.aecc.es). English-speaking hospice associations can be found on the Costa del Sol (Cudeca, ☎ 952 564 910, 🖳 http://www.cudeca.org) and the Costa Blanca – Costa Blanca Hospice Association (🖳 http://www.caring spain.com) and Sweet Charity Hospice (🖳 http://www.sweetcharity hospice.org);

- **Parkinsons** – Sarenet (🖳 http://www.sarenet.es/Parkinson), which several branches throughout the country;

Health Problems

- **Alcoholics Anonymous** – (💻 http://www.aa-europe.net/countries – Spain) has English-speaking groups in many areas;

- **Weight Watchers** – (☎ 902 300 210, 💻 http://www.weightwatchers.es) – has English-speaking groups on the Costa Blanca, the Costa del Sol and in the Canaries.

Nursing Care & Mobility Aids

Hospitals and health centres in Spain rarely provide mobility aids (e.g. wheelchairs and crutches) for long-term use. Mobility aids are available for hire or purchase from specialised shops (*Ortopedia* – see in the *Yellow Pages* under *Ortopedia, ayudas técnicas y material médico*) and from some charity organisations (e.g. Luz Mundi and the Cruz Roja). The following organisations provide mobility aids specifically for the expatriate population in resort areas:

- **Costa Blanca** – British Hire Service, based in Benidorm (☎ 629 985 801, 💻 http://www.britishhireservice.com), Mobility Abroad (💻 http://www.mobilityabroad.com);

- **Costa del Sol** – Independent Living, nursing care and equipment for the disabled (☎ 952 660 356, 💻 http://www.independentlivingspain.com), Mobility Abroad (💻 http://www.mobilityabroad.com);

- **Lanzarote** – Mobility Aids (☎ 928 346 005, 💻 http://www.mobilityaids-lanzarote.co.uk), Mobility Abroad (💻 http://www.mobilityabroad.com);

- **Majorca** – Mobility Abroad (💻 http://www.mobilityabroad.com);

- **Tenerife** – Mobility Aids (☎ 922 750 289, 💻 http://www.lero.net).

MEDICAL TREATMENT ABROAD

If you're entitled to state health benefits in Spain or another EU country, you can take advantage of reciprocal healthcare agreements in most other European countries. Everyone insured under Spanish social security is covered for medical expenses while travelling abroad, provided certain steps are taken to ensure reimbursement. In some cases, you must obtain a European Health Insurance Card (EHIC – *tarjeta sanitaria europea* – see page 201) from your local social security office before leaving Spain. This also applies to EU residents of Spain planning to visit their home country.

Full payment (possibly in cash) must usually be made in advance for treatment received abroad, although you will be reimbursed on your return to Spain. This applies to all EU countries except the UK, where everyone receives free emergency healthcare. You're also reimbursed for essential treatment in countries not mentioned above, although you must obtain detailed receipts. Note that reimbursement is based on the cost of comparable treatment in Spain. In certain countries, e.g. Canada, Japan, Switzerland and the US, medical treatment is very expensive and you're advised to have travel or holiday insurance (see page 274) when visiting these countries. This is advisable wherever you're travelling, as it provides more comprehensive medical cover than reciprocal healthcare agreements (and includes many other things such as repatriation). If you do a lot of travelling abroad, it's worthwhile having an international health insurance policy (see page 275).

Apart from the rich and famous who like to be photographed outside expensive clinics in the US, few Spaniards currently go abroad for medical treatment. Waiting lists have been reduced considerably in most of the country and the level of medical treatment is generally excellent so there's (as yet) little incentive to seek treatment abroad.

DYING IN SPAIN

Recording a Death

In Spain, a death must be registered within 24 hours at the town hall of the district where it took place. If the deceased was a foreigner, the town hall needs his passport or residence permit and the death must also be registered at the deceased's local consulate or embassy in Spain. A death certificate must be prepared and signed by the doctor who attended the death (in a hospital or elsewhere) and be legally certified by a judge. In the case of a foreigner, it must be presented to the deceased person's embassy or consulate in Spain in order to obtain a certificate valid in the deceased's home country. The certificates are required for insurance claims and to execute a will. The undertaker (*funeraria*) will usually take care of the registration and obtaining death certificates.

Burial & Cremation

A body can be buried or cremated in Spain or flown to another country for burial. If the deceased is to be buried or cremated in Spain, it usually takes place within 48 hours of the death. Funerals cost from €1,200 to €2,500. Cremation is cheaper than burial, although not all cemeteries have crematoriums, and costs from €300. Burial costs depend on the kind of grave and the length of rent – in most Spanish cemeteries, internment is above ground and bodies are placed in niches (*nichos*) set into walls, which are rented for a number of years, e.g. 5 to 50 (the rent is from €30 a year). The cheapest niches are in municipal cemeteries, where typical rentals are around €300 for five years, then €30 a year or up to €1,500 for 50 years. After the rental period has expired, bodies are interned in a common burial ground within the consecrated cemetery grounds. To avoid this you must buy a plot outright which can cost €3,000 or more. Malaga has a British cemetery and there's also an international cemetery in Benalmádena (Costa del Sol).

Flying a body to another country for burial is expensive (e.g. €1,000 to €2,000 within Europe), although the cost may be covered by an international insurance policy that includes repatriation. Cremating a body in Spain and taking the ashes in an urn to another country is a cheaper and more practical option.

Dying is an expensive business in Spain – expect to pay at least €1,500. It's possible to take out an insurance policy (*seguro de decesos*) for funeral expenses with a Spanish or foreign insurance company, although these are usually expensive. Note that consular and embassy authorities don't provide financial help for funeral costs or repatriation.

When a resident in Spain dies, all interested parties must be notified (see **Inheritance & Gift Tax** and **Wills** on pages 256 and 261). Note that inheritance tax must be paid within six months of the deceased's death. You need several copies of the death certificate which are required by banks and other institutions.

The death of a partner is one of the main reasons many retirees in Spain decide to return to their home country. Loneliness and financial hardship caused by the loss often mean that staying in Spain is no longer an attractive or practical option. See **Returning Home** chapter 12 for further information.

8.

FINANCE

Finance is one of the most important aspects of retiring in Spain and includes everything from transferring and changing money to mortgages and taxes. This chapter provides information about the foreigner's identification number, Spanish currency, importing and exporting money, banking, mortgages, aspects of taxation relevant to retirees and wills. For information about the cost of living and the entitlement to pensions and benefits, see **Chapter 3**.

IDENTIFICATION NUMBER

All foreign residents in Spain must have a foreigner's identification number (*Número de Identificación de Extranjero/NIE*). An *NIE* works as identification and a kind of tax number. Without an *NIE*, you won't be able to buy property, register a car on Spanish plates, arrange credit terms or use temporary employment agencies. An *NIE* must also be used in all dealings with the Spanish tax authorities, when paying property taxes and in various other transactions.

Forms for an *NIE* can be downloaded from the Ministry of Interior website (🖳 http://www.mir.es – *Extranjeros/Modelos de Solicitud*). Applications for an *NIE* must be made in person at a national police station (*comisaría*) with a foreigners' department (expect to queue for most of the morning). A representative can apply on your behalf only if you've given him a power of attorney made out abroad and translated into Spanish. (For reasons known only to a select few in the police, powers of attorney made out in Spain are no longer acceptable!) However, once you've applied, anyone can collect the *NIE* on your behalf. It can take up to three months to obtain an *NIE*.

SPANISH CURRENCY

Along with 11 other EU countries (Austria, Belgium, Finland, France, Germany, Greece, Ireland, Italy, Luxembourg, the Netherlands and Portugal), Spain's currency is the euro (€). Euro notes and coins became legal tender on 1st January 2002 replacing the peseta. The euro (€) is divided into 100 cents (*céntimo*) and coins are minted in values of 1, 2, 5, 10, 20, 50 cents, €1 and €2. The 1, 2 and 5 cent coins are copper-coloured and the 10, 20 and 50 cent coins are brass-coloured. The €1 coin is silver-coloured in the centre with a brass-coloured rim, and the €2 coin has a brass-coloured centre and silver-coloured rim.

Euro banknotes (*billetes*) are identical throughout the eurozone and are printed in denominations of €5, €10, €20, €50, €100, €200 and €500 (worth over £300, but surprisingly common – around a quarter of all €500 notes circulate in Spain!), with the size increasing with their value. Euro notes have been produced using all the latest anti-counterfeiting devices; nevertheless, you should be wary of €200 and €500 notes. When written, the euro symbol may appear before the amount (as in this book), after it (commonly used by the Spanish, e.g. 24,50€) or even between the euros and cents, e.g. 16€50. When writing figures (for example on cheques), a full stop/period (.) is used to separate units of millions, thousands and hundreds, and a comma to denote fractions, e.g. 1.234.567,89.

If possible, it's wise to obtain some euro coins and banknotes before arriving in Spain and to familiarise yourself with them. Bringing some euros with you (e.g. €50 to €100 in small notes) saves you having to change money on arrival. It's sensible not to carry a lot of cash and ideally you should avoid high value notes (above €50), which aren't widely accepted, particularly for small purchases or on public transport.

IMPORTING & EXPORTING MONEY

Exchange controls were abolished in Spain on 1st February 1992 and there are no restrictions on the import or export of funds. A Spanish resident is permitted to open a bank account in any country and to import (or export) unlimited funds in any currency. However, when a resident opens an overseas account, his Spanish bank must routinely inform the Bank of Spain within 30 days of any account movements over €3,000.

Declaration

Cash, notes and bearer-cheques in any currency, plus gold coins and bars up to the value of €6,000 may be freely imported or exported by residents and non-residents without approval or declaration. However, if you intend to re-export funds you should declare them, as this certifies that the foreign currency was imported legally and allows a non-EU person to convert euros back into a foreign currency. Residents receiving funds from non-residents or making payments to them of over €6,000 (or the equivalent in foreign currency) in cash or bearer cheques must declare them within 30 days. A form must be completed (B-3) giving the name, address and identification number (*Número de Identificatión de Extranjero/NIE* – see above) of the resident, the name and address of the non-resident, and the reason for the payment.

Sums of €6,000 to €30,000 (per person and journey) must be declared to the customs authorities (on form B-1) when entering or leaving Spain. Non-EU nationals wishing to import or export sums above €6,000 must obtain prior authorisation from the Dirección General de Transacciones Exteriores (DGTE) by completing form B-2 at your bank. These regulations are designed to curb criminal activities, particularly drug-trafficking, and also apply to transit travellers stopping in Spain for less than 24 hours. **If you don't declare funds, they're subject to confiscation.**

International Bank Transfers

When transferring money to Spain, shop around for the best exchange rate and the lowest costs. Banks are often willing to negotiate on fees and exchange rates when you're transferring a large amount of money.

SURVIVAL TIP
Be aware of fluctuations on the exchange rate, which can change at short notice and can mean you lose (or gain) when you transfer money to Spain.

For example, if you're transferring £10,000, this would be equal to €14,500 at an exchange rate of £1 = €1.45 (exchange rate in April 2006). However, if the £/€ exchange rate 'falls' to €1.40, the transfer is equal to €14,000 – a 'loss' of €500.

When transferring or sending money to (or from) Spain, you should be aware of the alternatives and shop around for the best deal. A bank-to-bank transfer can be made by a normal transfer or by a SWIFT electronic transfer. A normal transfer is supposed to take three to seven days, but in reality takes longer (particularly when sent by post), whereas a SWIFT telex transfer **should** be completed in as little as two hours (although SWIFT transfers aren't always reliable). It's usually quicker and cheaper to transfer funds between branches of the same bank or affiliated banks than between non-affiliated banks.

If you intend to send a large amount of money abroad for a business transaction such as buying a property, you should ensure that you receive the commercial rate of exchange rather than the tourist rate. Shop around and compare your bank's rate with that of at least one foreign exchange broker who specialises in sending money abroad (particularly large sums). The leading companies include Foreign Currency Direct (☎ 0800-328 5884 or 01494-725353, 💻 http://www.currencies.co.uk), Halewood (☎ 1753-859159, 💻 http://www.hifx.co.uk) and Moneycorp (☎ 020-7589 3000, Spain 966-771 068, 💻 http://www.moneycorp.com).

SURVIVAL TIP
Specialist currency brokers generally provide the cheapest way of transfering large funds, e.g. for a property purchase, from one currency to another.

Some foreign banks levy high charges on the transfer of funds to Spain to buy a home, which is the subject of numerous complaints, while others charge nothing if the transfer is made in euros. Always check charges and rates in advance and agree them with your bank (you can often negotiate a lower charge or a better exchange rate when transferring a large sum of money). The cost of transfers varies considerably, not only the commission and exchange rates, but also the transfer charges (such as the telex charge for a SWIFT transfer). Shop around a number of banks. Many Spanish banks deduct commission, whether a transfer is made in euros or a foreign currency. An EU directive limits banks to being able to pass on to customers the costs incurred by sender banks only and money has to be deposited in customers' accounts within five working days (however, this doesn't appear to apply to Spanish banks when transferring funds abroad – see the warning below).

Spanish banks (along with Portuguese) are reportedly the slowest in Europe to process bank transfers. It isn't unusual for transfers to get stuck in the pipeline (usually somewhere in Madrid), which allows the Spanish bank to use your money for a period interest-free. For example, transfers between British and Spanish banks occasionally take weeks and money can 'disappear' for months or even completely!

When exporting money from Spain to another country it's important to shop around for the best rate and lowest fees. Spanish banks can charge more or less what they like when making foreign transfers and they may charge up to 0.7 per cent of the amount transferred as a 'fee'. This can amount to a lot of money if you have sold a property in Spain and are transferring the money abroad.

It's cheaper to obtain a banker's draft and pay that into your foreign account, but check the fees first. Failing that you can withdraw cash from your Spanish account free of charge, but the amount may be limited and it is, of course, risky to carry too much cash with you. See also **Bank Charges** below.

Bank Drafts & Personal Cheques

Another way to transfer money is via a bank draft (*cheque bancario*), which should be sent by registered post. Note, however, that in the event that it's lost or stolen, it's impossible to stop payment and you must wait six months before a new draft can be issued. Bank drafts aren't treated as cash and must be cleared like personal cheques. It's also possible to send a creditor a cheque drawn on a personal account, although they can take a long time to clear (usually a matter of weeks) and fees are high. Some people prefer to receive a cheque direct (by post) from their overseas banks, which they then pay into their Spanish bank (although you must usually wait for it to clear). **The main problem with sending anything by post to or from Spain is that it leaves you at the mercy of the notoriously unreliable Spanish post office.**

It's possible to pay cheques drawn on a foreign account into a Spanish bank account, however, they can take weeks to clear (at least 21 days), as they must usually be cleared with the paying bank (although some Spanish banks credit funds to accounts immediately or within a few days).

OBTAINING CASH

One of the quickest methods of obtaining of cash is to draw cash on debit, credit or charge cards (but there's usually a daily limit, e.g. €600). Many foreigners living in Spain (particularly retirees) keep the bulk of their money in a foreign account (perhaps in an offshore bank) and draw on it with a debit card. This is an ideal solution for holidaymakers and holiday homeowners (although homeowners still need a Spanish bank account to pay their bills).

Most banks in major cities have foreign exchange windows where you can buy and sell foreign currencies, buy and cash travellers' cheques, and obtain a cash advance on credit and charge cards.

Most banks charge around 1 per cent commission with a minimum charge of between €3 to €6, so it's expensive to change small amounts. However, some banks charge a flat fee of €3 and no commission, irrespective of the amount, especially if you're a client of the bank. There are numerous private bureaux de change, many of which are open long hours.

They can be found at most travel agencies and even in some shops (such as El Corte Inglés department stores).

```
SURVIVAL TIP
Banks at airports and railway stations often offer the
worst exchange rates and charge the highest fees.
```

There are automatic change machines at airports and in tourist areas in major cities accepting major currencies, including US$, £Sterling and Swiss francs.

Most bureaux de change offer competitive exchange rates and charge no commission (but always check) and are also usually easier to deal with than banks. If you're changing a lot of money you may be able to negotiate a better exchange rate. However, the best exchange rates may still be found at a bank, even taking into consideration commission charges.

Posted exchange rates may apply only when changing high amounts, so ask before changing any money. The euro exchange rate (*cambio*) for most major international currencies is listed in banks and daily newspapers, and announced on Spanish and expatriate radio and television. **Always shop around for the best exchange rate and the lowest commission**.

BANKS

Spain are two main types of banks: clearing banks (*bancos*) and savings banks (*cajas de ahorros*). The clearing banks with the largest branch networks are the two giants, Banco Santander, now the fourth-largest in Europe after its takeover of the British bank Abbey National, and BBVA (Banco Bilbao Vizcaya-Argentaria), while the smallest are Banco Popular, Banesto and Sabadell Atlántico. All banks are listed in the *Yellow Pages* under *Bancos*.

Most banks also provide home banking services via telephone and/or the internet, and there are several internet/telephone-only banks such as ING Direct (☎ 901 020 901, 🖥 http://www.ingdirect.es) owned by ING Nationale-Nedenlanden, Openbank (☎ 902 365 366, 🖥 http://www.openbank.es) owned by Banco Santander and Uno-e (☎ 901 111 113, 🖥 http://www.uno-e.es) owned by BBVA and Telefónica. All three internet banks offer (relatively) high-interest current accounts with immediate access to your money, plus the usual services.

In addition to clearing banks, Spain also has around 50 savings banks (*cajas de ahorros*), which are similar to building societies in the UK and savings and loans in the US, and hold around 45 per cent of deposits and make some 25 per cent of personal loans. The two largest Spanish savings banks are La Caixa (some 3,600 branches) and Caja de Madrid (almost 1,900 branches). In general, savings banks provide a more personal friendly service than clearing banks and are excellent for local business (many have limited regional branch networks), but they aren't always best for international business.

Around 50 foreign banks operate in Spain, with most major foreign banks present in Madrid and Barcelona, but branches are rare in other cities. Among foreigners in Spain, the British are best served by their national banks in the major cities and resort areas. Barclays Bank (☎ 901 141 414, 🖳 http://www.barclays.es), Deutschebank (☎ 902 240 124, 🖳 http://www. deutsche-bank.es), Halifax (☎ 901 300 900, 🖳 http://www.halifax.es) and Lloyds TSB (🖳 http://www.lloydsbank.es) are the most prominent foreign banks in Spain. The Royal Bank of Scotland also operates at some Banco Santander branches.

Note, however, that foreign banks in Spain operate in exactly the same way as Spanish banks, so you shouldn't expect, for example, a branch of Barclays in Spain to behave like a branch in the UK or any other country.

Surprisingly, considering the size and spending power of foreign residents and tourists in Spain, most Spanish banks make few concessions to foreign clients, e.g. by providing general information and statements in foreign languages and having staff who speak foreign languages. However, Solbank specialises in banking for foreign residents and some branches of other national banks offer specific services with multi-language staff and information, including:

- **Bancaja** (☎ 902 204 020, 🖳 http://www.bancaja.es) – branches along the Mediterranean coast with the largest presence on the Costa Blanca;

- **Bankinter** (☎ 902 365 563, 🖳 http://www.bankinter.es) – branches nationwide;

- **CajaMar** (☎ 950 210 100, 🖳 http://www.cajamar.es) – branches mainly on the Mediterranean coast and Cadiz;

- **Solbank** (☎ 902 343 999, 🖳 http://www.solbank.es) – branches mainly in resort areas, particularly the Costa Blanca and the Costa del Sol;

- **Unicaja** (☎ 902 224 466, 🖳 http://www.unicaja.es) – branches mainly in Andalusia.

If you have a complaint regarding a bank, don't expect to receive a quick resolution or any resolution at all. A complaint should be addressed to the ombudsman (*defensor del cliente*, although the title may vary) of your bank. The Bank of Spain (Banco de España, Servicio de Reclamaciones, Alcalá, 50, 28014 Madrid, ☎ 913 385 068, 🖥 http://www.bde.es – '*Servicios al Público*') can provide further information about filing a complaint.

Unlike in some countries (e.g. the UK), banking is a personal affair in Spain and bank managers often know most of their clients by name. When you open an account at a bank, ask to be introduced to the manager and don't be afraid to negotiate special rates or a reduction in charges – most banks are keen to keep their customers.

Opening Hours

Normal bank opening hours are usually from 8.15 to 9am until around 1.30 or 2pm, Mondays to Fridays, and from 8.30 to 9.30am until 1pm on Saturdays in winter (banks are closed on Saturdays from around 1st April to 30th September). Savings banks open all day on Thursdays (until 7pm), but are closed on Saturdays. Some branches in major cities remain open continually from the morning until 4 or 4.30pm from autumn to spring, although they may close earlier on Fridays. Some banks are experimenting with longer hours at certain branches and opening from, for example, 8.15am until 8.30pm (or they may open from around 8.15am to 2pm and again from around 4.30 until 7.45pm). Banks in shopping centres may also open all day until late in the evening (some are open for the same hours as hypermarkets, e g from 10am until 10pm).

At major international airports and railway stations in major cities, there are also banks with extended opening hours, although they often have long queues. Banks are closed on public holidays, including local holidays (when banks in neighbouring towns often close on different days), and they may also close early during local *fiestas*. Many bureaux de change have long opening hours and some are even open 24 hours during the summer in resort areas.

Opening an Account

You don't need to be a resident to open a bank account in Spain. It's best to open a Spanish bank account in person, rather than by correspondence from abroad. Ask your friends, neighbours or colleagues for their recommendations and just go along to the bank of your choice and introduce yourself. You must be at least 18 and provide proof of identity (e.g. a passport), your address in Spain and your passport number or *NIE* (see page 230). If you wish to open an account with a Spanish bank while you're abroad, you must first obtain an application form, available from foreign branches of Spanish banks or direct from a Spanish bank in Spain. You must select a branch from the list provided, which should preferably be close to your new home in Spain (or where you plan to buy or rent a home). If you open an account by correspondence, you must provide a reference from your current bank.

Non-residents

Since Spain became a full member of the EU on 1st January 1993, banking regulations for resident and non-resident EU citizens have been identical. However, if you're a non-resident you're entitled to open a non-resident euro account (*cuenta de euros de no residente*) or a foreign currency account only. An important point for non-resident, non-EU citizens to note is that when importing funds for the purchase of a property (or any other major transaction), the transfer of funds must be verified via a certificate from your bank (*certificado de cambio de divisas*). This allows you to re-export the funds if (or when) you sell the property later. This is unnecessary for EU nationals.

Although it's possible for non-resident homeowners to do most of their banking via a foreign account using debit and credit cards, you will need a Spanish bank account (in euros) to pay your Spanish utility and tax bills (which are best paid by direct debit). If you own a holiday home in Spain, you can have your correspondence (e.g. cheque books, statements, payslips, etc.) sent to an address abroad.

Residents

You're considered to be a resident of Spain if you have your main centre of interest there, i.e. you live and work there almost permanently. To open a resident's account you must usually have a residence permit (*residencia* – see page 31) or evidence that you have a job in Spain. It isn't advisable to close your bank accounts abroad, unless you're sure you won't need them in the future. Even when you're resident in Spain, it's cheaper to keep money in local currency in an account in a country you visit regularly, rather than pay fees to change and transfer money. Many foreigners living in Spain maintain at least two current (cheque) accounts, a foreign account for international transactions and a local account with a Spanish bank for day-to-day expenses.

Bank Charges

Spanish banks are notorious for their high bank charges levied on almost all transactions – even the most insignificant of transactions such as paying cash into your own account at a branch other than your own can attract a charge of €3! Charges for transfers are particularly high and for large amounts transferred internationally can run into hundreds or even thousands of euros. Always obtain a list of charges before opening an account and compare the charges levied by a number of banks.

In early 2006, some Spanish banks (e.g. Banco Santander and Banesto) introduced 'no-commission accounts' for their customers with no charges levied on most transactions including transfers within the EU. It's expected that most banks will follow suit, but until they do, shop around and open an account at a bank with the lowest charges. You may be able to negotiate reduced bank charges with your bank manager, e.g. a certain number of transactions per month free of charge or charged at a reduced rate.

Offshore Banking

If you have a sum of money to invest or wish to protect your inheritance from the tax man, it may be worthwhile looking into the accounts and services (such as pensions and trusts) provided by offshore banking centres in tax havens (*paraísos fiscales*) such as the Channel Islands (Guernsey and Jersey), Gibraltar and the Isle of Man (around 50 locations worldwide are officially classified as tax havens). The main attractions of offshore banking are that money can be deposited in a wide range of currencies, customers are usually guaranteed complete anonymity, there are no double-taxation agreements, no withholding tax is payable, and interest is paid tax-free. Many offshore banks also provide telephone banking (usually seven days a week).

A large number of American, British and other European banks and financial institutions provide offshore banking facilities in one or more locations. Most institutions offer high-interest deposit accounts for long-term savings and investment portfolios in which funds can be deposited in any major currency. Many people living abroad keep a local account for everyday business and maintain an offshore account for international transactions and investment purposes.

SURVIVAL TIP
Most financial experts advise investors never to rush into the expatriate life and invest their life savings in an offshore tax haven until they know what their long-term plans are.

Accounts have minimum deposit levels that usually range from the equivalent of around €750 to €15,000 (e.g. £500 to £10,000), with some as high as €150,000 (£100,000). In addition to large minimum balances, accounts may also have stringent terms and conditions, such as restrictions on withdrawals or high early withdrawal penalties. You can deposit funds on call (instant access) or for a fixed period, e.g. from 90 days to one year (usually for larger sums). Interest on the sum invested is usually paid monthly or annually; monthly interest payments are slightly lower than annual payments, although they have the advantage of providing a regular income. There are usually no charges if a specified minimum balance is maintained. Many accounts offer a debit card (those linked with MasterCard or Visa are best) which can be used to obtain cash from ATMs throughout the world.

When selecting a financial institution and offshore banking centre, your first priority should be for the safety of your money. In some offshore banking centres, a percentage of bank deposits up to a maximum sum is guaranteed under a deposit protection scheme in the event of a financial institution going bust (the Isle of Man, Guernsey and Jersey all have such schemes). Unless you're planning to bank with a major international bank, you should check the credit rating of a financial institution before depositing any money, particularly if it doesn't provide deposit insurance. All banks have a credit rating (the highest is 'AAA') and a bank with a high rating will be happy to tell you (but get it in writing). You can also check the rating of an international bank or financial organisation with Moody's Investor Service (⌨ http://www.moodys.com).

 You should be wary of institutions offering higher than average interest rates, because if it looks too good to be true, it probably is – such as the Bank of International Commerce and Credit (BICC) which went bust in 1992.

MORTGAGES

Mortgages or home loans (*hipotecas*) are available from most Spanish banks (for residents and non-residents), foreign banks in Spain, and overseas and offshore banks. In recent years, there have been a record number of mortgages in Spain with the average amount borrowed around €140,000.

The amount you can borrow depends on various factors such as your age, income and whether you're married, and if so, whether your partner works. Lenders may also have a maximum lending limit based on a percentage of your income, but this isn't required by law.

SURVIVAL TIP
Some banks don't provide mortgages for those aged over 65 and many are reluctant to finance a home loan for the over 60s. Those that do usually only provide loans for a maximum period of 10 or 15 years.

Most banks offer mortgages of up to 80 per cent, although non-residents can usually borrow a maximum of 60 per cent only. To obtain a mortgage from a Spanish bank, you must usually provide proof of your monthly income and major outgoings (e.g. loans or commitments). There are no self-assessment mortgages such as in the UK and mortgages without proof of income (although advertised in the expatriate press) are difficult to find and virtually non-existent. Note that a mortgage can be assumed by the new owner (called *subrogación*) when a property is sold, which is a common practice in Spain.

Spanish mortgages are among the most competitive in Europe and in April 2006 variable interest rates were around 4 per cent. Around 90 per cent of home loans in Spain have a variable (*interés variable*) instead of a fixed interest (*interés fijo*) rate, and have traditionally been set at 1 to 2 per cent above the base rate (European inter-bank rate or EURIBOR). In April 2006, rates for variable mortgages ranged from 2.6 to 3.8 per cent and those for fixed mortgages from 5.4 to 6.4 per cent. Shop around and ask for the effective rate (*Tasa Anual Equivalente/TAE*) including commissions and fees. Further information on mortgage rates offered by Spanish banks can be found on the Ausbanc (Banking Ombudsman) website (🖥 http://www. ausbanc.com – some information in English).

If you finance your purchase of a Spanish home with a mortgage, bear in mind possible fluctuations in interest rates – a slight rise (even 0.25 per cent) can lead to substantial increase in monthly repayments.

SURVIVAL TIP
If you cannot afford an increase in your mortgage
repayments, think twice about financing an investment
through a mortgage.

Mortgages are granted on a percentage of the valuation, which itself is usually below the market value. The maximum mortgage in Spain is usually 80 per cent of the purchase price for a principal home (*vivienda habitual*) and 50 to 60 per cent for a second home (*segunda residencía*). The normal term is 10 to 15 years, although mortgages can be repaid over 10 to 40 years. Beware of long repayment terms: although monthly repayments are smaller on longer terms, interest payments are considerably higher. According to the bank association, Adicae, increasing the mortgage repayment term by ten years on a €150,000 mortgage results in a saving of €49 a month in repayments, but you will have to pay an extra €32,000 in interest!

Note that you must add expenses and fees totalling around 10 per cent of the purchase price, to the cost of a property. For example, if you're buying a property for €150,000 and obtain a 60 per cent mortgage, you must pay a 40 per cent deposit (€60,000) plus around 10 per cent fees (€15,000), making a total of €75,000. There are various fees associated with mortgages, e.g. most lenders levy an 'arrangement' fee (*comisión de apertura*) of 0.5 to 2.5 per cent. Although it's unusual to have a full survey carried out, most lenders insist on a 'valuation' (this usually costs between €150 to €300) before they grant a loan. Mortgages also usually have a cancellation fee of around 1 per cent.

It's customary for a property to be held as security against a home loan, i.e. the lender takes a first charge on the property, which is recorded at the property registry. If a loan is obtained using a Spanish property as security, additional fees and registration costs are payable to the notary (*notario*) for registering the charge against the property.

Spanish banks also often insist that you take out home insurance with them together with the mortgage, although you aren't legally required to do so. **Their rates are invariably higher than other insurers so it's wise to shop around.** See **Household Insurance** on page 271.

Remortgaging

If you have equity in an existing property, in Spain or abroad, then it may be more cost effective to re-mortgage (or take out a second mortgage) on that property, rather than take out a new mortgage for a second home in Spain. It involves less paperwork, and therefore lower legal fees, and a plan can be tailored to meet your individual requirements. Depending on your equity in your existing property and the cost of your Spanish property, this may enable you to pay cash for a second home. Note, however, that when a mortgage is taken out on a Spanish property it's based on that property and not the individual, which could be important if you get into repayment difficulties.

Foreign Currency Loans

It's also possible to obtain a foreign currency mortgage, other than in euros (in Spain or abroad), where repayments are made in your home country's currency, e.g. pounds sterling, with a UK bank. However, you should be wary about taking out a foreign currency mortgage, as interest rate gains can be wiped out overnight by currency swings and devaluations. It's generally recognised that you should take out a mortgage in the currency in which you're paid or in the currency of the country where a property is situated.

When choosing between a euro and a foreign currency loan, you should take into account all costs, fees, interest rates and possible currency fluctuations. If you have a foreign currency mortgage, you must usually pay commission charges each time you transfer foreign currency into euros or remit money to Spain. If you let a second home, you may be able to offset the interest (pro rata) on your mortgage against letting income. For example, if you let a property for three months of the year, you can offset a quarter of your annual mortgage interest against your letting income.

SURVIVAL TIP
Irrespective of how you finance your purchase, you should always obtain professional advice and shop around for the best deals.

TAXATION

An important consideration when retiring in Spain is taxation, which includes property tax, wealth tax, income tax on all your earnings including your pension, capital gains tax and inheritance tax.

Spain is no longer the tax haven it was in the '60s and '70s, when taxes were low and tax evasion was a way of life and almost encouraged! Spain's taxes have increased dramatically during the last few decades, particularly income tax; nevertheless, income tax and social security contributions remain among the lowest in the European Union, (EU) and income tax rates have been reduced in the last few years, while indirect taxes (e.g. on petrol) have increased.

Despite the efforts of the authorities, tax evasion is still widespread. Many foreign residents think they should be exempt from Spanish taxes, and some inhabit a twilight world as 'eternal tourists', not officially resident in any country; a few even have the effrontery to boast about not paying taxes. Needless to say, tax evasion is illegal and a criminal offence and offenders can be heavily fined or even imprisoned.

On the other hand, tax avoidance (i.e. legally paying as little tax as possible, if necessary by finding and exploiting loopholes in the tax laws) is highly recommended! Residents have a number of opportunities to legally reduce their taxes, while non-residents have few or none at all, and moving to Spain (or another country) often provides opportunities for legal 'favourable tax planning'.

To make the most of your situation, it's advisable to obtain income tax advice before moving to Spain, as there are usually a number of things you can do in advance to reduce your tax liability, both in Spain and abroad. Be sure to consult a tax adviser who's familiar with the Spanish tax system and that of your present country of residence. For example, you may be able to avoid paying tax on a business abroad if you establish residence and domicile in Spain before you sell it. On the other hand, if you sell a foreign home after establishing your principal residence in Spain, it becomes a second home and you may then be liable to capital gains tax abroad (this is a complicated subject and you should obtain expert advice). You should notify the tax authorities in your former country of residence that you're going to live permanently in Spain.

SURVIVAL TIP
Before you decide to settle in Spain permanently, you should obtain expert advice regarding Spanish taxes. This will (hopefully) ensure that you take maximum advantage of your current tax status and that you don't make any mistakes that you will regret later.

As you would expect in a country with millions of bureaucrats, the Spanish tax system is inordinately complicated, although the authorities have made a concerted effort over the last few years to make it easier to understand. However, individuals are liable for around 15 different taxes, including those associated with buying and selling property and motoring, levied by three tiers of government: central government, autonomous regional governments and local municipalities. Government taxes are administered by the Agencia Estatal de Administración Tributaria/*AEAT*, which has its headquarters in Madrid and assessment and tax collection centres in provincial capitals and large towns.

Most taxes are based on self-assessment (*auto-liquidación*), meaning that individual taxpayers are liable to report and calculate any tax due within the time limits established by law. Tax forms must be obtained by taxpayers, and most are downloadable from the AEAT website or can be purchased from a tobacconist's (*estanco*). Late payment of any tax bill usually incurs a surcharge of 20 per cent. Note that there's a five-year statute of limitations (*prescripción*) on the collection of taxes in Spain, i.e. if no action has been taken during this period to collect unpaid tax, it cannot be collected. Tax clearance permits aren't required by those leaving Spain to live abroad.

You can obtain free tax advice from the information section (*servicio de información* or *oficina de información al contribuyente*) at your local provincial tax office, where staff will answer queries and assist you in completing your tax declaration via their PADRE computer system. Some offices, particularly those located in resort areas, have staff who speak English and other foreign languages. The tax office provides a central telephone information service (☎ 901 335 533) from 9am to 9pm, Mondays to Fridays, and 9am to 2pm on Saturdays during May and June and from 9am to 7pm, Mondays to Fridays, the rest of the year.

If you require information about income tax and Value Added Tax (VAT) refunds or need to order tax labels, the tax office operates an automatic telephone service which is open 24 hours a day, seven days a week (☎ 901 121 224). There's also a useful website (🖥 http://www.aeat.es), although there are few pages in English, therefore your Spanish needs to be fluent to understand most of it.

Income Tax

Income tax (*impuesto sobre la renta de las personas físicas/IRPF*) in Spain is below the EU average and isn't supplemented by crippling social security charges, as in some other EU countries (e.g. France). Major tax reforms have been introduced in recent years, including the latest to take effect from 2007. Paying income tax in Spain rather than in another country can be advantageous, as there are more allowances than there are in many other countries. Nevertheless, if you're able to choose the country where you're taxed, you should obtain advice from an international tax expert.

Liability

Your liability for income tax in Spain depends on whether you're officially resident there. Under Spanish law you become a fiscal resident in Spain if you spend 183 days there during a calendar year or your main centre of economic interest, e.g. investments or business, is in Spain. Note that the 183-day rule also applies to other EU countries; for example, the UK limits visits by non-residents to 182 days in any one year or an average of 91 days per tax year over a four-year period. Irrespective of the 183-day rule, if your spouse and dependent minor children normally reside in Spain, have residence permits and you aren't legally separated, you're considered to be a fiscal resident in Spain (unless you can prove otherwise).

If you plan to retire permanently to Spain, you should notify the tax authorities in your previous country of residence. You may be entitled to an income tax refund (*devolución*) if you depart during the tax year, which usually requires the completion of a tax return. The authorities may require evidence that you're leaving the country, e.g. proof that you have a home in Spain. You may need to plan carefully the date of leaving your previous country of residence if the tax year is different from the Spanish tax year (calendar), e.g. the UK where the tax year runs from April to March. Consult a tax expert if this is the case.

If you're a pensioner and your earned, worldwide annual income (i.e. income from pensions plus a maximum of €1,600 from investments) is less than €8,000, you aren't required to make a tax declaration or pay Spanish income tax. If you're entitled to deductions for pension plans or housing, you must make a tax declaration irrespective of your earnings.

Double-taxation

Spanish residents are taxed on their worldwide income, whereas non-residents are taxed in Spain only on income arising in Spain, which is normally exempt from tax in their home countries, in accordance with double-taxation agreements. Spain has double-taxation treaties with around 50 countries, including all European Economic Area (EEA) countries (except Cyprus, Estonia, Latvia and Malta), Argentina, Australia, Bolivia, Brazil, Bulgaria, Canada, Chile, China, Cuba, Ecuador, India, Indonesia, Israel, Japan, Mexico, Morocco, the Philippines, Romania, Russia, South Korea, Switzerland, Thailand, Tunisia, Turkey, the US and Venezuela.

Treaties establish a tax credit or exemption on certain kinds of income, either in your country of residence or in the country where the income was earned. Taxpayers entitled to double-taxation relief must nevertheless make a Spanish tax declaration and, if their tax liability in another country is lower than that in Spain, they must pay the Spanish tax authorities the difference. Where applicable, a double-taxation treaty prevails over domestic law.

The US is the only country that taxes its non-resident citizens on income earned abroad (US citizens can obtain a copy of a brochure, *Tax Guide for Americans Abroad*, from American consulates).

Even if there's no double-taxation agreement between Spain and another country, you can obtain relief from double taxation through a direct deduction of any foreign tax paid or through a 'foreign compensation' (*compensación extranjera*) formula. In any case, citizens of most countries are exempt from paying taxes in their home country when they spend a minimum period abroad, e.g. a year. If you're in doubt about your tax liability in your home country, contact your nearest embassy or consulate (see page 330).

Taxable Income

Income tax is payable on earned and unearned income. Taxable income includes salaries, pensions, capital gains, property and investment income (dividends and interest), and income from professional, artistic, business or agricultural activities.

Allowances & Deductions

Before you're liable for income tax, you can deduct social security payments and certain costs from your gross income (allowances) and from the sum due after establishing your tax base (deductions). These include: a personal allowance, currently €3,400 plus an extra €800 for the over 65's or €1,000 for the over 75's (these amounts increase to €5,050, €900 and €1,100 respectively from 2007); disability deductions, currently €2,000 for a disability of between 33 and 65 per cent and €5,000 for disability above 65 per cent (these amounts increase to €2,270 and €6,900 from 2007); deductions for care if you have mobility problems; and Spanish pension plan deductions. For further details, see our sister publication **Living and Working in Spain** by David Hampshire (see page 383).

Taxation of Pensions

Pensions are taxed according to the source of the income, as detailed below:

SURVIVAL TIP
The taxation of investment capital and
insurance-based pensions can be complicated and you
should obtain expert professional advice from an
accountant or tax adviser before deciding where and
how to receive your pension.

Employment-based pensions: Employment-based pensions are taxed in the same way as salary income (see above). You're entitled to the same allowances and deductions, and the same tax rates apply. However, the situation isn't so straightforward if your pension is paid from a savings scheme such as a pension fund established by an employer with tax advantages in your home country.

Investment capital pensions: If you have an investment capital pension – i.e. you pay a sum of money or transfer assets such as property to another party in return for annuity payments (or a monthly income) for a fixed period or until death – this may give rise to capital gains and interest income, each of which is taxed differently.

Insurance-based pensions: Income from an insurance-based pension scheme, which allows you to choose between taking the whole amount accrued under a policy in a lump sum and having it paid in the form of annuities, is taxed as a capital gain (see page 255) or as ordinary income (see above).

Civil Service pensions: Civil Service pensions are usually tax-free and don't need to be declared to the Spanish authorities if they're your only source of income, although this depends on the country paying your pension and whether it has a double-taxation treaty with Spain (see page 246). However, you may need to provide the tax office with proof that your pension is taxed at source. Civil Service pensions don't include United Nations (UN) pensions, as the UN cannot tax its former employees (unlike individual countries). Note, however, that if you have other income that's taxable in Spain, your Civil Service pension is usually taken into account when calculating your Spanish tax rate and in that case must be declared. If you pay tax in error on a pension that wasn't in fact taxable, you can claim a refund only for the previous five years, which is Spain's statute of limitations (if they aren't collected, taxes also usually lapse after five years).

Calculation of Income Tax

The tax year in Spain is the same as the calendar year: from 1st January to 31st December. Income tax for non-resident individuals is levied at a flat rate of 25 per cent and rates for resident individuals (*personas físicas*) start at 15 per cent on income up to €4,161 rising to 45 per cent on income above €46,818, as shown in the table below. There are no longer different tax rates for couples who choose to be taxed individually or jointly.

Taxable Income	Tax Rate	Cumulative Tax
Up to €4,161	15%	€624.15
€4,161 to €14,357	24%	€3,071.19
€14,357 to €26,842	28%	€6,567
€26,842 to €46,818	37%	€13,958.12
Over €46,818	45%	

New Tax Rates: From 2007 (applicable to tax returns for 2007 made in 2008) the number of tax bands will be reduced from five to four and rates for resident individuals will start at 24 per cent on income up to €17,360, as shown below:

Taxable Income	Tax Rate	Cumulative Tax
Up to €17,360	24%	€4,166.40
€17,360 to €32,360	28%	€8,366.40
€32,360 to €52,360	37%	€15,766.40
Over €52,360	43%	

The total tax due is divided between the Spanish state (85 per cent) and the autonomous regions (15 per cent).

Tax Return

An annual income tax declaration (*declaración sobre la renta de personas físicas*) must be lodged between 1st May and 20th June by residents and non-residents with income in Spain (other than income from property letting). This deadline also applies to declarations for property tax and wealth tax for residents, although if you're entitled to a refund (*devolución*) it's extended until 30th June. Income tax is paid a year in arrears, e.g. the declaration filed in 2007 is for the 2006 tax year.

If your earned income is below €8,000 (for an individual declaration), it isn't necessary to complete an income tax declaration. Note that, if you're a Spanish resident, this limit applies to your worldwide income wherever it arises, but doesn't include income taxed in another country. If you're resident in Spain, the authorities will ask to see your income tax declaration when you renew your residence permit (*residencia*). Rather than try to explain why your income is below the tax threshold (and therefore possibly below the income necessary to obtain a *residencia*!), it's advisable to make a 'negative' tax declaration.

Unless your tax affairs are simple, it's advisable to employ an accountant or tax adviser (*asesor fiscal*) to complete your tax return and ensure that you're correctly assessed. There are 'foreign' tax assessors (*asesores de extranjero*) who specialise in filing returns for foreigners, particularly non-residents. The fees charged for filing tax returns vary and for residents are around €35 for a simple return and €60 for an ordinary return. The fee for filing a tax return for a non-resident is usually around €35. **Make sure that you have your tax return stamped as proof of payment by your adviser.**

There are four kinds of tax declaration form:

Draft declaration (*borrador*) – the simplest way of declaring your income whereby a draft declaration is sent to you by the tax authorities, with figures and calculations based on your income the previous year. Taxpayers who request a draft declaration in their previous year's declaration (via the tick box *petición de borrador/datos*) receive the draft by post in March or April; anyone else can request one before 15th June. Once you receive the draft, you must confirm or contest the figures.

Abbreviated declaration (*declaración abreviada*) – used by taxpayers whose income derives entirely from earnings or from pensions and investments that have already been subject to Spanish withholding tax. Note that, if your income consists of a pension that has had deductions made in another country and which you intend to subtract from your Spanish declaration, you cannot use this form, but must use a simple declaration (see below).

Simple declaration (*simplificada*) – used by those with the same sources of income as the abbreviated declaration (see above), plus income from letting, certain business and agricultural income, and capital gains from the sale of a permanent home where the total gain will be invested in a new home in Spain.

Ordinary declaration (*ordinaria*) – used by those with incomes from all sources other than those mentioned above, e.g. business or professional activities and capital gains.

Procedure

With the exception of a draft declaration, tax returns aren't sent out by the tax office and must be purchased from a tobacconist's (*estanco*) for around €0.50 each. If you're unable to obtain a tax return from a tobacconist's, you can get one from a tax adviser or your local tax office (*agencia tributaria*). An instruction booklet is provided with returns, and the tax office publishes a booklet, *Manual Práctico – Renta* (€0.75), containing examples of how to complete tax forms and an interpretation of the current Finance Act – a fascinating read **and** they charge you for it!

If you can use the abbreviated declaration, you should be able to complete your own tax form, perhaps with a little help from the tax office. However, most people require professional help to complete the *simplificada* and *ordinaria* tax forms. (Until the introduction of the abbreviated declaration, only some 15 per cent of Spain's 14m taxpayers completed their own tax declarations.) If you need assistance with an abbreviated or simple declaration, you can contact the information section (*servicio de información*) of your local tax office, which may have multi-lingual staff. However, tax offices won't help you complete an *ordinaria* tax form and you must make an appointment (☎ 901 223 344). When you go to the tax office, take along the following:

- Your end-of-year bank statements (*estado de cuenta*) showing any interest received and your average balance (*saldo medio*).

- Any papers relating to stocks, shares, bonds, deposit certificates or any other property owned, In Spain or abroad.

- Declarations and receipts for any taxes paid in another country (if you're seeking to offset payments against your Spanish taxes).

- Your passport, residence permit and *NIE*.

If tax is due, you can submit your return to the district tax office where you're resident for tax purposes or at a designated bank in the province. If no payment is due, you must file it at the tax office. If you delay filing your tax return by even a day, you must pay a surcharge on the tax due (see below), although it's possible to request a payment deferral.

You should retain copies of your tax returns for at least five years, which is the maximum period that returns are liable for audit by the Spanish tax authorities.

Payment

Unless deducted at source, income tax in Spain is paid at the same time as the tax declaration is made. You can pay the whole amount when the form is filed or 60 per cent with your declaration and the balance by the following 5th November. Payment must be made in cash; if you're filing at a bank where you hold an account, they will make an electronic transfer to the tax authorities.

Late payment of a tax bill usually incurs a surcharge of 20 per cent. Large fines can be imposed for breaches of tax law and in certain cases forfeiture of the right to tax benefits or subsidies for a period of up to five years. The fraudulent evasion of €30,000 or more in tax is punishable by fines of up to six times the amount defrauded and/or imprisonment.

Wealth Tax

Spain levies a wealth tax (*impuesto sobre el patrimonio*, commonly referred to simply as *patrimonio*) on residents and non-residents (unlike most other countries, which exempt non-residents). Your wealth is calculated by totalling your assets and deducting your liabilities. When calculating your liability for wealth tax, you must include the value of all your assets, including property, vehicles, boats, aircraft, businesses, cash (e.g. in bank accounts), life insurance, gold bars, jewellery, stocks, shares and bonds. The value of property for tax purposes is the highest figure of the following: the purchase price, the fiscal value (*valor catastral*) or the value assessed by the authorities, e.g. in the case of a house which hasn't yet been built or a property in an area where there are no property taxes. If you fail to declare your total assets, you can be fined.

It's no longer necessary for most people to declare their average bank balance (*saldo medio*) in Spain for wealth tax. However, if you're a non-resident and your country of residence has a double-taxation treaty with Spain (see page 246), bank balances and interest are taxable only in your country of residence.

Certain assets are exempt from wealth tax, including *objets d'art* and antiques (provided their value doesn't exceed certain limits), the vested rights of participants in pension plans and funds, copyrights (provided they remain part of your net worth), and assets forming part of Spain's historical heritage. Deductions are made for mortgages (for residents and non-residents), business and other debts, and any 'wealth' tax paid in another country. Other exemptions and allowances are detailed below.

Residents

Residents are entitled to two general allowances against wealth tax: €150,253 per person for a principal residence and €108,182.18 per person for all other assets. Therefore, if you're single and own your principal residence in Spain, you qualify for a wealth tax allowance of €258,435.18. If a property is registered in the names of both spouses (or a number of unrelated people), they should make separate declarations and are each entitled to claim the exemption. If you've bought a property with a loan or mortgage, there are deductions from your wealth tax liability. If your worldwide assets are below the taxable limit (€167,129) after allowances and you make an income tax declaration, you're exempt from making a wealth tax declaration.

Non-residents

There's no allowance for non-residents, who must pay wealth tax on **all** their assets in Spain, which for most non-resident property owners consists only of the property itself.

Tax Rates

In 2006, assets were taxed on a sliding scale as follows:

Asset Value Above Allowancee	Tax Rate	Cumulative Tax
Up to €167,129	0.2%	€334
€167,130 to €334,253	0.3%	€836
€334,254 to €668,499	0.5%	€2,507
€668,499 to €1,337,000	0.9%	€ 8,523
€1,337,001 to €2,673,999	1.3%	€25,904
€2,674,000 to €5,347,998	1.7%	€71,362
€5,347,999 to €10,695,996	2.1%	€183,670
Over €10,695,996	2.5%	

In the above table, the cumulative tax is the tax payable for each 'Asset Value' band, e.g. €2,507 is payable on assets of €668,499. If your assets are valued at €500,000 in excess of any allowances (i.e. as a resident – see above), you pay 0.2 per cent on the first €167,129 (€334), 0.3 per cent on the next €167,123 (€502) and 0.5 per cent on the balance of €165,746 (€829), making a total wealth tax bill of €1,665.

Declaration

Residents must make a declaration for wealth tax at the same time as they make their income tax declaration, i.e. between 1st May and 20th June. The declaration is made on Form 714 (*Impuesto Sobre el Patrimonio*), which is available from tobacconists and tax offices.

Non-residents owning a single property in Spain can make their declarations for tax on deemed letting income and wealth tax on a single form at any time during the year, e.g. the declaration for 2006 can be made any time until 31st December 2007. This is done on Form 214 (*Impuesto Sobre el Patrimonio y Sobre la Renta de No Residente*). Non-residents can have a financial representative in Spain make the declaration and arrange for payment on their behalf.

Property Tax

Property tax (*impuesto sobre bienes inmuebles urbana/rústica* or *IBI*) is payable by resident and non-resident property owners and goes towards local council administration, education, sanitary services (e.g. street and beach cleaning), social assistance, community substructure, and cultural and sports amenities. When you buy a property, you must register your ownership with the local town hall so that property tax can be applied. Registration must be made within two months of signing the deed and there are fines of up to €1,000 for non-registration.

Many local authorities also levy fees (*tasas*) for services such as rubbish collection, street and beach cleaning, issuing documents, local parking restrictions and fire-fighting services. These vary considerably from one authority to another (e.g. the charge for rubbish collection, which in some cases also includes sewerage, can be as little as €50 or as much as €400 per year). For further information about property taxes, see our sister publication **Buying a Home in Spain** by David Hampshire (see page 383).

> **SURVIVAL TIP**
> Before buying a property, check how much property tax
> and rubbish collection costs in the municipality – rates
> vary greatly and it may be cheaper to buy a property in
> the neighbouring municipality. For example, on the
> Costa del Sol rates payable for a villa in Mijas Costa are
> much cheaper than those in Marbella.

Capital Gains Tax

Capital Gains Tax (CGT – *impuesto sobre incremento de patrimonio*) is payable on the profit from the sale of certain assets in Spain, including antiques, art and jewellery, stocks and shares, property and businesses. Capital gains revealed as a result of the death of a taxpayer, gifts to government entities and donations of certain assets in lieu of tax payments are exempt from CGT. Spain's taxation system combines capital gains (*incremento de patrimonio*) and capital losses (*disminución de patrimonio*). Capital losses can be offset against capital gains, but not against ordinary income. Capital losses in excess of gains can be carried forward to offset against future gains for a five-year period.

Property

Capital gains tax (*impuesto sobre el incremento de patrimonio de la venta de un bien inmueble*) is payable on the profit from the sale of property and is based on the difference between the purchase price (as stated in the title deed) and the sale price of a property, less buying and selling costs (and the cost of improvements – provided you have bona fide invoices).

Exemptions

Residents aged over 65 are exempt from CGT on the profit made from the sale of their principal home, irrespective of how long they've owned it. However, the Spanish Tax Office defines a 'principal home' as the place where you've lived permanently for **at least three years**.

Residents aged below 65 are exempt from CGT on the profit made from the sale of their principal home, provided that all the profit is invested in the purchase of another principal home (not necessarily in Spain) within two years of the sale. Any profit that isn't reinvested is subject to CGT at the residents' tax rate (see below).

Tax Rates

Capital gains made by residents are treated as income, but taxed at a flat rate of 15 per cent (18 per cent from 2007). Non-residents are currently taxed at a flat rate of 35 per cent, but this is likely to be reduced in the near future to the same rate as residents.

For comprehensive information on the calculation of CGT liability, see our sister publication *Buying a Home in Spain* by David Hampshire (see page 383).

Inheritance & Gift Tax

As in most countries, dying doesn't free you (or, more correctly, your beneficiaries) from the clutches of the tax man. Spain imposes a tax on assets or money received as an inheritance or gift (*impuesto sobre sucesiones y donaciones*). The estates of residents and non-residents are subject to Spanish inheritance and gift tax if they own property or have other assets in Spain. Inheritance and gift tax is paid by the beneficiaries, e.g. a surviving spouse, and not by the deceased's estate.

The country in which beneficiaries must pay inheritance tax is usually decided by their domicile (see **Liability** on page 246). If they're domiciled in Spain, Spanish inheritance tax is payable on an inheritance, whether the inheritance is situated (or received) in Spain or abroad. There are currently numerous proposals for inheritance and gift tax reform, including the abolition of all inheritance tax or a substantial reduction on lower values. Many regions have already introduced inheritance tax reductions, although these are usually only for resident heirs or beneficiaries.

Tax is payable by beneficiaries within six months of a death if the deceased died in Spain (although it's possible to obtain a six-month extension) or within 30 days following the transfer of a lifetime gift. If the deceased died abroad, the inheritance tax declaration and the payment of inheritance tax duties must be made within 16 months.

Tax is assessed on the net amount received and accrues from the date of the death or the date of a gift. Some people have managed to avoid inheritance tax by failing to inform the Spanish authorities of a death (after five years and six months the tax can no longer be collected), although this is illegal.

Those who have been Spanish residents for at least three years receive an exemption of 95 per cent of inheritance tax when their principal residence or family business (in Spain) is bequeathed to a spouse, parent or child who has been living with them for at least two years before their death. The principal residence must be valued at less than €122,606 (there's no limit for a business) or the inheritance mustn't exceed €122,606 per heir, above which normal inheritance tax rates apply. For example, if the residence is worth €150,000, you pay tax at only 5 per cent on the first €122,606 and tax at the full rate on the balance of €27,394. The inheritor must retain ownership of the property for a minimum of ten years, although if he dies within the ten-year period no further tax is payable. However, if the property or business is sold during this period, tax may be levied at the discretion of the relevant authorities, e.g. the regional government.

The following regional variations apply: Andalusia has an exemption of 99 per cent on a principal residence; in the Balearics the exemption is 100 per cent up to the sum of €123,000; in Castile-La Mancha and Extremadura the exemption is 100 per cent; and Catalonia has an exemption of €125,060 per heir.

Liability

Inheritance and gift tax liability depends on your relationship to the donor, the amount inherited and your wealth before receipt of the gift or inheritance.

Relationship

Direct descendants and close relatives of the deceased receive an allowance before they become liable for inheritance tax, as shown below.

Group	Includes	Allowance
1.	Direct descendants under 21	€15,956.87 plus €3,990.72 for each year under 21 up to a maximum allowance of €48,000
2.	Direct descendants over 21,	€15,956.87 direct ascendants (parents and up), spouse or partner*

3. Relatives to third degree (and €7,993.46
   ascendants by affinity)
   including brother, sister, uncle,
   aunt, niece or nephew

4. Unrelated people and more None
   remote relatives (including
   common-law partners*)

* Some regions (Andalusia, Aragón, Balearics, Basque Lands, Catalonia, Madrid and Navarra) now recognise common-law partners as spouses for inheritance tax purposes, provided they are registered as such in the region.

Amount Inherited

Your inheritance tax liability is calculated as a percentage of the amount inherited (in excess of any allowance), as shown below:

Value Above Allowance	Tax Rate	Cumulative Tax Liability
Up to €7,993	7.65%	€611
€7,994 to €15,980	8.50%	€1,290
€15,981 to €23,968	9.35%	€2,037
€23,969 to €31,955	10.20%	€2,852
€31,956 to €39,943	11.05%	€3,735
€39,944 to €47,930	11.90%	€4,685
€47,931 to €55,918	12.75%	€5,703
€55,919 to €63,905	13.60%	€6,790
€63,906 to €71,893	14.45%	€7,944
€71,894 to €79,880	15.30%	€9,166
€79,881 to €119,757	16.15%	€15,606

€119,758 to €159,634	18.70%	€23,063
€159,635 to €239,389	21.25%	€40,011
€239,390 to €398,777	25.50%	€80,655
€398,778 to €797,555	29.75%	€199,291
Over €797,555	34.00%	

Note that Catalonia has a different inheritance tax scale.

Current Wealth

Your current wealth is the value of all your assets **before** the transfer.

Calculation

Once you've worked out your relationship group and calculated your inheritance tax liability, you can use the table below to calculate the inheritance tax payable based on your current wealth by multiplying your inheritance tax liability (shown in the above table) by the percentage shown under the relevant relationship group.

Current Wealth	Relationship Group		
	1/2	3	4
Up to €402,678	100%	158.82%	200%
€402,678 to €2,007,380	105%	166.76%	210%
€2,007,380 to €4,020,770	110%	174.71%	220%
Over €4,020,770	120%	190.59%	240%

For example, if you're in relationship group 3 (giving you a tax allowance of €7,993.46) and you've inherited €79,886.46, you must pay tax on €71,893, so your tax liability is €7,944; if your current wealth is between €402,678 and €2,007,380 (lucky you!), you pay inheritance tax at 166.76 per cent, which amounts to €13,247.41.

Avoiding Inheritance & Gift Tax

If you own (or are planning to buy) property in Spain it's importanat to decide in advance how you wish to dispose of it in order to reduce your tax liability. Ideally, this should be decided before buying a home in Spain. Property can be registered in a single name, both names of a couple or joint buyers' names, the names of children, giving the parents sole use during their lifetime, or in the name of a Spanish or foreign company or trust. It's advisable for a couple not only to register joint ownership of a property, but to share their other assets and have separate bank accounts, which helps to reduce their dependants' liability for inheritance tax. In some regions, Spanish law doesn't recognise the rights to inheritance of a non-married partner, although there are a number of solutions to this problem, e.g. a life insurance policy.

One way of reducing your liability to inheritance tax is to transfer legal ownership of property to a relative as a gift during your lifetime. However, this is treated as a sale (at the current market price) and incurs fees of around 10 per cent plus CGT (see page 255), above in this chapter which must be compared with your inheritance tax liability (see above). Whether you should will or 'sell' a property to someone depends on the value of the property and your relationship, and it may be cheaper for a beneficiary to be taxed under the inheritance laws. Take, for example, a couple jointly owning a property in Spain who wish to leave it to a child. When one of the parents dies, the child inherits half the property and pays inheritance tax on that amount. Inheritance tax on the other half of the property is paid when the other parent dies. In this way little tax is paid on a property with a low value. If you're elderly, it may pay you to make the title deed directly in the names of your children.

SURVIVAL TIP
Spanish inheritance law is a complicated subject and
professional advice should be sought from an
experienced lawyer who understands Spanish inheritance
law and the law of any other countries involved.

Your will (see below) is also a vital component in reducing Spanish inheritance and gift tax to the minimum or deferring its payment. Further information on this subject can be found in *Inheritance*, an information file published by the Foundation Institute of Foreign Property Owners (🖳 http://www.fipe.org) in various languages.

WILLS

It's an unfortunate fact of life that you're unable to take your hard-earned money with you when you make your final exit. All adults should make a will (*testamento*), irrespective of how large or small their assets (each spouse should make a separate will). If a foreigner dies without a will (intestate) in Spain, his estate may be automatically disposed of under Spanish law and the law regarding compulsory heirs (see below) applied.

A foreigner resident in Spain is usually permitted to dispose of his Spanish assets according to the law of his home country, provided his will is valid under the law of that country. If you've lived in Spain for a long time, it may be necessary for you to create a legal domicile in your home country for the purpose of making a will. A will made by a foreigner regarding Spanish assets isn't invalidated because it doesn't bequeath property in accordance with Spanish law, as Spanish law isn't usually applied to foreigners and the disposal of property (buildings or land) in Spain is governed by the law of the deceased's home country unless there's a dispute among the beneficiaries, in which case Spanish law is applied. See also **Inheritance & Gift Tax** above regarding ways to delay or circumvent the law of obligatory heirs and reduce inheritance tax.

Law of Obligatory Heirs

The following information applies to Spanish nationals only. Under Spanish law, a surviving spouse retains all **assets** acquired before marriage, half the assets acquired during the marriage, and all personal gifts or inheritances which have come directly to the spouse. The remaining assets must be disposed of under the law of 'obligatory heirs' (*herederos forzosos*), which is as follows. When a person dies leaving children, his estate is divided into three equal parts. One-third must be left to the surviving children in equal parts. Another third must also be left to the children, but the testator decides how it's to be divided. A surviving spouse has a life interest in this second third and the children who inherit it cannot dispose of it freely until the surviving parent dies. The final third can be freely disposed of. If a child has died leaving children of his own, they automatically inherit his share. If the deceased has no children, his surviving parents have a statutory right to one-third of his estate if he has a surviving spouse or half of his estate if he doesn't.

Types of Will

There are three kinds of Spanish will, each of which is described below. Note that, where applicable, the rules relating to witnesses are strict and, if they aren't followed precisely, can render a will null and void. Although it isn't necessary to have a Spanish will for your assets in Spain, it's advisable to have a separate will for **any** country in which you own property. If a person with a Spanish will dies his assets can be dealt with immediately under local law without having to wait for the granting of probate in another country (and the administration of the estate is also cheaper). Having a Spanish will for your Spanish assets speeds up the will's execution and saves the long and complicated process of having a foreign will executed in Spain. **If you have two or more wills, you must ensure that they don't contradict or invalidate one another.** You should periodically review your will to ensure that it reflects your current financial and personal circumstances.

Open Will

An open will (*testamento abierto*) is the standard and most suitable kind of will for most people. It's unnecessary to employ a lawyer to prepare an open will, although it's usually advisable. It must, however, be prepared by a notary who's responsible for ensuring that it's legal and properly drawn up. Its contents must be known to the notary and to three witnesses, who can be of any nationality; each witness must sign the will. The notary gives you a copy (*copia simple* or *copia autorizada*) and sends a copy to the general registry of wills (*Registro General de Actos de Ultima Voluntad*) in Madrid. The original remains at the notary's office. If you don't understand Spanish, you will need an official translation into a language that you speak fluently.

Closed Will

A closed will (*testamento cerrado*), whose contents remain secret, must be drawn up by a Spanish lawyer to ensure that it complies with Spanish law. You must take the will to a notary, who seals the envelope and signs it (plus two witnesses) and then files and records it as for an open will.

Holographic Will

A holographic will (*testamento ológrafo*) is a will made in your own handwriting or orally. If written, it must be signed and dated and must be clearly drafted to ensure that your wishes are absolutely clear. No witnesses or other formalities are required. It can be voluntarily registered with the registry of wills. On the death of the testator it must be authenticated before a judge, which delays the will's execution. An oral will must be made in the presence of five witnesses, who must then testify to a notary the wishes of the deceased. The notary then prepares a written will and certifies it. For anyone with a modest Spanish estate, e.g. a small holiday home in Spain, a holographic will is sufficient.

Cost & Procedure

The cost of preparing a simple open or closed will is around €125, plus the notary's fee (around €40). Spanish wills can be drawn up by Spanish lawyers and notaries abroad, although it's cheaper to do it in Spain.

Executors aren't normal in Spain and, if you appoint one, it may increase the inheritance tax payable. However, if you appoint an executor, you should inform your heirs so that they know who to notify in the event of your death. It isn't advisable to name a lawyer who doesn't speak Spanish as your executor, as he must instruct a Spanish lawyer (*abogado*), whose fees will be impossible to control. If you appoint a lawyer as your executor, he's permitted to charge a maximum of 5 per cent of the estate's value.

Your beneficiaries in Spain must produce an original death certificate or an authorised copy. If you die outside Spain, a foreign death certificate must be legally translated and notarised for it to be valid in Spain. The inheritance tax declaration and the payment of inheritance tax duties must be made within six months of your death if you die in Spain, and within 16 months if you die abroad (otherwise, a surcharge may result). Inheritance tax must be paid in advance of the release of the assets to be inherited in Spain, and beneficiaries may therefore need to borrow funds to pay the tax before they receive their inheritance. Note that the winding-up of an estate can take a long time in Spain.

Keep a copy of your will(s) in a safe place and another copy with your lawyer or the executor of your estate. Don't leave them in a safe deposit box, which in the event of your death is sealed for a period under Spanish law. You should keep information regarding bank accounts and insurance policies with your will(s), but don't forget to tell someone where they are!

Note that in Spain, marriage doesn't automatically revoke a will, as in some other countries.

 Spanish inheritance law is a complicated subject and it's important to obtain professional legal advice when writing or altering your will(s).

9.

ENSURE YOU'RE INSURED

An important aspect of retiring in Spain is insurance, not only for your home and its contents, but also health insurance for you (and your partner) when visiting Spain. If you live in Spain permanently you will require additional insurance. It's unnecessary to spend half your income insuring yourself against every eventuality, from the common cold to being sued for your last euro, although it's important to insure against any event that could precipitate a major financial disaster, such as a serious accident or your house falling down. The cost of being uninsured or under-insured can be astronomical.

SURVIVAL TIP
It's vital to ensure that you have sufficient insurance when visiting your home abroad, which includes health insurance (covered in Chapter 7), travel insurance, building and contents insurance, as well as continental car insurance (including breakdown insurance) and third party liability insurance.

As with anything connected with finance, it's important to shop around when buying insurance. Collecting a few brochures from insurance agents or making a few calls can save you a lot of money. Not all insurance companies are equally reliable or have the same financial stability and it may be better to insure with a large international company with a good reputation than with a small (e.g. Spanish) company, even if this means paying higher premiums. On the other hand, you may prefer to insure with a company with a local office where you know the staff personally rather than a national or international company where contact is by phone (and never to the same person!) or internet.

Read insurance contracts carefully and make sure that you understand the terms and the cover before signing them. Some insurance companies will do almost anything to avoid paying claims and use any available legal loophole, therefore it pays to deal with reputable companies only (not that this provides a foolproof guarantee). Spanish insurance companies can compel you to renew your insurance for a further year if you don't give adequate written notice (e.g. up to three months) of your intention to terminate, although most companies allow policyholders to cancel on renewal. Check in advance.

Bear in mind that if you wish to make a claim on a policy, you may be required to report an incident to the police within 24 hours (this may also be a legal requirement). The law in Spain may differ considerably from that in your home country or your previous country of residence and you should

never assume that it's the same. If you're uncertain of your rights, you're advised to obtain legal advice for anything other than a minor claim. Under European Union (EU) rules, an insurance company registered in an EU member country can sell its policies in any other EU country.

In matters regarding insurance, you're responsible for ensuring that you and your family are legally insured in Spain. Regrettably you cannot insure yourself against being uninsured or sue your insurance agent for giving you bad advice!

This chapter contains information about car, household, holiday and travel insurance. For information about health insurance, see **Chapter 7**.

CAR INSURANCE

All motor vehicles and trailers must be insured when entering Spain. It isn't, however, mandatory for cars insured in most European countries to have an international insurance 'green' card because motorists insured in an EU country, Hungary, Licchtenstein, Norway and Switzerland are automatically covered for third party liability in Spain. Nevertheless, if you have comprehensive cover and want to extend it to Spain you will need a green card and there will be a limit on how long you can drive in Spain on your foreign insurance, e.g. three to six months.

There are an estimated 2m drivers without insurance in Spain, where there's also more insurance fraud than in any other EU country. Note, however, that driving without obligatory insurance (*seguro obligatorio*) is a serious offence, for which you can be fined up to €3,000 or even imprisoned. You must carry your insurance documents when driving and can be fined €60 for not having them if you're stopped by the police.

Car insurance is available from many Spanish insurance companies and a number of foreign insurance companies in Spain, including direct insurance companies (who don't use agents). Always shop around and obtain a number of quotations.

Types of Insurance

The following categories of car insurance are available in Spain:

Third-party

Third-party insurance (*responsabilidad civil obligatoria* or *seguro obligatorio*) is the minimum required by law. It costs from around €300 a year to insure against the minimum third party claims (€360,000 for personal injury and €100,000 for damage to third party property). You should ensure that you fully understand the cover provided for the driver and passengers and that it meets your needs. You can choose to pay an extra premium for additional cover up to a specified or unlimited amount (*ilimitada*), which is highly recommended. Unlimited third party cover usually costs around €35 extra per year. Note that a driver and his family don't count as third parties and must be insured separately (see **Driver & Passenger Insurance** below).

Roadside assistance (*asistencia en viajes*), glass breakage (*rotura de lunas*) and legal expenses (*defensa penal*) in the event of a court case may be included in basic third party cover or can be added for an additional premium.

Third-party, Fire & Theft

Third-party, fire and theft insurance (*responsabilidad civil obligatoria, incendio y robo*), known in some countries as 'part comprehensive', includes cover against fire (*incendio*), natural hazards (e.g. rocks falling on your car), theft (*robo*), broken glass (e.g. windscreen), legal expenses (*defensa penal*), and possibly damage or theft of contents (although this is rare). Insurance against the theft of a stereo system is usually available only from the manufacturer (it may be included in the purchase price). You may be able to take out fire cover independently, although it's usually combined with theft cover.

Comprehensive

Comprehensive (sometimes called 'fully comprehensive') insurance, known in Spain as 'all risks' (*todo riesgo*), covers all the risks listed under third party, fire and theft (above) plus all other types of damage to your vehicle irrespective of how it's caused.

SURVIVAL TIP
Note that some insurance companies don't provide comprehensive cover for vehicles more than two or three years old (although it's possible to get comprehensive cover on vehicles up to ten years old).

Comprehensive insurance may be compulsory for lease and credit purchase contracts. Note that Spanish insurance doesn't usually pay for a replacement car when your car is being repaired after an accident.

Driver & Passenger Insurance

Driver and passenger insurance (*seguro de ocupantes*) is usually optional and can be added to insurance policies. Driver protection allows the driver of a vehicle involved in an accident to claim for bodily injury to himself, including compensation for his incapacity to work or for his beneficiaries should he be killed. There are usually various levels of driver and passenger accident insurance, e.g. from €5,000 to €25,000 for death and permanent disability.

Premiums

Insurance premiums in Spain are among the lowest in the EU, although they vary considerably depending on numerous factors, including the following:

- The type of insurance (see above).

- The type of car and its use. Cars are divided into eight categories, based on their performance (some companies don't insure high-performance vehicles), the cost of repairs, where and how much they are used (some premiums are based on the number of kilometres driven each year), whether they are garaged and whether theye are used for business and/or pleasure.

- Your age and accident record. Drivers with less than two or three years experience usually pay a 'penalty' (*multa*) and drivers over a certain age, e.g. 70, also pay higher premiums, although some companies offer low-cost policies for experienced older drivers, e.g. those aged over 50 or 55, with a good record. Other companies give discounts of 10 to 20 per cent for experienced drivers of any age.

- The area where you live. Premiums are highest in Madrid and other major cities and lowest in rural areas.

- Whether a car is garaged. Some insurance companies give an additional discount (e.g. 5 per cent) if a vehicle is garaged overnight.

Premiums vary from around €350 a year for third party insurance for a small family saloon to €1,500 or more a year for comprehensive insurance for a high-performance sports saloon. Short-term policies (for periods of less than a year) are available from some companies, although premiums are high, e.g. 50 per cent of the annual rate for three months and 70 per cent of the annual rate for six months. Value added tax (VAT/*IVA*) at 16 per cent is payable on insurance premiums. You can reduce your premium by choosing to pay an excess (*franquicia*), e.g. the first €150, €180, €300, €450 or €600 of a claim.

If you're convicted of drunk or dangerous driving, your premium will be increased considerably. In fact, if you're convicted of drunk driving, your insurance company will probably refuse to pay on a claim!

Insurance companies must give two months' notice of an increase in premiums.

No-claims Bonus

A foreign no-claims bonus (*bonificación/sistema bonus-malus*) is usually valid, provided you've had insurance within the last two years, but you must provide written evidence from your present or previous insurance company, not just an insurance renewal notice. You may need an official Spanish translation. **Always insist on having your no-claims bonus recognised, even if you don't receive the same percentage reduction as you received abroad (shop around).**

Most companies offer a 5 per cent discount for each year of no claims up to a maximum discount of 60 per cent, although some offer a maximum of only 50 per cent (or less). Foreign insurance companies may offer a more generous no-claims bonus than Spanish companies.

If you have an accident, you're usually required to pay a penalty (*multa*) or your bonus is reduced, e.g. one accident may lose you two years' no-claims bonus. You can usually pay an extra premium to protect your no-claims bonus. No-claims bonuses usually also apply to a second family car.

Claims

In the event of an accident, claims are decided on the information provided in accident report forms (*declaración de siniestro de automóvil*) completed by drivers, reports by insurance company experts and police reports. You must notify your insurance company of a claim within a limited period, e.g.

two to five days. Some companies have 24-hour helplines for claims. If you have an accident, the damage must usually be inspected and the repair authorised by your insurance company's assessor, although sometimes an independent assessor's report may be permitted. An inspection may be unnecessary for minor repairs. Note that when a vehicle is a total loss, a Spanish insurance company may pay only a percentage of its 'book' value, which is less than its actual value.

If your car is stolen, you must report it to the local police immediately and submit a copy of the police report with your claim. After reporting your car stolen, 30 days must elapse before an insurance company will consider a claim. Note that there's little communication or co-operation between insurance companies in Spain and trying to recover uninsured losses is a nightmare.

Cancellation

Spanish insurance companies are forbidden by law to cancel third party cover after a claim, except in the case of drunk driving or when a driver is subsequently disqualified from driving. A company can, however, refuse to renew your policy at the end of the current period, although they must give you 15 days' notice. Note also that if you have an accident while breaking the law, e.g. drunk driving, speeding or illegal parking, comprehensive insurance may be automatically downgraded to third party, which means that you must pay for your own repairs and medical expenses.

If you wish to cancel your car insurance at the end of the current term, you must notify your insurance company in writing by registered letter and usually give two months' notice. You may cancel your insurance before the term has expired if the premium is increased, the terms are altered, or your car has been declared a write-off or stolen. If you cancel your policy during the term of the insurance, e.g. you sell your car, and don't take out another policy, your insurance company isn't required to give you a refund.

HOUSEHOLD INSURANCE

Household insurance (*seguro de hogar*) in Spain generally includes the building, its contents and third party liability, all of which are contained in a multi-risk household insurance policy. Policies are offered by Spanish and foreign insurance companies and premiums are similar, although foreign companies may provide more comprehensive cover.

Building

Although not compulsory, it's wise to take out property insurance that covers damage to a building (*continente*) due to fire, smoke, lightning, water, explosion, storm, freezing, snow, theft, vandalism, malicious damage, acts of terrorism, impact, broken windows and natural catastrophes (such as falling trees). Insurance should include glass, external buildings, aerials and satellite dishes, gardens and garden ornaments. Note that if a claim is the result of a defect in the building or its design, e.g. the roof is too heavy and collapses, the insurance company won't pay up (yet another reason to have a survey before buying!).

Property insurance is based on the cost of rebuilding your home and should be increased each year in line with inflation. Make sure that you insure your property for the true cost of rebuilding. It's particularly important to have insurance for storm damage in Spain, which can be severe in some areas. If floods are one of your concerns, make sure you're covered for water coming in from ground level, not just for water seeping in through the roof. **Always read the small print of contracts.** Note that if you own a home in an area that has been hit by a succession of natural disasters (such as floods), your household insurance can be cancelled.

Contents

Contents (*contenido*) are usually insured for the same risks as a building (see above) and are insured for their replacement value (new for old), with a reduction for wear and tear for clothes and linen. Valuable objects are covered for their actual declared (and authenticated) value. Most policies include automatic indexation of the insured sum in line with inflation. Contents insurance may include accidental damage to sanitary installations, theft, money, replacement of locks following damage or loss of keys, alternative accommodation cover, and property belonging to third parties stored in your home. Some items are usually optional, e.g. credit cards, frozen foods, emergency assistance (plumber, glazier, electrician, etc.), redecoration, garaged cars, replacement pipes, loss of rent, and the cost of travel to Spain for holiday homeowners. Many policies include personal third party liability, e.g. up to €300,000, although this may be an option.

Items of high value must usually be itemised and documentation (e.g. a valuation) and photographs provided. Some companies even recommend or insist on a video film of belongings. When claiming for contents, you should produce the original bills if possible (always keep bills for expensive items) and bear in mind that replacing imported items in Spain may be more expensive than buying them abroad. Contents' policies contain security clauses and if you don't adhere to them a claim won't be considered. If you're planning to let a property, you may be required to inform your insurer. Note that a building must be secure with iron bars (*rejas*) on ground-floor windows and patio doors, shutters and locks. Most companies offer a discount if properties have steel reinforced doors, high security locks and alarms (particularly alarms connected to a monitoring station). See **Home Security** on page 162.

An insurance company may send someone to inspect your home and advise on security measures. Policies pay out for theft only when there are signs of forced entry, and you aren't covered for thefts by a tenant (but may be covered for thefts by domestic staff). All-risks policies offering a worldwide extension to a household policy covering jewellery, cameras and other items aren't usually available from Spanish insurance companies, but are available from a number of foreign companies.

Community Properties

If you own a property that's part of a community development (see page 150), the building is usually insured by the community (although you should make sure that it's comprehensively insured). You must, however, be insured for third party risks (*riesgo a terceros*) in the event that you cause damage to neighbouring properties, e.g. through flood or fire. Household policies usually include third party liability up to a maximum amount, e.g. €300,000.

Insuring Abroad

It's possible and legal to take out building and contents insurance in another country for a property in Spain (some foreign insurance companies offer special policies for holiday homeowners), although you must ensure that a policy is valid under Spanish law. The advantage is that you have a policy you can understand and you're able to handle claims in your own language. This may seem like a good option for a holiday home, although it can be more expensive than insuring with a Spanish company and can lead to conflicts if, for example, the building is insured with a Spanish-registered company and the contents with a foreign based company. Most experts advise that you insure a Spanish home and its contents (*continente y contenido*) with a Spanish insurance company through a local agent.

Premiums

Premiums are usually calculated on the size (constructed area in square metres) of a property, its age, the value of the contents and the security protection, e.g. window protection (e.g. bars) at ground level, the number of entrance doors and their construction. As a rough guide, building insurance costs around €10 a year per €5,000 of value insured, e.g. a property valued at €200,000 will cost €400 a year to insure. Contents insurance costs from around €15 a year per €5,000 of value insured (e.g. a premium of €30 for contents valued at €10,000) and may be higher for a detached villa than an apartment, e.g. up to €20 per €5,000 insured. Detached, older and more remote properties often cost more to insure than apartments and new properties (especially if located in towns), due to the higher risk of theft.

Claims

If you wish to make a claim, you must usually inform your insurance company in writing (by registered letter) within two to seven days of an incident or 24 hours in the case of theft. Thefts should also be reported to the local police within 24 hours, as the police report (*denuncia* – see page 313), of which you receive a copy for your insurance company, constitutes irrefutable evidence of your claim. Check whether you're covered for damage or thefts that occur while you're away from your property and are therefore unable to inform the insurance company immediately.

Take care that you don't under-insure your house contents and that you periodically reassess their value and adjust your insurance premium accordingly. You can arrange to have your insurance cover automatically increased annually by a fixed percentage or amount. If you make a claim and the assessor discovers that you're under-insured, the amount due is reduced by the percentage by which you're under-insured (e.g. if you're insured for €5,000 and you're found to be under-insured by 50 per cent, your claim for €1,500 is reduced by 50 per cent to €750).

HOLIDAY & TRAVEL INSURANCE

Holiday and travel insurance (*seguro de viajes*) is highly recommended for anyone who doesn't wish to risk having their holiday or travel ruined by financial problems or to arrive home broke. As you probably know, anything can and often does go wrong with a holiday, sometimes before you even get started (particularly when you **don't** have insurance). The following information applies equally to residents and non-residents, whether you're travelling to or from Spain or within Spain. Nobody should visit Spain without travel (and health) insurance! See **Chapter 7.**

Travel insurance is available from many sources, including travel agents, insurance companies and agents, banks, automobile clubs and transport companies. Package holiday companies and tour operators also offer insurance policies, some of which are compulsory, too expensive and don't provide adequate cover. You can also buy 24-hour accident and flight insurance at major airports, although it's expensive and doesn't provide the best cover. Before taking out travel insurance, carefully consider the range and level of cover you require and compare policies. Short-term holiday and travel insurance policies should include cover for holiday cancellation or interruption; missed flights; departure delay at the start **and** end of a holiday (a common occurrence); delayed, lost or damaged baggage; personal effects and money; medical expenses and accidents (including evacuation home); personal liability and legal expenses; flight insurance, and default or bankruptcy insurance, e.g. against a tour operator or airline going bust.

Health Cover

Medical expenses are an important aspect of travel insurance and you shouldn't rely on insurance provided by reciprocal health arrangements (see page 202), charge and credit card companies, household policies or private medical insurance (unless it's an international policy), none of which usually provide adequate cover (although you should take advantage of what they offer). The minimum medical insurance recommended by experts is €300,000 in Spain and the rest of Europe, and €1.2m for the rest of the world (many policies have limits of between €1.8m to €2.4m). If applicable, check whether pregnancy related claims are covered and whether there are any restrictions for those over a certain age, e.g. 65, as travel insurance is becoming increasingly more expensive for those aged over 65.

Always check any exclusion clauses in contracts by obtaining a copy of the full policy document, as not all the relevant information is included in an insurance leaflet. High-risk sports and pursuits should be specifically covered and **listed** in a policy (there's usually an additional premium). Winter sports policies are available and are more expensive than normal holiday insurance ('dangerous' sports are excluded from most standard policies). Third-party liability cover should be €2.4m in North America and €1.2m in the rest of the world. Note that this doesn't cover you when you're using a car or other mechanically propelled vehicle.

Cost

The cost of travel insurance varies considerably, depending on where you buy it, how long you intend to stay in Spain and your age. Generally, the longer the period covered, the cheaper the daily cost, although the maximum period covered is usually limited, e.g. six months. With some policies an excess must be paid for each claim. As a rough guide, travel insurance for Spain (and most other European countries) costs from around €35 for one week, €60 for two weeks and €100 for a month for a family of four (two adults and two children under 16). Premiums may be higher for those aged over 65.

Annual Policies

For those who travel abroad frequently, whether on business or pleasure, an annual travel policy provides the best value, but carefully check exactly what it includes. Many insurance companies offer annual travel policies for a premium of around €200 for an individual (the equivalent of around two months insurance with a standard travel insurance policy), which are excellent value for frequent travellers. Some insurance companies also provide an 'emergency travel policy' for holiday homeowners who need to travel abroad at short notice to inspect a property, e.g. after a severe storm. The cost of an annual policy may depend on the area covered, e.g. Europe, worldwide (excluding North America) and worldwide (including North America), although it doesn't usually cover travel within your country of residence. There's also a limit on the number of trips a year and the duration of each trip, e.g. 90 or 120 days. An annual policy is usually a good choice for owners of a retirement home in Spain who travel there frequently for relatively short periods.

SURVIVAL TIP
You should check carefully exactly what's covered by (or omitted from) an annual policy, as it may not provide adequate cover or may not cover you for an extended holiday abroad.

10.

KEEPING YOURSELF OCCUPIED

Retirement opens up a whole new world of leisure possibilities and for many people provides the chance to experience new activities and pastimes that they previously didn't have time for. However, some retirees find it difficult to know what to do with their increased free time and life can be lonely as you no longer have the daily contact with colleagues in your workplace and you will probably (initially at least) have a much smaller circle of friends. Your leisure time during retirement needs planning and you should make the most of your free time to keep healthy and active, stimulate your mind and, most importantly, enjoy yourself. You might even find that you would like to continue to work – a part time job is an attractive possibility for many people or you may wish to work as a volunteer.

Spain offers a wealth of leisure possibilities for retirees, ranging from a wealth of sports to arts and crafts classes, most of which aren't expensive. This chapter examines the main leisure options open to retirees in Spain including employment opportunities, outdoor activities, sports, entertainment, social clubs and church groups, and information about travelling around Spain.

EMPLOYMENT OPPORTUNITIES

For some retirees, the whole point of retiring in Spain is to forget all about their previous working life and start a new life of leisure, while others miss the daily contact with their former colleagues and find their days are empty without the discipline and routine of employment (a common experience). For them, a part time job could be the solution, which is also a good way to meet people and supplement your pension.

Regulations

In most countries, including Spain and the UK, remuneration received for part-time employment has no effect on state-pension payments, but it's worth checking your tax liabilities. Additional income from part-time work may increase your tax liability. See **Income Tax** on page 245 for further information.

Once you start work, your employer should register you with the social security system and may need to make monthly contributions on your behalf (retirees who have contributed to the social security system for at least thirty-five years are exempt).Your employer also makes monthly deductions from your salary for income tax.

Many pensioners in Spain have part-time jobs where they're paid cash in hand by the employer – both parties save on tax payments and possibly social security contributions. Be aware, however, that this is illegal and penalties are high if you're caught.

Which Job?

Your employment opportunities depend on where you live and your skills, not least your Spanish language proficiency. Some popular part-time jobs include shop assistants, gardeners, odd-job men, babyminders and other casual employment. There are also plenty of opportunities for seasonal work, e.g. helping out in bars and cafés during the busy summer months.

It's also worth considering turning a hobby into a paying concern; for example, if you're interested in furniture restoration, computing (English-speaking 'PC doctors' are always in demand in resort areas) or car mechanics. Buying and selling on the internet, e.g. via Ebay, or at a local market can also be lucrative as well as a way of making use of your free time. Job-share is another possibility, although job sharing is much less common in Spain than other countries such as the UK, and you also might like to consider consultancy work in your area of expertise, which can often be done via the internet.

Voluntary Work

An excellent way to fill your day while helping others at the same time, is to become a volunteer. Wherever you live in Spain, there are organisations who would be more than grateful for a few hours of your time: charities, self-help organisations and support groups are continually seeking helpers.

Volunteer work consists of a variety of jobs such as helping out at a charity shop (Cudeca's 11 shops in aid of the cancer hospice on the Costa del Sol are run entirely by volunteer workers); driving sick, disabled or non-car owners to hospital or medical appointments; listening to and providing advice to those in need; providing company to the lonely; or helping to run charity events.

Spanish speakers are always needed to provide interpretation and translation services for other expatriates, e.g. at health centres or town halls. If you speak good Spanish, it's also worth offering to assist at local Spanish charities, e.g. the Red Cross (Cruz Roja).

For information about local charities and organisations, check your local newspapers or enquire at your town hall or health centre.

Starting a Business

Setting up a business in Spain isn't for the faint-hearted, although thousands of foreigners have successfully launched businesses, and the paperwork and red tape alone will take up hours of your time even if you hire the services of a *gestor* (see page 311) to help. Once you've completed the paperwork, long working hours are required in order to establish a business and get it firmly off the ground. In short, this is probably not the ideal activity for retirement! However, if you're set on starting your own business in Spain, our sister publication **Making a Living in Spain** by Anne Hall (see page 383) provides comprehensive information and advice, as well as many business ideas.

SPORTS & ACTIVITIES

Spain's year-round pleasant climate lends itself to an outdoor life – few activities are 'rained off' here – and there are ample opportunities to make the most of this.

Bowls

Lawn bowls has grown in popularity in resort areas and most have bowling clubs and leagues run by expatriates. See your local press for contact details or the website 🖳 http://www.bowlinginspain.com. The Spanish equivalent to lawn bowls, *petanca* or *bolos*, is played throughout Spain at all levels and many parks have an area reserved for *petanca*.

Cycling

Cycling is very popular in Spain where the mountainous terrain provides some of Europe's most challenging ascents. If you're a serious cyclist there are around 5,000 annual cycling races and events held throughout the country including the tour of Spain (Vuelta de España – 🖳 http://www.lavuelta.com), the third-most important world cycle race after the tours of France and Italy.

For the less energetic, cycle tracks can be found throughout Spain including many along Spain's 'Greenways', converted railways tracks which provide virtually flat cycling through spectacular countryside (see 🖥 http://www.viasverdes.com). Several specialist holiday companies organise cycling holidays in different regions of Spain including the Balearics.

Bikes are available for hire in many resorts and towns and can be purchased at specialist shops and hypermarkets (see the *Yellow Pages* under *Bicicletas*).

Fishing

Spain is a paradise for fishermen with its over 2,000km (1,250mi) of coastline, over 75,000km (46,000mi) of rivers, and thousands of lakes and reservoirs. Sea fishing is very popular, particularly among locals, and you can fish without a licence from the shore (but, note that fishing isn't allowed from many beaches) or rent a boat and go out to sea. Common seawater fish include grouper, mackerel, sardines and sea-bream. The Canaries are home to the great fishing grounds of the Atlantic, where some of sport fishing's largest prey, e.g. marlin, tuna and shark, are found in abundance. Deep-sea fishing trips are also organised from most Spanish ports and competitions are held regularly.

Freshwater fishing requires a licence, valid for one, three or five years, issued by regional governments. Licences are available from various places including town halls, savings banks and regional offices, and some regional governments issue them online. You need to present proof of identity, evidence of civil liability insurance (in some regions only, e.g. Andalusia) and pay the fee, which varies from €4 to €12 for one year. In many regions fishing licences are free for the over 65s. The website *Su Licencia* (🖥 http://www.sulicencia.com) processes licence applications online for the regions of Aragon, Asturias, Castile & Leon, Castile-La Mancha, Catalonia, Extremadura and Navarra for a fee of around €20. Penalties for fishing without a licence are high and if you're caught you will probably have your rod confiscated.

The fishing season varies depending on the species of fish, e.g. the salmon season commences on the first Sunday in March. On most rivers there are limits on the numbers of licences issued each day and on the size of fish (and often the number) that may be caught, and the bait and technique that can be used. The most common freshwater fish include carp, perch, pike, salmon and trout. Salmon are found in the streams and rivers in the Cantabrian range and in Galicia, and trout are common in the upper reaches of rivers throughout Spain.

Material

Tackle and bait are available from specialised shops, often located within the port in coastal towns. Look in the *Yellow Pages* under *Armerías* and *Deportes: Artículos* for contact details.

Two useful books for fishermen are *Angling in Spain* and *Flyfishing in Spain*, both written and published by Phil Pembroke.

Gardening

Much of Spain's coastline is a gardener's paradise and for most of the year, many gardens are full of colour. Not surprisingly, gardening is a popular pastime and a rewarding one. Northern Europeans are often surprised at the size and variety of plants that can be grown in Spain.

Few places on the coast have ideal climates, however, and it's often too hot and dry for some plants to flourish without extensive watering. Frosts are a problem inland and salty winds on the coast often kill many plants. The Costa Brava probably has one of the best gardening climates with sunny conditions and enough rain. In some parts of Spain, e.g. the Costa de Almería and the Canaries, maintaining a green garden is almost impossible. To keep costs and maintenance down, it's best to choose plants that thrive in the area – typical Mediterranean plants are slow-growing and love dry soil, e.g. herbs such as rosemary and thyme, oleanders and pines.

Don't be taken in by all you see at the garden centre as many plants are forced at the nursery for display purposes and rarely survive in 'real' conditions, and it's easy to waste money on unsuitable plants. You may spend €30 on a hydrangea, only to find it dies in the dry air in your Costa del Sol garden. In the Canaries and dry parts of the mainland, choose low-maintenance plants such as succulents and cacti, and pave or gravel areas instead of having lawn (grass needs almost daily watering in the summer to survive).

If you aren't a keen gardener or don't have the energy, consider buying a small property without a garden but with a balcony, terrace or patio. Even the smallest area can be decorated with colourful pot plants such as geraniums and Busy Lizzies (*Impatiens*), which flower for most of the year.

Clubs & Societies

Many areas have gardening clubs where visits to local gardens and talks by specialists are organised. Check your local press for details.

Gardeners

If you find your garden too much to manage and need the assistance of a gardener, expect to pay from €100 a month for basic chores such as grass cutting and pruning, and up to €200 a month for full-time maintenance of the whole garden. There are also specialist companies providing gardening services in most resort areas, although their services can be expensive.

Materials

Garden centres (*viveros*) have sprung up all over Spain, selling plants, trees, garden ornaments, garden furniture and just about everything else you need to create and maintain a garden. Prices vary considerably and it's worth shopping around to find somewhere with reasonable prices that can also offer good advice about the most suitable plants. Plants can also be bought cheaply at stalls at weekly markets (*mercadillos*) held in most towns. DIY stores and hypermarkets stock gardening materials and furniture, but garden machinery (e.g. lawn mower) is usually only available at specialist shops.

There are a number of specialist books on gardening in Spain including *Gardening in Spain* by Marcelle Pitt (Santana Books) and *Your Garden in Spain* by C. and D. Handscombe (Santana Books).

Golf

Golf is one of Spain's main sporting attractions and it's home to around 250 golf courses, mostly located in coastal areas and around Madrid. The Costa del Sol (also known as the Costa del Golf) has over 45 courses including the world-class Valderrama in Sotogrande, which hosts the annual Volvo Masters Tournament and where the Ryder Cup was played in 1997. The Costa Blanca has a good choice of courses, particularly in the south, and El Saler south of Valencia is one of Spain's top courses and host to the Spanish Open. The Costa Brava and Costa de la Luz on the Spanish Algarve are also good golfing destinations. Golfing opportunities are more limited on the islands, although Majorca and Tenerife have a good choice.

Spanish golf courses are invariably excellent and beautifully maintained. Most courses are situated in picturesque settings (sea, mountain or forest), many designed by world's top designers such as Severiano Ballesteros and Robert Trent Jones, and linked with property development (some of Spain's most expensive homes are on golf courses). Many golf clubs are combined with country or sports clubs and offer a wide variety of sports and social facilities, including swimming pools, spas, racket sports, and a bar and restaurant. Golf clubs also provide golf instruction and several have driving ranges, while a growing number of independent golf schools stage regular courses for all standards from beginner to expert.

Spain has courses to suit all standards, although unlike some other countries, there are few municipal courses and it's an expensive sport. Most courses are owned by syndicates and have annual membership fees starting at around €1,500 (€2,000 for a couple) and seasonal and daily fees for non-members. Green fees vary depending on the club and the season (summer is the low season in the south). Expect to pay from €30 for 9 holes and from €50 for 18 holes (from €60 on the Costa del Sol), although top courses charge considerably more. You can rent golf clubs (from around €15), golf trolleys/carts (from around €5 a round or €15 for an electric trolley) and electric golf buggies (€25 to €50 a round) at most clubs.

A detailed list of Spanish golf courses and their vital statistics is available from the Royal Spanish Golf Federation (Real Federación Española de Golf – ☎ 915 552 682, 🖳 http://www.golfspainfederacion.com). There are numerous websites dedicated to golf in Spain, including Golf in Spain (🖳 http://www.golfinspain.com) where you can book a round online. Several golf magazines are published in Spain including *Andalucía Golf* and the *Costa del Sol Golf News*.

Hiking & Rambling

Spain has some of the finest hiking and rambling areas in Europe and few countries can offer its combination of good weather and spectacular, unspoilt countryside. Spain is unrivalled in Europe for its diversity of landscape, profusion of flora and fauna, and its variety of native animals and birds, many of which are unique to Spain. Many areas have marked paths or trails and there are walks to suit all levels. The best times for walking are spring and autumn, when the weather isn't too hot, although summer walking is pleasant in much of northern Spain, e.g. in the Picos de Europa and the Pyrenees. Winter walking is possible in inland regions in southern and eastern Spain, but beware of very cold weather conditions in high areas.

Many regions of Spain offer excellent hiking and there are several outstanding routes, the most famous of which is the 'pilgrim's way' from Le Puy in France to Santiago de Compostela in Galicia, known as the *Camino de Santiago* and designated a *Grande Randonnée* (GR65) by the French. Several other pilgrim's ways run through Spain to Santiago including the *Camino de la Plata*, which starts in Seville. Spain's longest circular route, known as the Sulayr (🖳 http://www.sulayr.net), has recently been opened and covers 340km (212mi) around the base of the Sierra Nevada range and takes around 19 days. Serious (insane?) walkers may be interested in the European hiking route, GR7, extending from Tarifa (Spain's southernmost tip) along the Mediterranean coast all the way to Greece, some 2,100km (1,300mi) away. Easier walks, but no less beautiful, can be found on Spain's 'Greenways' (Vías Verdes), which follow disused railway lines through spectacular countryside (see 🖳 http://www.viasverdes.com for more information).

Maps and specialist publications (such as those published by Editorial Alpina) are available from tourist offices and national park visitor centres. A number of books about hiking in Spain are published in English, including *Trekking in Spain* by Marc Dubin (Lonely Planet), *Walking Through Spain* by Robin Neillands (Queen Anne Press) and several area-specific guides published by Cicerone (🖳 http://www.cicerone.co.uk).

There are local rambling and hiking clubs in most parts of Spain, many run by expatriates. Ask at your town hall or see the local press for details. Specialist walking holidays are also organised throughout Spain.

Horse Riding

Horse riding is popular throughout Spain, where there's a long history of horse breeding and horsemanship. The Spanish or Andalusian thoroughbred is among the most famous breeds in the world and the art of horsemanship is demonstrated in many equestrian schools, such as the Real Escuela Andaluza del Arte Ecuestre in Jerez. Spain has numerous ranches, riding centres and schools (*picaderos*) where you can hire a horse by the hour or day, and/or have riding lessons (many are run by foreigners in resort areas). Riding holidays (weekend or longer) are available in many parts of Spain. For details of your nearest riding centre, look in the *Yellow Pages* under *Equitación: escuelas* or *picaderos*.

Keep Fit Classes & Gymnasiums

Gymnasiums (gyms) and health clubs can be found all over Spain, although the range of equipment and facilities varies greatly. Some include a pool, tennis courts, sauna, spa and bar services, whereas others just provide gym apparatus. Many councils operate municipal gyms and provide a range of keep fit classes (e.g. aerobics, Pilates, spinning and yoga), some of which are specifically designed for older 'keep-fitters'.

Most gyms and health clubs offer weekly, monthly or annual membership or you can pay for individual classes on a pay-as-you-go basis. Fees vary considerably and start at around €40 a month in a resort area. Council-run gyms and classes are considerably cheaper, but places may be limited to registered residents only (see **Local Council Registration** on page 192). There are usually reduced fees for couples.

Before you start any strenuous fitness classes or gym routine, it's advisable to have a medical check-up. When using apparatus for the first time, ask the fitness coach to demonstrate the correct way to use it. Muscle strains and injury can cause permanent damage, particularly as you get older. Always warm-up at the start of any exercise and warm-down at the end.

Racket Sports

Racket sports are popular, particularly tennis, and there are thousands of tennis courts throughout Spain where the weather permits outdoor tennis to be played all year round. Many tennis clubs provide a variety of other facilities, including pools and a gymnasium. Court surfaces are usually clay (*arcilla*) or cement (*hormigón*).

Court hire costs from €5 to €50 an hour, depending on the venue and facilities offered. Membership of a tennis club costs from around €35 a month, although some clubs are considerably more expensive. All clubs organise regular tournaments and provide professional coaching (individual and group lessons), and many clubs and hotels run resident tennis schools throughout the year. Individual lessons cost from €25 an hour. Information regarding tennis clubs and competitions can be obtained from the Royal Spanish Tennis Federation (Real Federación Española de Tenis – ☎ 932 005 355, 🖳 http://www.rfet.es).

Other racket sports such as squash and badminton are relatively rare in Spain, although there are badminton clubs in areas that are popular with foreign residents.

Skiing

Skiing is popular in Spain where there are around 30 ski resorts, located mainly in the Pyrenees. The skiing season runs from December to April or May. Downhill skiing (*esquí de descenso*) is the most popular form of skiing, although cross-country (*esquí nórdico* or *esquí de fondo*) is also catered for at some resorts. Snowboarding (known simply as *snow*) is increasingly popular. Spain provides excellent conditions for beginners and intermediate skiers, but advanced skiers will find that Spanish pistes don't provide sufficient challenges.

Skiing holidays in Spain (and neighbouring Andorra) are relatively cheap compared to the Alps, but nevertheless skiing isn't a cheap sport. Expect to pay around €300 for the equipment (skis, boots and clothes) and at least €30 for a day's skiing pass. Cheaper equipment can be purchased in department stores and sports shops during the January sales (when discounts of up to 60 per cent are offered) and shops in resorts also offer discounts at the end of the season. Ski rental costs around €20 a day and boots around €10 a day.

Most resorts have a range of ski lifts, including cable cars, chair-lifts and drag-lifts. Pistes in Spain are rated as green (very easy – *muy fácil*), blue (easy – *fácil*), red (difficult – *difícil*) or black (very difficult – *muy difícil*). A variety of accommodation is available, including hotels, self-catering apartments and chalets. Accommodation is more expensive during holiday periods (Christmas, New Year and Easter), when ski-lift queues are interminable and pistes are often overcrowded. Weekends are also busy times – weekdays outside school holiday periods are the best times to ski.

The latest weather and snow conditions are broadcast on Spanish television (usually on Thursday and Friday evenings) and radio, published in daily newspapers, and are available direct from resorts themselves (see below).

Resorts

Southern Spain: Europe's southern-most ski resort, Pradollano situated in the perpetually snow-capped mountains of Sierra Nevada in Granada, is just over two hours drive from the Costa del Sol and has over 70km (43mi) of pistes. Snow is generally guaranteed, as the resort has an extensive network of snow-making machines. The resort, host to the World Cup in 1996, has excellent accommodation and facilities. A one-day ski pass costs from €27 (€35 in the high season) and season tickets are available. Further information including current weather conditions is available from ☎ 958 249 100 and 🖳 http://www.sierranevadaski.com.

Pyrenees: Catalonia (Barcelona, Costa Brava and Costa Dorada) has easy access to no less than 17 ski resorts within the region itself, as well as other resorts in the Pyrenees in Aragon and Andorra. Catalonia's largest resorts include La Masella, with 57km (35mi) of pistes, and Baqueira Beret with 104km (65mi). As well as alpine ski and snowboarding, a variety of winter sports are available including cross-country ski, heli-ski, dog sledging and skating. Day ski passes start at €24 and season tickets are available. Information about ski resorts in the Pyrenees (including weather conditions) can be found at 💻 http://www.catski.net and 💻 http://www.nievede aragon.com (Spanish only) and information about skiing in Andorra from 💻 http://www.skiandorra.ad.

Northern Spain: Asturias, Cantabria and Galicia have three ski resorts, although they are all relatively small and crowded at weekends and during holiday periods. Alto Campoo in the heart of Los Picos mountains has 17km (11mi) of pistes and stunning surroundings (💻 http://www.altocampoo.com). San Isidro (💻 http://www.estacionsanisidro.com), 66km (41mi) south-east of Oviedo, currently has 24km (15mi) of pistes, but has an additional 15-20km (9-12mi) under construction. Valgrande-Pajares (💻 http://www.valgrande-pajares.com), south of Oviedo and on the border with the province of León, has 30km (19mi) of pistes.

Water Sports

Not surprisingly considering Spain's vast coastline, many islands and numerous lakes and reservoirs, the country is a Mecca for water sports enthusiasts.

Sailing

Spain's Mediterranean, and to a lesser extent, Atlantic coastlines provide excellent conditions for sailing, and some parts of the country, e.g. the Costa Brava and many parts of the islands' coastlines, are accessible only by sea. Yatching is part and parcel of daily life in some areas of Spain, particularly the Balearics (which, some say, were made to be seen from a boat), and there are numerous annual sailing competitions. The Conde de Barcelona's Trophy and the King Juan Carlos' Cup competitions held around Majorca are the most prestigious. Valencia hosts the world's oldest yachting competition, the America's Cup (💻 http://www.infoguia2007.com) in 2007.

Boats: Yacht prices are competitive in Spain and good second-hand deals can be found. New yachts are liable for 16 per cent VAT. All vessels keep permanently in Spain must be registered there in the Maritime Registry (*Registro Marítimo*) controlled by the local maritime authority (*Capitanía Marítima*), and the Mercantile Registry (*Registro Mercantil*). Boats (crewed and uncrewed) can be hired from harbours in resort areas, although to rent an uncrewed boat you need a skipper's certificate (*título de patrón*).

Marinas: Spain has a wealth of marinas and harbours, many with over 1,000 berths (including Puerto Marina and Puerto Banús on the Costa del Sol), which are scattered liberally along Spain's coastline. Many marinas on the Costa Blanca (particularly near Valencia) are currently being expanded or upgraded in preparation for the America's Cup in 2007. Marinas range from a few mooring posts with basic facilities to huge complexes such as Puerto Banús, Spain's answer to St Tropez, full of vast ostentatious yachts, luxury cars and beautiful people.

Despite Spain's large number of marinas, finding a berth in summer can be difficult and mooring is expensive, particularly at fashionable resorts. Costs in the low season start at €15 a day for an 8 x 3 metre berth to from €50 a day for a 20 x 5 metre berth. There are discounts for monthly and annual mooring. The cost of keeping a boat on the Atlantic coast is cheaper than on the Mediterranean.

Sailing clubs: Most marinas and coastal towns have sailing clubs (*club náutico*), which offer tuition and courses for all levels and ages.

Scuba-diving

Spanish waters are home to a number of marine reserves where scuba-diving opportunities are among the best in Europe. The Cabo de la Nao peninsula off the north coast on the Costa Blanca, Cabrera Island in the Balearics, El Cabrón to the east of Gran Canaria and Minorca's north coastline are of particular note. To dive in Spanish waters, you need a diving permit (costing around €10), available from diving clubs and schools (usually located in marinas).

Scuba-diving can be dangerous and safety is of paramount importance. Divers should be aware of strong currents, stick to designated diving areas and never dive alone.

Swimming

No surprisingly, swimming is a popular pastime in Spain and swimming pools are found everywhere on the Spanish coastline and most towns have a municipal pool, indoor and/or outdoor. Most municipal indoor pools have swimming clubs and organise swimming lessons and life-saving courses.

The beach bathing season lasts from Easter to October along most of the coastline, although the season is shorter on the northern coast and longer in some parts of the southern Mediterranean. The Canaries have year-round beach and bathing weather. During the high season, beaches in resort areas have lifeguard services who operate a flag system to indicate when swimming is safe: a green flag indicates safe conditions, yellow possible hazards, while red (danger) means swimming is prohibited. However, swimming can be dangerous at any time on beaches that have lethal currents and several swimmers drown each year.

Windsurfing

Some of Europe's finest surfing waters are found in Spain. Tarifa on the Costa de la Luz (Europe's windiest place) is a windsurfer and kitesurfers' paradise, and hosts several world-class competitions each year. Other top surfing spots include Fuerteventura and El Mádano (Tenerife) in the Canaries and Fornells on the north coast of Minorca. Several websites (e.g. 🖳 http://www.surferos.net and 🖳 http://www.windtarifa.com) provide weather reports and news of competitions, and the monthly magazine, *Surf a Vela*, is a must for windsurfing aficionados.

ENTERTAINMENT

Spain offers numerous possibilities for entertainment, ranging from amateur productions to world-class acts, and even the smallest towns usually have a programme of cultural events.

Finding Out What's On

An excellent source of information about activities and what's on is the local tourist office, where you will find a wealth of information and leaflets about local attractions and events. Tourist offices are usually open from 9.30am to 2pm and from 4pm to 7.30 or 8pm, Mondays to Saturdays. Offices in cities and resort areas usually have longer opening hours. Large tourist offices have websites where events and cultural programmes are listed.

The local press also publishes daily entertainment listings such as cinema programmes, exhibitions and talks. In large cities there are weekly or monthly magazines dedicated to entertainment and numerous websites (e.g. 🖳 http://www.guiadelocio.com and 🖳 http://www.lanetro.com) also provide a wealth of information. Many town councils publish cultural programmes and some foreigners' departments also produce newsletters listing local cultural events.

Cinemas

Cinema remains a popular pastime in Spain and in recent years, many multi-screen centres have opened in resort areas. Tickets are usually good-value (from €5) and many cinemas offer discounts to pensioners for weekday performances. There are several screening a day on weekdays with more at weekends. Foreign films are usually dubbed into Spanish, but some cinemas in resort areas (the Costa del Sol is particularly well catered for) show films in English. Some cinemas in large cities also show original soundtrack films (indicated by V.O. – *versión original*) and some towns have film clubs where non-Spanish soundtrack films are shown.

Fairs & Festivals

Festivals (*fiestas*) and fairs (*ferias*) form an essential part of cultural and social life in Spain, where even the smallest village celebrates at least one big party a year. Spanish festivals are colourful events, usually noisy with plenty of fireworks and loud music, lasting several days during which the locality comes almost to a standstill. Essential ingredients include processions (often religious), music, dancing and feasting (including large amounts of alcohol). Festivals in some areas also include bulls – bull-running and bullfighting. Festivals are a chance for everyone to join in, foreigners included, and there's rarely any violence or serious crime, although pickpockets and bag snatchers are fairly common at the largest events.

Spain's largest festivals include the following:

- **Carnival** – held in February around Mardi Gras and celebrated throughout Spain. The most famous carnival celebrations are held in Gran Canaria and Tenerife, where the festivities are similar to those in Rio de Janeiro, and in Cadiz.

- **Holy Week** – solemn religious processions are held throughout Spain, although those in Andalusia (e.g. Seville) are particularly famous.

- **San José** – Valencia stages one of the Spain's most colourful (and loudest) celebrations in honour of San José (St Joseph). Huge papier-mâché effigies are erected around the city and burnt on the night of the 19th March amid huge celebrations and tonnes of fireworks.

● **San Juan** – many Mediterranean towns and villages hold all-night parties on the night of the 22nd June in honour of San Juan (St John) to celebrate the arrival of summer. Bonfires are lit on beaches and rituals include leaping through fire as a means of purification.

● **Virgen del Carmen** – most coastal localities celebrate the patron of fishermen's day on 16th July when the saint's image is paraded in boats along the coast.

Local festivals are usually celebrated on the local saint's day or mark a significant local event, e.g. a wine harvest or deliverance from the Moors. Torremolinos on the Costa del Sol even celebrates its tourists with an annual 'Tourism Day' in early June.

Museums & Galleries

In recent years, the choice of world-class museums and galleries in Spain has improved, and many have become more visitor-friendly with better guides and information. Most large museums now have cafés and/or restaurants and a museum shop. Museum fees are reasonable and most offer discounts for pensioners (the Prado is free for the over 65's). Opening times are usually from 9am to 7pm (smaller museums may open only from 10am to 2pm and most close on Mondays.

Madrid is home to the so-called Art Triangle, consisting of the Prado (🖳 http://www.museoprado.es), home to one of the world's richest art collections; the Thyssen-Bornemisza (🖳 http://www.museothyssen.org), housing a premier art collection; and the Reina Sofía (🖳 http://www.museo reinasofia.es), Europe's leading museum of contemporary art. Barcelona boasts a number of important art collections including the Picasso Museum (🖳 http://www.museupicasso.bcn.es), the Miró Foundation (🖳 http://www. bcn.fjmiro.es) and the Barcelona Museum of Contemporary Art (🖳 http:// www.macba.es).

Other important museums include the Dali-Theatre Museum in Figueres (🖳 http://www.salvador-dali.org), second only to the Prado in popularity, the Picasso Museum in Malaga (🖳 http://www.museopicassomalaga.org), Madrid's Archaeological Museum (🖳 http://www.man.es) and Valencia's City of Arts and Sciences (🖳 http://www.cac.es). Most towns have at least one museum, often housing some real treasures, and churches, cathedrals and monasteries are invariably home to great works of art.

Music

Music of all kinds, from flamenco to rock, jazz to classical, can be heard in Spain, and most large towns and cities have regular performances. Several cities have orchestras (e.g. Madrid, Malaga and Murcia) that perform a season of concerts (usually from October to June) and foreign orchestras and choirs regularly tour Spain. There are also several prestigious annual music festivals: the international guitar festival in Cordoba in July; Granada's international festival of music and dance (Spain's most important musical event) in July; and the Santander international festival of music, dance and drama in July/August. Jazz festivals are held in many large cities, e.g. Barcelona, Bilbao, Madrid and Malaga, as well as in smaller venues such as San Javier (Mar Menor) and Sitges (Costa Dorada).

Rock and pop concerts are staged by both Spanish and international stars throughout the year, although few big stars (e.g. Bruce Springsteen and U2) have more than one concert venue in Spain. Bars and clubs throughout Spain regularly have live music, and expatriate crooners singing cover versions of hit songs are popular in resort areas. If you're into making your own music, many bars and clubs have jam sessions and karaoke.

Theatre, Opera & Dance

Most large towns and cities have at least one theatre (usually in Spanish) and offer a year-round cultural programme. However, productions can be seen in English in many resort areas where there are numerous theatre groups and clubs, e.g. the Salon Varietés in Fuengirola, Costa del Sol (🖥 http://www.salonvarietestheatre.com) and the Castle Theatre Group in Denia, Costa Blanca (🖥 http://www.deniacastletheatre.com). Tickets for a play usually range from €5 to €60, and discounts for pensioners are sometimes offered.

Opera is popular in Spain and regular performances are held in major cities, although Barcelona is the only Spanish city with a 'proper' opera house, the Gran Teatro del Liceu. Dance is also popular and Spain has a national ballet company and several prestigious dance companies, particularly flamenco.

SOCIAL CLUBS & ORGANISATIONS

Even the smallest village in Spain has at least one social club and most towns have several, while in major cities and resort areas there's a wealth of expatriate clubs and societies catering for a wide range of activities. The Costa Blanca and Costa del Sol have a particularly good choice with just about every activity covered, from bridge to square dancing, cycling to football. There are also chapters of global clubs such as the Lions International, Rotary Clubs, International Men's and Women's Clubs, American Women's and Men's Clubs, and Toastmasters International. Charitable and self-help organisations such as Alcoholics Anonymous (see page 223), the British Legion and numerous animal protection societies also operate in popular resort areas.

Many clubs advertise their activities and venues in the local press (see **Appendix B** for a list of English-language publications) or on local notice boards. Some town councils have a database of clubs and associations in their area. Some clubs have their own facilities such as a clubhouse, library, bar and restaurant. Membership fees vary considerably, e.g. €10 to €100, and some offer daily, weekly and monthly membership for visitors.

Joining a local club or society is one of the best ways to meet people and clubs are also useful sources of information and help. Spanish speakers have the option of joining a local club, which are often subsidised by the local council and provide low-cost sports activities and social events. Pensioners are particularly well catered for and most towns and large villages have a pensioners' social centre (*Hogar del Jubilado* or *del Pensionista*).

Church Groups

If you're a church-goer, the chances are that there will be a congregation near you and if you retire to an area popular with expatriates, there may well be services in English. The Costa Blanca and Costa del Sol have the best choice of services in English and most religions are catered for. Barcelona and Madrid also have services in English. The Royal British Legion and Salvation Army also have groups in several parts of Spain. For details of venues and times, consult your local newspaper or ask at your town hall.

Many expatriate church groups in Spain run social groups and support services, and are often an excellent way of making new friends and contacts when you first arrive.

DAY & EVENING CLASSES

It's important to keep your mind active during retirement and evening and day classes offer an ideal opportunity to learn new skills and activities. There are several possibilities for 'mature' students, including the following:

Local Councils

Local councils run numerous courses such as Spanish and other foreign languages, sporting activities, art and crafts, cookery, computing and internet skills, and dance. Courses are provided for all ages and are generally run twice or three times a week from October to June. Advantages of courses run by local councils include subsidised fees and the chance to integrate with the local community and speak Spanish. Courses are usually popular and you need to book early to get a place, although you should note that priority is given to registered residents (see **Local Council Registration** on page 192).

University Courses

Spanish speakers: Retirees with a good level of spoken and written Spanish may be interested in a university course, possibly leading to a degree. Several universities in Spain including Alicante, the Balearics (based in Palma de Majorca), Barcelona, the Canaries (La Laguna in Tenerife and Las Palmas de Gran Canaria), Malaga, Murcia and Valencia offer courses for students aged over 55 under the 'Univerity Programme for Older Adults' ('Programa Universidad para Mayores'). A variety of courses is offered over at least three terms. Further information is available from ▣ http://www.aepumayores.org, which has some information in English.

English speakers: The Open University (▣ http://www.open.ac.uk), based in the UK, provides distance learning in over 600 courses, many of which lead to a degree. Fees are reasonable and you need a computer with internet access. Many courses include optional residential weekends where you get the chance to meet your fellow students.

'University of the Third Age'

Residents over 50 who aren't in full-time employment may be interested in the University of the Third Age (U3A), which has centres on the Costa Blanca (Calpe, Denia and Jávea), the Costa Brava (Lloret de Mar and Roses) and the Costa del Sol (Fuengirola and Marbella). Courses are offered in English in a huge variety of subjects including computer literacy, history, photography and Spanish, as well as lectures and travel activities. Members pay a small annual fee (e.g. €12).

Further information is available from:

- **Costa Blanca**

  - Calpe (🖳 http://www.u3acalpe.com)

  - Denia (🖳 http://www.u3adenia.org)

  - Jávea (🖳 http://www.u3ajavea.org)

- **Costa Brava** – 🖳 http://www.u3acostabrava.org

- **Costa del Sol** – 🖳 http://www.u3acostadelsol.org

Courses are also run privately by professionals and local clubs.

TRAVELLING AROUND SPAIN

Spain is the second-largest country in Europe (after France) and offers infinite variety with something for everyone, including magnificent beaches; spectacular unspoilt countryside from deserts to snow-capped mountain peaks, dense wooded valleys to wide river deltas; stunning historic monuments; architectural gems from Neolithic burial chambers to avant-garde tower blocks; vibrant nightlife; bustling sophisticated cities; superb wine and cuisine; a surfeit of art, culture and serious music – in short, 'Everything under the sun', as proclaimed by the national tourist board's slogan.

Wherever you choose to retire in Spain, whether it's one of the *costas* or an inland village, make sure you take every opportunity to visit the rest of Spain. One of its foremost attractions is its outstanding countryside and a rugged beauty that's almost unparalleled in Europe with more (and larger) unspoilt areas than any other European country, many preserved as national parks and nature reserves. Many national parks are within easy reach of cities and the *costas*, making it easy to get away from the hustle and bustle of everyday life.

Among Spain's great cities are Madrid and Barcelona, which enjoy intense rivalry. Barcelona is Spain's most cosmopolitan and avant-garde city with the added attraction of being on the Mediterranean. Madrid is larger with a wealth of elegant monuments and museums, and one of Spain's greenest cities. Madrid is also one of the country's friendliest cities and home to some of Europe's liveliest nightlife. Other gems include Avila, Burgos, Cáceres, Cadiz, Cordoba, Cuenca, Girona, Granada, Malaga, Mérida, Palma de Mallorca, Pamplona, San Sebastian, Salamanca, Santander, Santiago de Compostela, Segovia, Seville, Toledo and Valencia, to name just a handful.

Many smaller towns are also worth visiting and even large villages are often home to a surprising number of historic monuments.

Travel to and from Spanish cities is generally straight-forward (see **Getting Around** on page 48 for further information) and public transport is good-value, but if you plan to visit the countryside or towns and villages, it's best to travel by car. Be aware that distances in Spain are huge and driving can be tiring. The best time to visit inland Spain is from October to June when daytime temperatures aren't too hot for sightseeing.

Accommodation

Many types of accommodation are available in Spain, catering for all tastes and pockets, from sumptuous, grand luxury (*gran lujo*) to budget.

Hotels

Hotels in Spain are generally excellent and often much better value than many of their European counterparts. They're classified with one to five stars (*estrellas*), depending on the facilities offered rather than their price. Expect to pay from €30 for a double room with a bathroom in a one-star hotel to over €250 in a five-star hotel. VAT at 7 per cent (4.5 per cent in the Canaries) is added to all hotel bills. Breakfast isn't usually included in the price. Reservations can be made by telephone or via the internet, and you should arrive at the hotel before 6pm unless you inform the hotel you will arrive later.

The *Michelin Red Guide: España, Portugal* (Michelin) and *Hoteles y Restaurantes de España* (El País Aguilar) provide listings of hotels throughout Spain (both updated annually) and the Spanish National Tourist Board website (🖳 http://www.spain.info) also provides information about hotels. Local tourist board websites also usually include information about accommodation.

'Special Hotels'

'Special hotels', known as *hoteles con encanto*, are found throughout Spain and include the following:

Paradores: *Paradores* (☎ 902 547 979 or 🖳 http://www.parador.es) are historic buildings such as castles, palaces, convents and monasteries, converted into unique hotels often with luxurious rooms and facilities. There are around 85 *paradores* throughout Spain, often situated in or near a historic city. Prices for a double room start at around €75 and discounts are available outside the high season, e.g. the over 60s are entitled to 35 per cent discount on half-board stays. A comprehensive book, *Paradores de Turismo*, by José Mª Iñigo (Everest) is available from bookshops.

Rusticae: Rusticae (☎ 902 103 892 or 💻 http://www.rusticae.es) is a company specialising in select hotels, currently totalling around 150 hotels usually with luxury accommodation in exquisite surroundings (often rural), with prices for a double room starting at around €120.

Rural Accommodation

Rural tourism is currently one of Spain's boom industries and also one of the best ways to enjoy the unique countryside. Almost everywhere in Spain there are rural cottages, farmhouses and typical regional houses, offering room rental with meals (known as *alquiler de habitaciones* and similar to a British 'bed and breakfast') or rental of a property with self-catering facilities (*alquiler de la casa*). Prices start at €50 for a double room and breakfast or €100 per night for a house sleeping four people.

Several books are published on rural tourism, e.g. *Guía de Alojamiento de Turismo Rural* (Anaya Touring) and *Anuario de Turismo Rural* (Susaeta), and there are numerous websites (usually with an English-language option) such as 💻 http://www.azrural.com and 💻 http://www.toprural.com. Many establishments have online booking facilities. Rural tourism is popular with Spaniards at weekends and during holiday periods, therefore you should book well in advance if you plan to travel at these times.

'Special hotels' in rural settings are listed in *Alastair Sawday's Special Places to Stay: Spain* (Alastair Sawday Publishing), *Karen Brown's Spain* (Karen Brown Guides) and *Small Hotels and Inns of Andalusia: Charming Places to Stay in Southern Spain* by Guy Hunter-Watts (Santana Books).

Budget Accommodation

Hostels (*hostales* or *pensiones*) provide the main budget accommodation in towns and cities and, although accommodation is usually clean, you get what you pay for and ensuite bathrooms are rare. Prices start at around €25 for a double room.

Camping is popular in Spain where there are over 800 campsites, the majority of which are found on the coast. Campsites are classified in four categories: Luxury (*lujo*), 1st, 2nd and 3rd class (*primera, segunda, tercera clase*), according to their amenities. Fees are around €3 per person per day plus €2.50 to €3 for a car and around the same for a caravan or camping space. Motor caravans or campervans (*autocaravanas*) cost between €5 and €7.50 a day.

Many campsites open from April to October only and it's advisable to book during the high season, particularly for sites in coastal areas. Several guides to campsites are available including *Guía Oficial de Campings* (TurEspaña), the *Guía Ibérica de Campings y Bungalows* (Ocitur), which includes campsites in Portugal, and the *Guía de Campings* (Federación Española de Empresarios de Camping).

SURVIVAL TIP
Note that wild camping (including campervans) is forbidden in most of Spain, particularly on beaches, river banks and in the mountains, and you can be fined for camping illegally.

TRAVELLING FURTHER AFIELD

If you want to explore further afield, there are numerous possibilities, most of which aren't expensive. Travel agents have offers year-round and many are excellent value, particularly if you're prepared to travel at short notice. Numerous websites also offer cheap holidays, e.g. 🖳 http://www.last minute.com and 🖳 http://www.vlajar.com.

Morocco

Morocco is an exciting travel option within easy reach of the south of Spain. Day trips to Tangier are feasible – ferries leave from Algeciras and Tarifa (the catamaran ferry takes just 30 minutes) – and a choice of tours leave daily from the Costa del Sol to Chaouen, a mountain village in the north and Tangiers. Day trips cost around €50 and trips lasting several days around €300. Most travel agents and tour operators offer longer trips to Morocco visiting the cities of Casablanca, Fez, Marrakech and Rabat. Flights are available from Malaga to Rabat and Casablanca. Trips to Morocco from the Canaries are popular and there are regular flights from Gran Canaria and Tenerife to Rabat and Marrakech.

DNAC is a travel company specialising in unique personalised trips to Morocco with top class accommodation, gourmet food and visits to both tourist haunts and places off the beaten track. DNAC organises à la carte trips to many destinations in Morocco, including the main cities and the Sahara. Further information is available from 💻 http://www.dnac.net.

Europe

Residents in the south of Spain are within easy driving distance of Portugal (the Algarve is around four hours from the Costa del Sol), which offers plenty to do and see for the visitor. Numerous budget airlines operate cheap flights to many European destinations from several Spanish airports, including the following:

- Air Berlin (☎ 902 320 737, 💻 http://www.airberlin.com) – flies from numerous Spanish airports to destinations in Austria, Denmark, Germany, Italy, the Netherlands and Switzerland.

- Air Madrid (☎ 902 515 251, 💻 http://www.airmadrid.com) – flies from Barcelona and Madrid to Bucarest, Milan, Nice, Paris and Rome.

- EasyJet (☎ 902 299 992, 💻 http://www.easyjet.com) – flies from several Spanish airports to destinations in Germany, Italy and Switzerland.

- Ryanair (☎ 807 220 032, 💻 http://www.ryanair.com) – flies from several Spanish airports to destinations in Belgium, France, Germany, Italy and Sweden.

- Spanair (☎ 902 929 191, 💻 http://www.spanair.com) – flies to destinations in Denmark, Sweden and Switzerland.

- Vueling (☎ 902 333 933, 💻 http://www.vueling.com) – flies from Barcelona, Madrid and Valencia to destinations in Belgium, Holland and Italy.

In autumn 2006, Iberia is launching a new low-cost airline, Catair, offering flights to numerous European destinations from several Spanish airports.

11.

MISCELLANEOUS

This chapter contains miscellaneous information of interest to retirees in Spain, including crime and security, culture shock, fast facts about Spain, legal and general advice, religion, the Spanish police and social customs.

For comprehensive information about just about all aspects of living in Spain, see our sister publication *Living and Working in Spain* by David Hampshire (see page 383).

CRIME

Spain's crime rate is among the lowest in Europe: according to figures released by the Spanish Interior Ministry, in 2006 Spain has an incidence of nearly 50 crimes per 1,000 inhabitants, the lowest in the EU apart from Portugal and Ireland. In the UK, figures are 105 crimes per 1,000 inhabitants and in Germany, 80. However, the crime rate in Spain has increased dramatically over the past decade, although statistics released in June 2006 show a slight decrease (3.4 per cent) in crime generally throughout the country.

The Spanish generally have a lot of respect for law and order, although 'petty' laws are often ignored. In villages away from the tourist areas, crime is almost unknown and windows and doors are usually left unlocked. Major cities have the highest crime rates and Alicante, Barcelona, Madrid, Malaga, Seville and Valencia are among the worst. Many cities are notorious for 'petty' crime such as handbag snatching, pickpockets and thefts of and from vehicles. Stealing from cars, particularly those with foreign registrations, is endemic throughout Spain.

The most common crime in Spain is theft, which embraces a multitude of forms. One of the most common is the ride-by bag snatcher on a motorbike or moped. Known as the 'pull' (*tirón*), it involves grabbing a hand or shoulder bag (or a camera) and riding off with it, sometimes with the owner still attached (occasionally causing serious injuries). Motorcycle thieves also smash car windows at traffic lights to steal articles left on seats, so stow bags on the floor or behind seats. Tourists and travellers are the targets of some of Spain's most enterprising criminals, including highwaymen, who pose as accident or breakdown victims and rob motorists who stop to help them.

Foreigners are often victims of burglary, particularly holiday homeowners, which is common in some resort areas, and according to statistics there's a burglary every six minutes. In some areas, it isn't unusual for owners to return from abroad to find their homes ransacked. It's advisable to arrange for someone to check your property periodically when it's left unoccupied.

Petty theft by gypsies, who wander into homes when the doors are left open, is common in some parts of Spain (see also **Home Security** on page 162).

Violent crime is relatively rare in Spain, although armed robbery has increased considerably and sexual crime is also on the increase, particularly in Madrid. Muggings at gun or knife-point are also rare in most towns, although they're becoming increasingly common in some areas.

The Costa del Sol has earned an unsavoury reputation as a refuge for criminals and fugitives from justice, hence its nickname the 'Costa del Crime', although in recent years the Costa Blanca and Costa Brava have also attracted the wrong sort of 'tourists'. Much organised crime (particularly money laundering and drug trafficking) on the Costa del Sol is centred on Marbella – the 'White Whale' money-laundering scandal uncovered in 2005 involved millions of euros. The government has set up a special police body in the attempt to reduce it; however, although money-laundering scandals provide an interesting and eye-opening diversion for locals, they have little effect on residents' lives.

One of the biggest dangers to most foreigners in Spain isn't from the Spanish, but from their own countrymen and other foreigners. It's common for expatriate 'businessmen' to run up huge debts, either through dishonesty or incompetence, and cut and run owing their clients and suppliers thousands of euros.

In resort areas, confidence tricksters and fraudsters lie in wait around every corner. Fraud of every conceivable kind is a fine art in Spain and is commonly perpetrated by foreigners on their fellow countrymen – so beware!

See also **Household Insurance** on page 271 and **Home Security** on page 162.

CULTURE SHOCK

The story's all too familiar among retirees to Spain: the sun is continuously shining and you've got a tan to prove it, dining out and the *vino* are cheap, and all your fellow retirees at home are green with envy. However, after those initial blissful weeks the novelty starts to wear off: the plumber who promised he would fix the bathroom tap last week still hasn't appeared, the queues for residence permits are miles long, the shops shut after lunch and your gardener doesn't speak a word of English. You even find yourself missing the drizzle and wondering why you ever retired to Spain. At this point you have two options: you can make a success of your retirement and new life in Spain or you can give up and go home.

The above pattern of emotions form part of a well-documented condition, officially known as 'culture shock', but you may find it reassuring to know that most expatriates go through the same pendulum of feelings when they move abroad. Some retirees (the minority) give in to the negative feelings and return to their home country, but the majority choose to persevere with their new life abroad and go on to enjoy a fulfilling and happy retirement. There's a lot you can do to help yourself settle in and ensure that you're among the retirees whose retirement to Spain is a triumph rather than a failure. Below are some tips to smooth your move to Spain and help make settling in to retirement in Spain easier.

Before You Go

- Do as much research as possible about Spain and the area you're moving to before leaving home. It helps to obtain some copies of local newspapers and magazines (many have online editions) to get a feel for what's going on; study guidebooks and relocation guides (Survival Books publish a number of other useful books – see page 383); and visit some of the many websites (See **Appendix B**) about Spain which have expatriate forums. Forewarned is forearmed and settling into a new place is much easier if you have a good idea of what to expect.

- Take a course in Spanish; English is widely spoken in many parts of Spain, but not by everyone and if you can speak some Spanish you will feel less helpless and local people will warm to you more. See **Learning the Language** on page 62 for further information.

- Keep your expectations realistic: the Costa Blanca and Costa del Sol have wonderful climates for most of the year, but it can (and frequently does) pour with rain for days on end in winter and many properties don't have central heating and are cold and damp. In complete contrast, the summer months can be swelteringly hot.

Accommodation

- When you first move to Spain, it's better initially to rent a property (rather than buy), which allows you time to get a feel for an area without the commitment and expense of buying a property – then, if you don't like the location, you can move somewhere else relatively easily.

● Don't burn your bridges and, if you can afford it, maintain your home abroad until you're sure you want to spend your retirement in Spain. Even if you're sure you don't want to return to your home country, it's comforting to know that you have an escape route if you need it. Retirees who sell up and cut all ties with their home country can feel trapped in Spain, particularly if things go wrong.

● Move to somewhere with good flight connections with your home town so that you can pop back easily and cheaply if you wish to. Alicante and Malaga have the most frequent and widest range of flights. See **Getting There** on page 33 for more information.

Arrival

● Make an extra effort to get out and meet people. Join a local club or society (there are hundreds on the most popular *costas*), even if there isn't an activity you're particularly interested in – at least you will have the opportunity to meet other people and talk to them.

● Be as flexible as possible and try to accept unusual and frustrating aspects of Spanish life: make allowances for the *mañana* approach (see **Social Customs** on page 315) and remember that Spanish paperwork is relentless and the red tape frustrating for everyone, including the Spanish – you can save yourself time and stress by paying a *gestor* (see page 311) to sort it out.

● **Finally, allow yourself time to adapt – expect it to take at least six months – but most of all, enjoy it!**

See also **Finding Help** on page 193 for further advice and tips on settling in.

FAST FACTS ABOUT SPAIN

Capital: Madrid

Population: around 44m, which is steadily increasing largely due to the influx of foreign residents, including retirees (some 8.5 per cent of the population are foreigners).

Largest cities: Madrid (pop. 3.2m), Barcelona (1.6m), Valencia (800,000), Seville (700,000) and Zaragossa (650,000).

Geography: Spain is the second-largest country in Western Europe and occupies the Iberian Peninsula along with Portugal. It covers an area of 492,463km² (190,154mi²) including the Balearics and the Canary Islands. The mainland stretches from 805km (500mi) from north to south and 885 (550mi) from east to west. Mainland Spain's coastline totals 2,119km (1,317mi) along the Mediterranean (east and south coasts) and Atlantic (southwest, west and north coasts).

Government: parliamentary democracy with general elections held every four years (the next are due in early 2008). Spain has 17 autonomous regions (see map in **Appendix E**), which have far-reaching powers and responsibility for everyday matters such as health, education, environment, economic development and public works.

Time difference: In mainland Spain and the Balearics, the time is GMT plus one hour, all year round. In the Canaries, however, the time is GMT, all year round. Times in Spain are usually written using the 24-hour clock, e.g. 3pm is 15h.

LEGAL SYSTEM

If you're seeking legal advice, ask around among local residents and obtain recommendations. This way you will usually find out not only who to employ, but more importantly who to avoid (the wrong legal advice is often more expensive in the long term than having none at all). Always obtain an estimate (*presupuesto*) of costs in advance, if possible in writing, and shop around and compare fees from a number of lawyers, as they can vary considerably. The estimate should detail exactly what the lawyer will do for his fees. Bear in mind, however, that if you consult a number of legal 'experts' about the same matter, you're highly unlikely to receive exactly the same advice.

The Spanish legal system is excruciatingly slow (i.e. largely at a standstill) and there's a backlog of hundreds of thousands of cases throughout Spain, which means that it takes years for many cases to come to court. Even local courts can take five years to hear a case, although delays are usually up to two years for minor offences and up to four years for serious offences. **If possible, you should do everything to avoid going to court**.

Lawyers

If you're buying property, starting a business or making a will in Spain, you should employ the services of an experienced Spanish lawyer (*abogado*).

You may be able to obtain a list of lawyers from your local embassy or consulate (see **Appendix A**). Suggested lawyers' fees are set by provincial professional bodies (*Ilustre Colegio de Abogados*), although individual lawyers often set much higher fees. However, fees are usually lower than those charged by lawyers in northern European countries, with a simple consultation of less than half an hour costing from €30. When preparing contracts involving a sum of money, e.g. property or land purchase, fees are calculated as a percentage of the sum involved. 'No win, no fee' lawsuits are illegal in Spain.

Always try to engage a lawyer who speaks your mother tongue. In some areas, lawyers who speak English and other foreign languages are common and they're used to dealing with foreigners and their particular problems. If you don't receive satisfactory service from your lawyer, you can complain to the local professional college (see **Lawyers' Associations** on page 157 for a listing). Common complaints include long delays, poor communication, high fees and overcharging (particularly with regard to property transactions involving foreigners).

Notaries

A notary (*notario*) is a public official authorised by the government, who's most commonly engaged in property transactions. He doesn't deal with criminal cases or proffer advice concerning criminal law. *Notarios* have a monopoly in the areas of transferring real property, testamentary (e.g. of wills) and matrimonial acts, which by law must be in the form of an authentic document, verified and stamped by a *notario*. In Spain, property conveyancing is strictly governed by Spanish law and can be performed **only** by a *notario*. In respect to private law, a *notario* is responsible for administering and preparing documents relating to property sales and purchases, inheritance, wills, establishing limited companies, and buying and selling businesses. He also certifies the validity and safety of contracts and deeds. If you need irrefutable proof of delivery of a letter or other documents, they should be sent via a *notario*, as nobody can deny receiving a document delivered through his offices.

Gestores

A *gestor* is an official agent licensed by the Spanish government as a middleman between you and the bureaucracy (this speaks volumes for the stifling and tortuous Spanish bureaucracy!). While it isn't compulsory to employ a *gestor*, it can save you a lot of time and stress. A *gestor's* services aren't expensive and most people find it worthwhile employing one.

They usually work in a *gestoría*, where a number of experts may be employed dealing with different matters, including residence permits; establishing and registering a business; obtaining a driving licence, tourist plates or registering a car; social security; and property contracts. A *gestor* can help you in your dealings with any government body or state-owned company. Note, however, that the quality of service provided by *gestores* varies considerably, therefore you should obtain a recommendation from your lawyer.

MAKING A COMPLAINT

Consumer Complaints

Most large towns and all provinces have a consumer affairs department or consumer complaints office (Oficina Municipal de Información al Consumidor/OMIC). These offices can provide information about consumer regulations and file complaints on the consumer's behalf. If you have any sort of consumer complaint, the local OMIC is the best place to start and even if they cannot solve the problem themselves they will be able to find the right official body to help you.

When you make a consumer complaint you must complete an official complaint's form (*hoja de reclamación*), which all businesses in Spain are required to have by law. Once the form is complete, you take a copy to your local OMIC where action will be taken on your behalf against the offending business. If the business is found to be in the wrong, it will be penalised.

SURVIVAL TIP
Complaint forms are often powerful consumer tools and sometimes just asking for one in a shop will result in your complaint being resolved immediately!

The main consumer association in Spain is the Organización de Consumidores y Usuarios (OCU, ☎ 902 300 187 or 🖳 http://www.ocu.org for details of your local provincial office), which has watchdog and educational roles.

If you have a complaint about municipal services (e.g. a poor refuse collection service or lack of streetlights), you can complain directly to your town hall. If this has no effect it may be worth making an appointment with the councillor (*concejal*) in charge of the relevant department. This action is reasonably effective in small towns and villages, but less so in larger localities.

All professionals in Spain must be registered with the appropriate provincial association, e.g. doctors must be registered with the provincial *Colegio de Médicos* and lawyers with the *Colegio de Abogados*. If you have a complaint about a professional it's worth contacting the corresponding association and filing an official complaint. In extreme cases, professionals have been struck off the list for malpractice. Complaints about banking should be addressed in the first instance to the branch office and then to the bank's ombudsman (*defensor del cliente*). The Bank of Spain has a central banking ombudsman, Ausbanc (🖥 http://www.ausbanc.es).

Reporting a Crime

Loss or Theft

If you lose anything or are the victim of a theft, you must report it (*hacer una denuncia*) in person, by phone or via the internet to the local or national police. This must usually be done within 24 hours if you plan to make a claim on an insurance policy. The report form, of which you receive a copy with an official stamp for your insurance company, may be printed in English and Spanish. **If you don't speak Spanish, you should have a fluent Spanish speaker with you**, although in some tourist areas there are interpreters so you may be able to make a complaint in your own language (English is usually available).

Complaints can also be made by telephone (☎ 902 102 112) or online (🖥 http://www.policia.es – *Denuncias* at the bottom left). Once you've made your complaint you're given a number that you must take to the nearest police station after 10am the following day and within 72 hours. When you arrive you present the number to the official and you're given a signed and stamped copy of the complaint. Telephone and internet complaints are given priority and it saves having to queue for hours at a police station.

Other Crimes

Complaints about any crime other than loss or theft, must be made in person at your nearest police station.

SPANISH POLICE

Spain has a high ratio of police officers to inhabitants and three police forces, often with confusing and overlapping roles, although the government plans to amalgamate the three forces to improve co-ordination and make better use of skills and resources. Note that all police in Spain are armed, usually with revolvers, but sometimes with machine guns. The main forces are:

- The local municipal police (*policía municipal/local* or *guardia urbana*) who wear a navy uniform and deal with minor crime such as traffic control, protection of property, civil disturbances and the enforcement of municipal laws. Local police are the most approachable of Spanish policemen;

- The national police (*policía nacional*), who also wear navy uniforms, deal with serious crime such as theft, rape and muggings, and also control demonstrations and crowds. The national police also issue residence and work permits;

- The civil guard (*guardia civil*) wear green uniforms and handle traffic on roads outside urban areas, serious crime and immigration.

Some autonomous regions have their own police forces, such as the *Ertzaintza* in the Basque Country and the *Mosses d'Esquadra* in Catalonia.

RELIGION

The Spanish state is officially a lay country, but Spain is historically and culturally a Catholic country. A nationwide survey carried out in 2006 found that 77 per cent of Spaniards claim they're Catholics (compared to 83.5 per cent in 1998), although of this percentage, half claim they never go to church except on special occasions.

The majority of the world's religious and philosophical movements have religious centres or meeting places in the major cities and resort areas, including English (e.g. Anglican) and American churches (see **Churches** on page 296 for further information). The right to freedom of religion is guaranteed under the Spanish constitution, although some extreme sects are prohibited.

Religion is gradually losing its importance in Spanish society, particularly among young people and in cities, although the majority of Spaniards get married in church and most families celebrate christenings and first communions. However, these occasions are social rather than religious and thousands of euros are spent on celebrations.

If you choose to retire to a small town or village, the Catholic religion is likely to play an important part in local life and in many areas of Spain, the local priest is a key figure in the community. Be aware of this and sensitive to it, particularly if you aren't Catholic or are an atheist.

SOCIAL CUSTOMS

All countries have their own particular social customs and Spain is no exception. As a foreigner you will probably be excused if you accidentally make a *faux pas*, but you should take note of social etiquette and do your utmost to follow it. This is particularly true if you choose to retire to a small Spanish community, where everyone's actions are carefully noted by everyone else!

Daily Timetable

In general, the Spanish tend to do most things later in the day than their European counterparts.

Eating Times

Meals, in particular, are eaten later: people breakfast around 9 or 10am (many employees have a 30-minute breakfast break during the morning); lunch is eaten between 2 and 3.30pm (4pm in the summer); and dinner or supper from 9pm. It isn't uncommon to find people sitting down to dinner at 11pm or even later in summer.

Shopping Hours

Most shops open from 10am to 1.30 or 2pm and from 4.30 or 5pm to 7.30 or 8pm (6 to 9pm in the summer). Larger shops such as supermarkets and department stores, and shops within shopping centres open from 10am to 10pm. Indoor markets open from 8am to 2 or 3pm.

Working Hours

Working hours are generally from 10am to 2pm and from 4 or 5pm to 7 or 8pm, although many employees including civil servants work from 8am to 3pm.

Most of Spain 'shuts down' between *siesta* hours (3 to 4.30pm), particularly during the summer when even city streets are deserted at this time.

The Spanish timetable takes a little getting used to, particularly the later mealtimes and shopping hours. However, most foreigners find it makes sense to have a *siesta* during the hottest hours of the day when temperatures can reach 40°C (104°F) in the shade and leave activities such as shopping for when it's cooler.

Dress

The Spanish are almost invariably well groomed and dressed, and style and fashion are important, although they often dress casually. Men in particular dress smartly on most occasions. Spaniards consider that swimwear, skimpy tops and flip-flops are strictly for the beach or pool, and not for example, the streets, restaurants or shops. Indeed, many Spaniards find the foreigners' attire of shorts and no t-shirts or mini-skirts and bikini tops offensive when worn outside the beach. Some shops and restaurants refuse entry to those 'inappropriately attired'. Churches and other places of worship refuse entry to people dressed inappropriately, e.g. in shorts. It's also advisable to dress conservatively when doing business or visiting government offices on official business.

Formality

The Spanish language makes a strong distinction between the formal (*usted*/*Vd*) and informal (*tú*) means of address. *Usted* should be used when addressing adults you don't know, particularly older people. *Tú* should be used for friends and young people, including children. You should address older people as *Don* (for male) or *Doña* (female), followed by their Christian name, e.g. Don Antonio, or simply, Señor or Señora.

Be aware that some Spaniards find it offensive if you address them informally when you hardly know them, although most will make allowances for foreigners. If in doubt, use the formal address. Note that in the Canaries (and much of South America), the informal form of address is rarely used except between children – even parents and children address each other as *usted*.

Greetings

When you're introduced to a Spaniard you should shake hands at the beginning and the end of the meeting when it's polite to say '*encantado/a*' ('nice to meet you'). Male and female acquaintances kiss each other, usually on both cheeks (on one cheek in the Canaries), although the kiss is more of a brush on the cheek. Close family and male friends embrace.

Informal greetings are '*hola*' ('hello' or 'hi') or '*buenas*' (an informal 'good day'). Otherwise, you should use '*buenos días*' ('good morning') until midday or 1pm, '*buenas tardes*' ('good afternoon') from lunchtime until around 9 or 10pm, and '*buenas noches*' after that. '*Adiós*' is 'goodbye', although the more informal '*hasta luego*' ('see you later') or '*hasta pronto*' ('see you soon') are more frequently used.

Punctuality

Punctuality isn't one of the Spaniards' virtues, although arriving late for meetings is now frowned on in many business circles. If you have an appointment with a Spaniard don't expect him to arrive on time, although being more than 15 minutes late is considered bad manners. If you're going to arrive late for an appointment you should telephone and apologise.

The epitome of unpunctuality is the '*mañana*' ('tomorrow') syndrome, where assurances of delivery, work or results are promised '*mañana*'. Bear in mind that '*mañana*' can mean anytime in the future, but almost certainly not tomorrow! This lackadaisical approach to life is more common in small towns and villages, although it's present throughout Spain. The '*mañana*' attitude is one of the aspects foreigners find most frustrating and difficult to adapt to when they move to Spain. However, it's best (and less stressful) to accept this as part and parcel of Spanish daily life and to sit back and relax while you're waiting for '*mañana*' to arrive.

12.

RETURNING HOME

While many retirees dream of permanent retirement to sunny Spain, it's a harsh fact of life that many of those who retire there will be forced (or choose) to return permanently to their home country at some time. The reasons are many and varied, mostly due to personal circumstances which can change dramatically overnight. Exact statistics are difficult to obtain because many people never register as residents in Spain or their home country and therefore don't 'exist' on official statistics, but it's estimated that around one-third of those who retire to Spain return to their home country after a period.

Financial problems are the most common reason for leaving Spain. These may include being unable to meet capital gains or inheritance tax bills when their partner dies, struggling to make ends meet on a widow's pension, discovering that your monthly income doesn't cover care during ill health or disability, and investments that perform badly and dramatically reduce your income.

The death of a partner is also a widespread cause of retirees leaving Spain and returning home. The widow or widower not only has to cope with possible financial hardship but also with the paperwork associated with inheritance (for many people, this is the first time they have to deal directly with Spanish bureaucracy) and with loneliness. Many people find the situation impossible to bear and need the support of their family in their home country.

Ill health and disability are another reason retirees are forced to return to their home country. Home help and care provided by the state in Spain are poor and private care is often the only provision, an expensive option, particularly if you need round-the-clock care. Residential homes are in short supply and, again, state provisions are poor. Retirees' home countries often provide considerably better facilities and for many retirees it's a logical decision to return home.

Other retirees who make the decision to go home, cite family ties as their main motive and it's easy to underestimate how much you will miss your close family (particularly grandchildren) and friends when you're in Spain.

If you do find your retirement in Spain hasn't worked out or that there are no longer compelling reasons to stay, don't regard it as a failure on your part, but simply as an adventure that didn't turn out as you originally planned. Once you've decided to leave Spain and return to your home country, however, it's important to plan ahead to ensure that you make the right financial and practical decisions.

This chapter is designed to help you plan your return home and includes information about timing, selling your home, settling your affairs in Spain, and practical tips for your return to a country you left many years ago and which may have changed considerably.

CAN YOU AFFORD IT?

Many northern European countries have a higher cost of living than Spain and you may find that your pension income isn't sufficient when you return home. The cost of property in your home country is another major financial concern, although if you sell your home in Spain at a profit (see **Selling Your Home** below), this may not be a problem.

Before you return, check whether you're entitled to allowances and benefits in your home country. Returning nationals are usually entitled to state-benefits, but there may be conditions and requirements, e.g. a certain number of years social security contributions in your home country. British nationals returning to the UK should contact the International Pension Centre (IPC), Tyneview Park, Newcastle-upon-Tyne, NE98 1BA (☎ 0191-218 7777, 🖳 http://www.dwp.gov.uk) for information about benefits and allowances. The IPC publish a useful free booklet, *GL28 Coming from abroad and social security benefits*, which can be downloaded from their website.

TIMING

As with any life-changing decision, the timing of your departure from Spain is the key to success. Start planning your departure from Spain as far in advance as you can – at least six months, if possible. Whatever your reasons for having to leave and however distressing you find it to stay, try to avoid leaving in a rush.

Taxation

If you're a resident in Spain, obtain expert advice on the timing of your move for tax purposes. In most countries, the annual tax year is the calendar year (i.e. from 1st January to 31st December), but some countries, e.g. the UK, have different tax years. Depending on your tax circumstances, it may be more advantageous to move at a certain time of the year.

Before leaving Spain, foreigners should pay any tax due for the previous year and the year of departure by applying for a tax clearance. A tax return should be filed before departure and include your income and deductions from 1st January of the departure year up to the date of departure. Your local tax office will calculate the tax due and provide a written statement. When departure is made before 31st December, the previous year's taxes are applied. If this results in overpayment, a claim must be made for a refund.

SELLING YOUR HOME

Most retirees returning to their home country are homeowners and wish to sell their property before they leave. If this is your case, then it's worth considering the following points.

Price & Property Market

Your most important consideration is the price you need or can get for your Spanish home. It's important to bear in mind that all property has a market price and the best way of ensuring a quick sale (or any sale) is to ask a realistic price. This will naturally depend on the property market in your area at the time you wish to sell and also the property market in the area you plan to move to in your home country. This is important, because the price you obtain from the sale of your property in Spain will probably determine what sort of property you can buy when you return to your home country.

> **SURVIVAL TIP**
> **It may pay you to keep your Spanish home for a while until the market improves and rent a property in your home country.**

The national property market in Spain in 2006 was generally stable with steady rises in most regions, although some (e.g. the Costa del Sol) were slower than others. Unlike in previous years, the Spanish property market is currently a buyer's market rather than a seller's and in many areas there's a surfeit of property for sale. If you bought your property before say 2002 you're likely to make a substantial profit, even if you sell below the current market value. If, however, you bought after 2002 the chances of making a profit are smaller and in some cases (particularly if you bought in the last few tears), negligible, particularly when you take buying and selling costs into account. For detailed information about the Spanish property market, see page 151.

Your first step is to find out the market value of your property. You can ask an estate agent to do this – most will provide a free appraisal of a home's value or compare your home with others on the market or that have recently been sold. You should be prepared to drop the price slightly (e.g. 5 to 10 per cent) and should set it accordingly, but don't over-price it as it will deter buyers. You also need to decide how quickly you need to sell your home: if you're in a hurry it might be worth dropping the price for a quick sale. On the other hand, if you can wait six months there may be no need to reduce the price. In today's market, expect to wait at least three months for a definite offer and sale (six months in some areas).

If your home is in an area where the resale market is slow, you have the following options:

- Sell the property for significantly below the market price; this will probably speed up the sale allowing you to leave Spain sooner, and will also reduce your liability for capital gains tax (see page 255), but you could lose money and be unable to afford a property in your home country.

- Sell the property at slightly below the market price; this means you will get a realistic price for your property, but you may still have to wait several months for a sale.

- Rent your property until the market improves. This option buys you time, although there's no guarantee that you will get a higher price for your home in one or two years' time. If you let your Spanish home short-term, you will be able to use it for holidays and the money can go towards renting a home in your home country or supplementing your pension. However, on the negative side you won't have the money from the sale at your disposal, there may be problems with tenants and you'll need to employ someone to look after your property.

Presentation

As well as the right price, another secret to a quick sale lies in the presentation of the property. First impressions (inside and out) are essential when potential buyers view your property, therefore it's important to present it in its best light and make it as attractive as possible. It pays to invest in a coat of paint (interior and exterior), a few touches of decoration (e.g. fresh flowers and plants) and a kitchen facelift (e.g. new cupboard doors).

SURVIVAL TIP
Be conservative in your decoration, avoid 'loud' colours and make sure your home isn't cluttered.

You may wish to employ the services of a so-called 'house doctor' for advice on optimising your home's appearance and therefore its chances of a quick sale. Several companies provide these services in popular resort areas. It isn't always worth modernising your kitchen and bathroom unless you're sure the cost will be recouped in the sale price. It may be cheaper (and definitely less stressful) to reduce the asking price rather than pay for modernisation. Note that you have a duty under Spanish law to inform a prospective buyer of any defects that aren't readily apparent and which materially affect the value of a property.

Who Sells Your Home?

Most foreigners use the services of an estate agent, while Spaniards prefer to sell their homes themselves. The option you choose depends largely on your time and personal circumstances – if you find yourself in a stressful situation or are unwell, it's best to leave the sale in the hands of professionals and save yourself unnecessary distress. Other advantages of using an estate agent include access to better marketing and a wider market, meaning increased chances of selling. On the other hand, not all estate agents are trustworthy and all charge commission of at least 5 per cent. If you decide to use an agent ask around for recommendations for one who specialises in your local area, check the agent's conditions carefully (beware of signing exclusive contracts), and never pay an agent's commission until the sale is completed and you've received the money from the sale.

Selling your home yourself saves money on the agent's commission and gives you control over the sale without pressure from an agent. However, it's a time-consuming option and you may find it distressing to be continually showing your home to strangers.

Capital Gains Tax

The main cost involved in the sale of a home is capital gains tax (CGT), which is levied on the profit made on the sale. The amount you're liable to pay depends on the purchase and selling prices, how long you've owned the property, your residency status and the deductions you're entitled to. Calculations of CGT are complicated and you should consult a tax advisor or lawyer specialising in property law to find out your CGT liability.

Exemptions from CGT

● Residents over 65 are exempt from CGT on the profit made from the sale of their principal home, irrespective of how long they've owned it.

However, the Spanish tax authorities defines a 'principal home' as the place where you've lived permanently for at least three years before you sell.

● Residents aged under 65 are exempt from CGT on the profit made from the sale of their principal home, provided that all the profit is invested in the purchase of another principal home within two years of the sale. The new principal home must be in your new country of residence, i.e. not necessarily Spain. Any profit that isn't reinvested is subject to CGT at 15 per cent (18 per cent from 2007).

● Property owners who bought their home before 31st December 1986 are exempt from CGT, irrespective of their residency status.

If none of the above exemptions apply to you, you're liable for CGT. Residents are subject to CGT at 15 per cent (18 per cent from 2007) and non-residents at a rate of 35 per cent (this is expected to fall to 18 per cent from 2007).

For comprehensive information regarding the calculation of CGT including up to date figures, see our sister publication **Buying a Home in Spain** by David Hampshire (see page 383).

TERMINATING A RENTAL CONTRACT

If you don't own a property in Spain and live in rental accommodation, it's relatively easy to sort out your accommodation affairs. Most rental contracts state that the tenant should give the landlord a calendar month's notice of the termination of the contract. Inform your landlord **in writing** of the date of your intended departure and send the notification by registered post (*acuse de recibo*).

Find out about the conditions for the return of your deposit. Some landlords accept the deposit in lieu of the last month's rental payment, but others require a month's rental payment and only return the deposit (or part of it) once they've checked the accommodation for damage and missing items. Some landlords charge tenants for cleaning at the end of the tenancy. It's usually cheaper to clean the property yourself or pay a cleaner to do it for you. Be aware, however, that some landlords don't accept this and will present a bill for cleaning regardless of whether you've cleaned or not.

When your tenancy ends, ensure you pay all outstanding utility bills and cancel any direct debits – it isn't uncommon for old tenants to find themselves paying the new tenants' bills!

SETTLING YOUR AFFAIRS IN SPAIN

When leaving Spain, there are many things to be considered and sorted out. The following checklist provides a guide to the essential tasks and should help make them easier (provided you don't leave everything to the last minute). It's worth employing the services of a *gestor* (see page 311) to do some of the tasks below on your behalf.

Checklist

● Arrange shipment of your furniture and belongings – book a removal or shipping company well in advance;

● Arrange to sell or dispose of anything you aren't taking with you;

● Check the immigration procedure for non-resident nationals in your home country;

● Cancel your residence permit (*baja de permiso de residencia*) at the nearest police station (*comisería de policía*);

● Inform the tax office that you're no longer resident and pay any outstanding income or capital gains tax or apply for a rebate. It's advisable to obtain expert advice regarding this (see **Timing** on page 321).

● Inform your utility companies (e.g. electricity, gas, water and telephone) in writing of your departure well in advance, particularly if you need to get a deposit refunded;

● Cancel your registration (*baja de empadronamiento*) at your local council;

● Cancel your registration with the social security authorities (*baja de seguridad social*);

● Cancel all insurance policies unless they're valid in your home country;

● Close your bank account in Spain (unless you need to keep it open to pay bills or receive future payments) and cancel your direct debits;

● Check that you've paid all outstanding bills (e.g. utility, community);

● Ensure that you will have adequate healthcare cover in your home country. You may need to take out a private health insurance policy;

● Return any library books or anything borrowed;

- If you need to leave some loose ends when you depart (e.g. you haven't sold your house), you can give 'power of attorney' to a lawyer or professional you trust in Spain. This can be 'general purpose' or for a specific purpose only and can for a fixed period or open-ended.

Be <u>very, very careful</u> before giving anyone a power of attorney over your financial affairs in Spain (or anywhere else), as it isn't unknown for a lawyer or other professional to sell assets illegally and abscond with the money. If you must do it, it should be for a specific reason only and for a limited period.

ARRIVAL IN YOUR HOME COUNTRY

Although your circumstances or personal preferences may have brought it about, returning home to a country you left a number of years ago can be a daunting prospect. Since you left your home country many things will have changed and the return home may not be an easy experience. It will hopefully be a happy one, but at the same time may be fraught with difficulties as you adjust to a new lifestyle that you may have idealised, particularly if you've left Spain because of problems there. You may also have financial problems, especially if the cost of living in your home country is higher than in Spain and you cannot afford to buy a home.

You will probably suffer from reverse culture shock (see **Culture Shock** on page 307) with much the same symptoms as you experienced when you first retired to Spain, and you may be surprised to find how long it takes for you to re-adapt to life in your home country. Expect to find your family and friends interested in your life in Spain at first, but bear in mind that most will lose interest after a while.

To make your return home as smooth as possible, you should follow the same advice for retiring abroad (see pages 195 and 307). Above all, try not to look on your return as a failure, but the end of an adventure or a chapter in your life. Don't dwell on the past (although if you must look back, try to remember the good times!) but look forward to getting acquainted with your home country all over again – like meeting an old friend after many years – and facing new and rewarding experiences.

APPENDICES

Appendix A: FURTHER INFORMATION

Embassies & Consulates

Embassies are located in the capital Madrid; many countries also have consulates in other cities (British provincial consulates are listed on page 335). Embassies and consulates are listed in the yellow pages under *Embajadas*. Some countries have more than one office in Madrid and, before writing or calling in person, you should telephone to confirm that you have the correct office.

Algeria: C/General Oraá, 12, 28006 Madrid (☎ 915-629 705).

Angola: C/Serrano, 64, 28001 Madrid (☎ 914-356 166).

Argentina: C/Pedro de Valdivia, 21, 28006 Madrid (☎ 917-710 500, 🖳 http://www.portalargentino.net).

Australia: Pza Descubridor Diego Ordás, 3, 28003 Madrid (☎ 913-536 600, 🖳 http://www.spain.embassy.gov.au).

Austria: Paseo de la Castellana, 91, 28046 Madrid (☎ 915-565 315, 🖳 http://www.bmaa.gv.at/madrid).

Belgium: Paseo de la Castellana, 18, 28046 Madrid (☎ 915-776 300, 🖳 http://www.diplobel.org/spain).

Bolivia: C/Velázquez, 26, 28001 Madrid (☎ 915-780 835, 🖳 http://www.mcei-bolivia.com).

Bosnia & Herzegovina: C/ Lagasca, 24, 28001 Madrid (☎ 915-750 870).

Brazil: C/ Fernando el Santo, 6, 28010 Madrid (☎ 917-004 650, 🖳 http://www.brasil.es).

Bulgaria: C/Travesia de Santa Maria Magdalena, 15, 28016 Madrid (☎ 913-455 761).

Cameroon: C/Rosario Pino, 3, 28020 Madrid (☎ 915-711 160).

Canada: C/Núñez de Balboa, 35, 28001 Madrid (☎ 914-233 250, 🖳 http://www.canada-es.org).

Chile: C/Lagasca, 88, 28001 Madrid (☎ 914-319 160).

China: C/Arturo Soria, 113, 28043 Madrid (☎ 915-194 242, 🖳 http://www.embajadachina.es).

Colombia: C/General Martínez Campos, 48, 28010 Madrid (☎ 917-004 770).

Costa Rica: Paseo de la Castellana, 164, 28046 Madrid (☎ 913-459 622).

Croatia: C/Claudio Coello, 78, 28001 Madrid (☎ 915-776 881).

Cyprus: Paseo de la Castellana, 45, 28046 Madrid (☎ 915-783 114).

Czech Republic: Avda. Pío XII, 22-24, 28016 Madrid (☎ 913-531 880, 🖳 http://www.mfa.cz/madrid).

Cuba: Paseo de la Habana, 194, 28036 Madrid (☎ 913-592 500, 🖳 http://www.ecubamad.com).

Denmark: C/Claudio Coello, 91, 28006 Madrid (☎ 914-318 445, 🖳 http://www.embajadadinamarca.es).

Ecuador: C/Velázquez, 114, 28006 Madrid (☎ 915-627 215).

Egypt: C/Velázquez, 69, 28006 Madrid (☎ 915-776 308).

El Salvador: C/General Oraá, 9, 28006 Madrid (☎ 915-628 002, 🖳 http://www.embasalva.com).

Estonia: C/Claudio Coello, 91, 28006 Madrid (☎ 914-261 671, 🖳 http://www.estemb.es).

Finland: Paseo de la Castellana, 15, 28046 Madrid (☎ 913-196 172, 🖳 http://www.finlandia.es).

France: C/Salustiano Olózaga, 9, 28001 Madrid (☎ 914-238 900, 🖳 http://www.ambafrance-es.org).

Gabon: C/Francisco Alcántara, 3, 28002 Madrid (☎ 914-138 211).

Germany: C/Fortuny, 8, 28010 Madrid (☎ 915-579 000, 🖳 http://www.embajada-alemania.es).

Greece: Avda. Doctor Arce, 24, 28002 Madrid (☎ 915-644 653).

Guatemala: C/Rafael Salgado, 3, 28036 Madrid (☎ 913-440 347).

Haiti: C/Marqués del Duero, 3, 28001 Madrid (☎ 915-752 624).

Honduras: Paseo de la Castellana, 164, 28046 Madrid (☎ 915-790 251, 💻 http://www.embahonduras.es).

Hungary: C/Fortuny, 6, 28010 Madrid (☎ 914-137 011, 💻 http://www.embajada-hungria.org).

India: Avda. Pío XII, 30-32, 28016 Madrid (☎ 902-901 010, 💻 http://www.embajadaindia.com).

Indonesia: C/Agastia, 65, 28043 Madrid (☎ 914-130 294, 💻 http://www.embajadaindonesia.es).

Iran: C/Jerez, 5, 28016 Madrid (☎ 913-450 112, 💻 http://www.embajadairan.es/madrid).

Iraq: C/Ronda de Sobradiel, 67, 28043 Madrid (☎ 917-591 282).

Ireland: Paseo de la Castellana, 46, 28046 Madrid (☎ 914-364 093).

Israel: C/Velázquez, 150, 28002 Madrid (☎ 917-829 500, 💻 http://www.embajada-israel.es).

Italy: C/Lagasca, 98, 28006 Madrid (☎ 914-233 300).

Ivory Coast: C/Serrano, 154, 28006 Madrid (☎ 915-626 916).

Japan: C/Serrano, 109, 28006 Madrid (☎ 915-907 600, 💻 http://www.embjapon.es).

Jordan: Paseo General Martinez Campos, 41, 28010 Madrid (☎ 913-191 100).

Korea: C/González Amigó, 15, 28033 Madrid (☎ 913-532 000, 💻 http://www.korea.net).

Kuwait: Paseo de la Castellana, 141, 28046 Madrid (☎ 915-792 467).

Latvia: C/Alfonso XII, 52, 28014 Madrid (☎ 913-691 362).

Lebanon: Paseo de la Castellana, 178, 28046 Madrid (☎ 913-451 368).

Libya: C/Pisuerga, 12, 28002 Madrid (☎ 915-635 753).

Lithuania: C/ Pisuerga, 5, 28002 Madrid (☎ 917-022 116, 🖳 http://www.emblituania.es).

Luxembourg: C/Claudio Coello, 78, 28001 Madrid (☎ 914-359 164, 🖳 http://www.mae.lu/espagne).

Malaysia: Paseo de la Castellana, 91, 28046 Madrid (☎ 915-550 684).

Malta: Paseo de la Castellana, 45, 28046 Madrid (☎ 913-913 061).

Mauritania: C/Velázquez, 90, 28006 Madrid (☎ 915-757 006).

Mexico: Carrera de San Jerónimo, 46, 28014 Madrid (☎ 913-692 814, 🖳 http://www.embamex.es).

Monaco: C/Villanueva, 12, 28001 Madrid (☎ 915-782 048).

Morocco: C/Serrano, 179, 28002 Madrid (☎ 915-631 090, 🖳 http://www.maec.gov.ma/madrid).

The Netherlands: Avda. del Comandante Franco, 32, 28016 Madrid (☎ 913-537 500, 🖳 http://www.embajadapaiseshajos.es).

New Zealand: Plza. de la Lealtad, 2, 28014 Madrid (☎ 915-230 226, 🖳 http://www.nzembassy.com/spain).

Nicaragua: Paseo de la Castellana, 127, 28046 Madrid (☎ 915-555 510).

Nigeria: C/Segre, 23, 28002 Madrid (☎ 915-630 911).

Norway: Paseo de la Castellana, 31, 28046 Madrid (☎ 913-103 116, 🖳 http://www.noruega.es).

Pakistan: Avda. Pío XII, 11, 28016 Madrid (☎ 913-458 986, 🖳 http://www.embajada-pakistan.org).

Panama: C/Claudio Coello, 86, 28006 Madrid (☎ 915-767 668).

Paraguay: Paseo Eduardo Dato, 21, 28010 Madrid (☎ 913-082 746).

Peru: C/Príncipe de Vergara, 36, 28001 Madrid (☎ 914-314 242).

Philippines: C/Eresma, 2, 28002 Madrid (☎ 917-823 830, 💻 http://www.philmadrid.com).

Poland: C/Guisando, 23 bis, 28035 Madrid (☎ 913-736 605, 💻 http://www.polonia.es).

Portugal: C/Pinar, 1, 28006 Madrid (☎ 917-824 960).

Romania: Avda. Alfonso XIII, 157, 28016 Madrid (☎ 913-504 436, 💻 http://www.embajadarumana.com).

Russia: C/Velázquez, 155, 28002 Madrid (☎ 915-622 264).

Saudi Arabia: C/Doctor Alvarez Sierra, 3, 28033 Madrid (☎ 913-834 300, 💻 http://www.arabiasaudi.org).

Slovakia: C/Pinar, 20, 28006 Madrid (☎ 915-903 861).

Slovenia: C/Hermanos Bécquer, 7, 28006 Madrid (☎ 914-116 893).

South Africa: C/Claudio Coello, 91, 28006 Madrid (☎ 914-363 780, 💻 http://www.sudafrica.com).

Sweden: C/Caracas, 25, 28010 Madrid (☎ 917-022 000, 💻 http://www. swedenabroad.com).

Switzerland: C/Núñez de Balboa, 35, 28001 Madrid (☎ 914-363 960, 💻 http://www.eda.admin.ch/madrid).

Syria: Pza. Platerías Martínez, 1, 28014 Madrid (☎ 914-203 946).

Thailand: C/Joaquín Costa, 29, 28002 Madrid (☎ 915-632 903).

Tunisia: Avda Alfonso XIII, 64, 28016 Madrid (☎ 914-473 508).

Turkey: C/Rafael Calvo, 18, 28010 Madrid (☎ 913-198 064, 💻 http://www.tc madridbe.org).

Ukraine: C/ Ronda de la Abubilla, 52, 28043 Madrid (☎ 917-489 360, 💻 http://www.embucrania.org.es).

United Arab Emirates: C/Capitán Haya, 40, 28020 Madrid (☎ 915-701 003).

United Kingdom: C/Fernando el Santo, 16, 28010 Madrid (☎ 917-008 200, 💻 http://www.ukinspain.com).

United States of America: C/Serrano, 75, 28006 Madrid (☎ 915-872 200, 🖳 http://www.embusa.es).

Uruguay: Paseo Pintor Rosales, 32, 28008 Madrid (☎ 917-580 475).

Venezuela: C/Capitán Haya, 1, 28020 Madrid (☎ 915-981 200).

Vietnam: C/ Arturo Soria, 201, 28043 Madrid (☎ 915-102 867, 🖳 http://www.embavietnam-madrid.org).

British Provincial Consulates in Spain

British consulates can provide British nationals with lists of English-speaking professionals such as lawyers and doctors and help them with the following: contacting next of kin in case of illness or bereavement; information on burial and repatriation; transferring money; dealing with legal problems.

Alicante: British Consulate, Plaza Calvo Sotelo, 1/2, 03001 Alicante (☎ 965-216 190, ✉ enquiries.alicante@fco.gov.uk).

Barcelona: British Consulate-General, Edif. Torre de Barcelona, Avda. Diagonal, 477-13, 08036 Barcelona (☎ 933-666 200, ✉ barcelonaconsulate@ ukinspain.com).

Bilbao: British Consulate, Alamada de Urquijo, 2-8, 48008 Bilbao (☎ 944-157 600, ✉ bilbaoconsulate@ ukinspain.com).

Ibiza: British Vice-Consulate, Avenida de Isidoro Macabich, 45, 07800 Ibiza (☎ 971-301 818, ✉ britishconsulate.ibiza@fco.gov.uk).

Las Palmas de Gran Canarias: British Consulate, Edif. Cataluña, Luis Morote, 6-3, 35007 Las Palmas (☎ 928-262 508, ✉ LAPAL-Consular@ fco.gov.uk).

Madrid: British Consulate-General, Paseo de Recoletos, 7/9, 28004 Madrid (☎ 915-249 700, ✉ madridconsulate@ ukinspain.com).

Malaga: British Consulate, Edif. Eurocom, C/Mauricio Moro Pareto, 2-2°, 29006 Malaga (☎ 952-352 300, ✉ malaga@fco.gov.uk).

Menorca: Honorary British Vice-Consulate, Sa Casa Nova, Cami de Biniatap, 30, Es Castell, 07720 Menorca (☎ 971-367 818).

Palma de Mallorca: British Consulate, Plaza Mayor, 3D, 07002 Palma de Mallorca (☎ 971-712 445, ✉ consulate@palma.mail. fco.gov.uk).

Santa Cruz de Tenerife: British Consulate, Plaza Weyler, 8-1, 38003 Santa Cruz de Tenerife (☎ 922-286 863, ✉ tenerife. enquiries@fco.gov.uk).

Property Exhibition Organisers

Property exhibitions are common in the UK and Ireland, and are popular with prospective property buyers who can get a good idea of what's available in a particular area and make contact with estate agents and developers. Below is a list of the main exhibition organisers in the UK and Ireland. Note that you may be charged a small admission fee.

Home Buyer Show (UK ☎ 020-7069 5000, 🖳 http://www. homebuyer.co.uk). The Home Buyer Show holds an annual property exhibition in London.

Homes Overseas (UK ☎ 020-7002 8300, 🖳 http://www.homes overseas.co.uk). Homes Overseas is the largest organiser of international property exhibitions and stages a number of exhibitions each year at a range of venues in both the UK and Ireland.

International Property Show (UK ☎ 01252-720652, 🖳 http:// www.internationalpropertyshow.com). The International Property Show is held several times a year at a range of venues in the UK and Ireland.

A Place in the Sun Live! (UK ☎ 0870-352888, 🖳 http:// www.aplaceinthesunlive.com). A Place in the Sun organises two large property shows a year in London and Birmingham.

Spain on Show (UK ☎ 0500-780878, 💻 http://www.spain
onshow.com). Spain on Show organises several annual property
exhibitions at venues around the UK.

World of Property (UK ☎ 01323-726040, 💻 http://www.outbound
publishing.com). The *World of Property* magazine publishers (see
Appendix B) organise several large property exhibitions a year in
the UK.

Appendix B: FURTHER READING

English-language Newspapers & Magazines

Unless otherwise stated, addresses and telephone numbers are in Spain.

Absolute Madrid, Palacio de Miraflores, Carrera de San Jerónimo 15, 2, 28014 Madrid (☎ 914-547 268, 🖳 http://www.absolute magazine.com). Free monthly magazine.

Absolute Malaga, Office 21, Edif Tembo, Avda Rotary International, 29660 Puerto Banús, Malaga (☎ 902-301 130, 🖳 http://www.absolutemagazine.com). Free monthly magazine.

Absolute Marbella, Office 21, Edif Tembo, Avda Rotary International, 29660 Puerto Banús, Malaga (☎ 902-301 130, 🖳 http://www.absolutemagazine.com). Free monthly magazine.

Barcelona Connect, (☎ 933-170 474, 🖳 http://www.barcelona connect.com). Free monthly magazine.

Barcelona Metropolitan (☎ 934-514 486, 🖳 http://www. barcelona-metropolitan.com). Free monthly magazine.

The Broadsheet (☎ 915-237 480, 🖳 http://www.thebroad sheet.com). Free monthly magazine.

Costa Blanca News, C/ Alicante 9, Polígono Industrial La Cala, Finestrat, Alicante (☎ 965-855 286, 🖳 http://www.costablanca-news.com). Weekly newspaper published on Fridays.

Costa del Sol News, CC Las Moriscas Local 10, Avda Juan Luis Peralta, 29629 Benalmádena Pueblo, Malaga (☎ 952-448 730, 🖳 http://www.costadelsolnews.es). Weekly newspaper published on Fridays.

Euro Weekly (☎ 952-561 245, 🖳 http://euroweeklynews.com). Weekly free newspaper with editions for the Costa Blanca, Costa del Sol, Costa de Almería, the Heart of Andalusia and Majorca.

Essential Marbella (☎ 952-766 344, 🖳 http://www.essential magazine.com). Free monthly magazine.

Homes Overseas, Blendon Communications, 1st Floor, 1 East Poultry Avenue, London EC1A 9PT, UK (UK ☎ 020-7002 8300, 🖳 http://www.homesoverseas.co.uk). Monthly property magazine.

The Ibiza Sun (🖳 http://www.theibizasun.net). Free weekly newspaper.

In Madrid (☎ 915-226 780, 🖳 http://www.in-madrid.com). Free monthly magazine.

Island Connections (☎ 922-750 609, 🖳 http://www.news canarias.net). Fortnightly newspaper published in the Canary Islands.

La Chispa (🖳 http://www.lachispa.net). Free monthly magazine on natural living in Andalusia.

Lanzarote Gazette (☎ 902-250 750, 🖳 http://www.gazette live.com). Free monthly magazine covering Lanzarote and Fuerteventura.

Living Spain, Albany Publishing, Tunns Cottage, Olney, Bucks MK46 4AE, UK (UK ☎ 01234-710992, 🖳 http://www.livingspain.co.uk). Bimonthly lifestyle and property magazine.

The Mallorca Daily Bulletin (☎ 971-788 400, 🖳 http://www. majorcadailybulletln.es). Daily newspaper for the Balearics.

Property News, Jarales de Alhamar, Calahonda, 29647 Mijas-Costa, Malaga (☎ 952-931 603, 🖳 http://www.property-spain.com). Free monthly newspaper.

Spain Magazine, Media Circus Publications Ltd, 21 Royal Circus, Edinburgh EH3 6TL, UK (UK ☎ 0131-226 7766, 🖳 http://www.spain magazine.co.uk). Monthly lifestyle and property magazine.

Spanish Homes Magazine, 5th Floor, Low Rise Building, Kings Reach Tower, Stamford St, London SE1 9LS (UK ☎ 020-7633 3333, 🖳 http://www.spanishhomesmagazine.com). Monthly property magazine.

Spanish Magazine, Merricks Media Ltd, Units 3 & 4, Riverside Court, Lower Bristol Rd, Bath BA2 3DZ, UK (UK ☎ 01225-786844,

⌨ http://www.spanishmagazine.co.uk). Monthly lifestyle and property magazine.

Sur in English, Diario Sur, Avda. Doctor Marañón, 48, 29009 Malaga (☎ 952-649 741, ⌨ http://www.surinenglish.com). Free weekly newspaper.

Tenerife News (☎ 922-346 000, ⌨ http://www.tenerifenews.com). Free fortnightly newspaper.

The Paper (☎ 922-735 659, ⌨ http://www.thepaper.net). Free fortnightly magazine covering Tenerife.

Valencia Life, (⌨ http://www.valencialife.net). Quarterly magazine.

West Coast Magazine (☎ 902-310 313, ⌨ http://westcoast magazine.es). Free monthly magazine covering the western Costa del Sol from Marbella to Sotogrande.

World of Property, 1 Commercial Road, Eastbourne, East Sussex BN21 3XQ, UK (UK ☎ 01323-726040, ⌨ http://www.outbound publishing.com). Bi-monthly property magazine.

Books

The books listed below are just a selection of the hundreds written about Spain. For example, in addition to the general tourist guides listed, there are numerous guides covering individual cities and regions of Spain. The publication title is followed by the author's name and the publisher's name (in brackets). Note that some titles may be out of print, but may still be obtainable from book shops or libraries. Books prefixed with an asterisk are recommended by the author.

Living & Working in Spain

**The Best Places to Buy a Home in Spain, Joanna Styles (Survival Books)

**Costa Blanca Lifeline, Joanna Styles (Survival Books)

Costa del Sol Lifeline, Joanna Styles (Survival Books)

Earning Money from your Spanish Home, Joanna Styles (Survival Books)

Introducing Spain, B.A. McCullagh & S. Wood (Harrap)

Life in a Spanish Town, M. Newton (Harrap)

Living and Working in Spain, David Hampshire (Survival Books)

*Madrid Inside Out**, Arthur Howard & Victoria Montero (Frank)

Making a Living in Spain, Anne Hall (Survival Books)

Simple Etiquette in Spain, Victoria Miranda McGuiness (Simple Books)

Spain: Business & Finance (Euromoney Books)

Traditional Houses of Rural Spain, Bill Laws (Collins & Browns)

*You and the Law in Spain**, David Searl (Santana)

General Tourist Guides

AA Essential Explorer Spain (AA)

Andalucía Handbook, Rowland Mead (Footprint)

*Andalucía: The Rough Guide** (Rough Guides)

*Baedeker's Spain** (Baedeker)

Berlitz Blueprint: Spain (Berlitz)

Berlitz Discover Spain, Ken Bernstein & Paul Murphy (Berlitz)

*Blue Guide to Spain: The Mainland**, Ian Robertson (Ernest Benn)

*Cadogan Guides: Spain**, Dana Facaros & Michael Pauls (Cadogan)

Collins Independent Travellers Guide Spain, Harry Debelius (Collins)

Daytrips Spain & Portugal, Norman Renouf (Hastings House Pub)

Excursions in Eastern Spain, Nick Inman & Clara Villanueva (Santana)

Excursions in Southern Spain, David Baird (Santana)

*Eyewitness Travel Guide: Spain, Deni Bown (Dorling Kindersly)

Fielding's Paradors in Spain & Portugal, A. Hobbs (Fielding Worldwide)

*Fodor Spain (Fodor)

*Fodor's Exploring Spain (Fodor's Travel Publications)

*Frommer's Spain's Best-Loved Driving Tours, Mona King (IDG Books)

Guide to the Best of Spain (Turespaña)

*Inside Andalusia, David Baird (Santana)

The Insider's Guide to Spain, John de St. Jorre (Moorland)

*Insight Guides: Spain (APA Publications)

Lazy Days Out in Andalucía, Jeremy Wayne (Cadogan)

*Let's Go Spain & Portugal (Macmillan)

*Lonely Planet Spain (Lonely Planet)

*Madrid, Michael Jacobs (George Philip)

Madrid: A Traveller's Companion, Hugh Thomas (Constable)

*Michelin Spain Green Guide (Michelin)

*Michelin Red Guide: España, Portugal (Michelin)

Off the Beaten Track: Spain, Barbara Mandell & Roger Penn (Moorland)

*Paupers' Barcelona, Miles Turner (Pan)

Rick Steves' Spain & Portugal, Rick Steves (John Muir Publications)

*Rough Guide to Andalucía, Mark Ellingham & John Fisher (Rough Guides)

The Shell Guide to Spain, David Mitchell (Simon & Schuster)

Spain: A Phaidon Cultural Guide (Phaidon)

Spain at its Best, Robert Kane (Passport)

Spain: Everything Under the Sun, Tom Burns (Harrap Columbus)

Spain on Backroads, Duncan Petersen (Hunter Publishing)

*Spain: The Rough Guide, Mark Ellingham & John Fisher (Rough Guides)

*Special Places to Stay in Spain, Alistair Sawday (ASP)

Time Off in Spain and Portugal, Teresa Tinsley (Horizon)

*Time Out Madrid Guide (Penguin)

Travellers in Spain: An Illustrated Anthology, David Mitchell (Cassell)

Welcome to Spain, R.A.N. Dixon (Collins)

*Which? Guide to Spain (Consumers' Association and Hodder & Stoughton)

Travel Literature

*As I Walked Out One Midsummer Morning, Laurie Lee (Penguin)

*Between Hopes and Memories: A Spanish Journey, Michael Jacobs (Picador)

*The Bible in Spain, George Borrow (Century Travellers Series)

*Cider with Rosie, Laurie Lee (Penguin)

Gatherings in Spain, Richard Ford (Dent Everyman)

*Handbook for Travellers in Spain, Richard Ford (Centaur Press)

Iberia, James A. Michener (Fawcett)

*Jogging Round Majorca, Gordon West (Black Swan)

In Search of Andalucía, Christopher Wawn & David Wood (Pentland Press)

*In Spain, Ted Walker (Corgi)

*A Rose for Winter, Laurie Lee (Penguin)

*Spanish Journeys: A Portrait of Spain, Adam Hopkins (Penguin)

*South from Granada, Gerald Brenan (Penguin)

*A Stranger in Spain, H.V. Morton (Methuen)

Two Middle-aged Ladies in Adalusia, Penelope Chetwode (Murray)

*A Winter in Majorca, George Sands

Food & Wine

*AA Essential Food and Drink Spain (AA)

*The Best of Spanish Cooking, Janet Mendel (Santana)

The Complete Spanish Cookbook, Jacki Passmore (Little Brown)

*Cooking in Spain, Janet Mendel (Santana)

Delicioso: The Regional Cooking of Spain, Penelope Casas (Knoff)

A Flavour of Andalucía, Pepita Aris (Chartwell)

*Floyd on Spain, Keith Floyd (Penguin)

The Food and Wine of Spain, Penelope Casas (Alfred A. Knopf)

404 Spanish Wines, Frank Snell (Santana)

Great Dishes of Spain, Robert Carrier (Boxtree)

*The 'La Ina' Book of Tapas, Elisabeth Luard (Schuster)

Mediterranean Seafood, Alan Davidson (Penguin)

**Rioja and its Wines, Ron Scarborough (Survival Books)

Shopping for Food and Wine in Spain (Santana)

*Spanish Cooking, Pepita Aris (Apple Press)

*The Spanish Kitchen, Pepita Aris (Wardlock)

The Spanish Table, Marimar Torres (Ebury Press)

*Spanish Wines, Jan Read (Mitchell Beazley)

The Spanishwoman's Kitchen, Pepita Aris (Cassell)

The Tapas Book, Adrian Linssen & Sara Cleary (Apple Press)

Tapas, Silvano Franco (Lorenz)

*The Wine and Food of Spain, Jan Read & Maite Manjón (Wedenfeld & Nicolson)

The Wine Roads of Spain, M&K Millon (Santana)

Miscellaneous

The Art of Flamenco, D.F. Pohren (Musical News Services Ltd)

*Battle for Spain: The Spanish Civil War 1936-1939, Anthony Beevor (Weidenfeld & Nicolson)

*Blood Sport: A History of Spanish Bullfighting, Timothy Mitchell (University of Pennsylvania Press)

Cities of Spain, David Gilmour (Pimlico)

Dali: A Biography, Meredith Etheringon-Smith (Sinclair-Stevenson)

*A Day in the Life of Spain (Collins)

*Death in the Afternoon, Ernest Hemingway (Grafton)

Gardening in Spain, Marcelle Pitt (Santana)

The Gardens of Spain, Consuela M. Correcher (Abrams)

Ghosts of Spain, Giles Tremlett (Faber & Faber)

*In Search of the Firedance, James Woodall (Sinclair-Stevenson)

The King, Jose Luis de Vilallonga (Weidenfeld)

Liz Parry's Spanish Phrase Book, Liz Parry (Santana Books)

*Nord Riley's Spain, Nord Riley (Santana)

*On Foot Through Europe: A Trail Guide to Spain and Portugal, Craig Evans (Quill)

*Or I'll Dress You in Mourning, Larry Collins & Dominique Lapierre (Simon & Schuster)

La Pasionaria, Robert Low (Hutchinson)

Spain: A Literary Companion, Jimmy Burns (John Murray)

Spain's Wildlife, Eric Robins (Santana)

Trekking in Spain, Marc S. Dubin (Lonely Planet)

*Walking Through Spain, Robin Neillands (Queen Anne Press)

*Wild Spain, Frederic Grunfeld & Teresa Farino (Ebury)

*Your Garden in Spain, D. and C. Handscombe (Santana Books)

*Xenophobe's Guide to the Spanish (Ravette)

APPENDIX C: USEFUL WEBSITES

The following list contains some of the many websites dedicated to Spain as well as websites containing information about a number of countries. Websites about particular aspects of life and work in Spain are mentioned in the relevant chapters.

Spanish Websites

About Spain (🖥 http://www.aboutspain.net). Information about specific regions.

All About Spain (🖥 http://www.red2000.com). General tourist information.

Andalucia (🖥 http://www.andalucia.com). Comprehensive information about the region of Andalusia in English.

Barcelona (🖥 http://www.xbarcelona.com). Information including job opportunities and useful tips for foreigners living in Barcelona.

Expatica (🖥 http://www.expatica.com). An excellent compendium of general information about living and working in Spain.

Ideal Spain (🖥 http://www.idealspain.com). Information about many aspects of living in Spain.

Madrid Man (🖥 http://www.madridman.com). A wealth of useful and continually updated information about living and working in Madrid including an 'ask the expert' facility.

Spain Expat (🖥 http://www.spainexpat.com). Information about living in Spain, including an 'ask the legal expert' facility. The site has particularly good links.

Spain for Visitors (🖥 http://spainforvisitors.com). Good general information about visiting Spain.

Spanish Living (🖥 http://www.spanish-living.com). Useful general and property information.

Spanish Property Insight (🖥 http://www.spanishproperty insight.com). One of the best websites on property with the emphasis on up-to-date, useful and impartial information. The site includes a forum and a free monthly e-newsletter.

Survival Books (🖳 http://www.survivalbooks.net). Survival Books are the publishers of this book and *Buying a Home in Spain*, *The Best Places to Buy a Home in Spain* and *The Wines of Spain*. The website includes useful tips for anyone planning to buy a home, live, work, retire or do business in Spain.

This is Spain (🖳 http://www.thisisspain.info). Useful general information about moving to Spain.

TurEspaña – Spanish National Tourist Office (🖳 http://www.tourspain.co.uk or 🖳 http://www.spain.info).

TuSpain (🖳 http://www.tuspain.com). General information with the emphasis on buying property and residential matters.

UK in Spain (🖳 http://www.ukinspain.com). The British embassy's official site includes a wealth of useful information about aspects of living and working in Spain. Go to the 'Consular Information' section and click on the 'Living in Spain' section.

General Websites

Escape Artist (🖳 http://www.escapeartist.com). An excellent website and probably the most comprehensive, packed with resources, links and directories covering most expatriate destinations. You can also subscribe to the free monthly online expatriate magazine, *Escape from America*.

Expat Exchange (🖳 http://www.expatexchange.com). Reportedly the largest online community for English-speaking expatriates, provides a series of articles on relocation and also a question and answer facility through its expatriate network.

Expat World (🖳 http://www.expatworld.net). 'The newsletter of international living.' Contains a wealth of information for American and British expatriates, including a subscription newsletter.

Expatriate Experts (🖳 http://www.expatexpert.com). A website run by expatriate expert Robin Pascoe, providing invaluable advice and support.

Family Life Abroad (🖳 http://www.familylifeabroad.com). A wealth of information and articles on coping with family life abroad.

Just Landed (🖳 http://www.justlanded.com). Useful relocation information for 26 countries.

MASTA (🖳 http://www.masta.org). An advisory service for travel abroad including useful factsheets and personalised health briefs available by telephone (UK ☎ 0906-822 4100).

Real Post Reports (🖳 http://www.realpostreports.com). Provides relocation services, recommended reading lists and plenty of interesting 'real-life' stories containing anecdotes and impressions written by expatriates in just about every city in the world.

Travel Documents (🖳 http://www.traveldocs.com). Useful information about travel, specific countries and documents needed to travel.

Travel Health Zone (🖳 http://www.travelhealthzone.com). Health portal for international travellers.

World Travel Guide (🖳 http://www.wtgonline.com). A general website for world travellers and expatriates.

Worldwise Directory (🖳 http://www.suzylamplugh.org/worldwise). This website, run by the Suzy Lamplugh charity for personal safety, providing a useful directory of countries with practical information and special emphasis on safety, particularly for women.

British Websites

Brits Abroad (🖳 http://www.britsabroad.co.uk). Online shopping for all those items of typically British food you just can't do without abroad.

British Expatriates (⌨ http://www.britishexpat.com). This website with country-specific sections keeps British expatriates in touch with events and information about the UK.

UK Trade Partners (⌨ http://www.uktradeinvest.gov.uk). A government sponsored website whose main aim is to provide trade and investment information on just about every country in the world. Even if you aren't planning to do business abroad, the information is comprehensive and up to date.

American Websites

Americans Abroad (⌨ http://www.aca.ch). This website offers advice, information and services to Americans abroad.

An American Abroad (⌨ http://www.anamericaabroad.com). Useful resources for Americans living outside the US.

US Government Trade (⌨ http://www.export.gov). A huge website providing a wealth of information principally for Americans planning to trade and invest abroad, but useful for anyone planning a move abroad.

Australian & New Zealand Websites

Australians Abroad (⌨ http://www.australiansabroad.com). Information for Australians concerning relocating plus a forum to exchange information and advice.

Southern Cross Group (⌨ http://www.southern-cross-group.org). A website for Australians and New Zealanders providing information and the exchange of tips.

Websites for Women & Children

Foreign Wives Club (⌨ http://www.foreignwivesclub.com). An online community for women in bicultural marriages.

Third Culture Kids (🖥 http://www.tckworld.com). A website designed for expatriate children living abroad.

Travel for Kids (🖥 http://www.travelforkids.com). Advice on travelling with children around the world.

Women of the World (🖥 http://www.wow-net.org). A website designed for female expats anywhere in the world.

Travel Information & Warnings

The websites listed below provide daily updated information about the political situation and natural disasters around the world, plus general travel and health advice and embassy addresses.

Australian Department of Foreign Affairs and Trade (🖥 http:// www.smartraveller.gov.au).

British Foreign and Commonwealth Office (🖥 http://www. fco.gov.uk).

Canadian Department of Foreign Affairs (🖥 http://www.dfait-maeci.gc.ca). They also publish a useful series of free booklets for Canadians moving abroad.

New Zealand Ministry of Foreign Affairs and Trade (🖥 http://www.mft.govt.nz).

SaveWealth Travel (🖥 http://www.savewealth.com/travel/warnings).

The Travel Doctor (🖥 http://www.tmvc.com.au). Contains a country by country vaccination guide.

US State Government (🖥 http://www.state.gov/travel). US Government website.

World Health Organization (🖥 http://www.who.int).

Appendix D: WEIGHTS & MEASURES

Spain uses the metric system of measurement. Those who are more familiar with the imperial system of measurement will find the tables on the following pages useful. Some comparisons shown are only approximate, but are close enough for most everyday uses. In addition to the variety of measurement systems used, clothes sizes often vary considerably with the manufacturer.

Women's Clothes

Continental	34	36	38	40	42	44	46	48	50	52
UK	8	10	12	14	16	18	20	22	24	26
US	6	8	10	12	14	16	18	20	22	24

Pullovers

	Women's						Men's					
Continental	40	42	44	46	48	50	44	46	48	50	52	54
UK	34	36	38	40	42	44	34	36	38	40	42	44
US	34	36	38	40	42	44	sm	med	lar	xl		

Men's Shirts

Continental	36	37	38	39	40	41	42	43	44	46
UK/US	14	14	15	15	16	16	17	17	18	-

Men's Underwear

Continental	5	6	7	8	9	10
UK	34	36	38	40	42	44
US	sm	med		lar	xl	

Note: sm = small, med = medium, lar = large, xl = extra large

Children's Clothes

Continental	92	104	116	128	140	152
UK	16/18	20/22	24/26	28/30	32/34	36/38
US	2	4	6	8	10	12

Children's Shoes

Continental	18	19	20	21	22	23	24	25	26	27	28	29	30	31	32
UK/US	2	3	4	4	5	6	7	7	8	9	10	11	11	12	13

Continental	33	34	35	36	37	38
UK/US	1	2	2	3	4	5

Shoes (Women's and Men's)

Continental	35	36	37	37	38	39	40	41	42	42	43	44
UK	2	3	3	4	4	5	6	7	7	8	9	9
US	4	5	5	6	6	7	8	9	9	10	10	11

Weight

Imperial	Metric	Metric	Imperial
1oz	28.35g	1g	0.035oz
1lb*	454g	100g	3.5oz
1cwt	50.8kg	250g	9oz
1 ton	1,016kg	500g	18oz
2,205lb	1 tonne	1kg	2.2lb

Length

Imperial	Metric	Metric	Imperial
1in	2.54cm	1cm	0.39in
1ft	30.48cm	1m	3ft 3.25in
1yd	91.44cm	1km	0.62mi
1mi	1.6km	8km	5mi

Capacity

Imperial	Metric	Metric	Imperial
1 UK pint	0.57 litre	1 litre	1.75 UK pints
1 US pint	0.47 litre	1 litre	2.13 US pints
1 UK gallon	4.54 litres	1 litre	0.22 UK gallon
1 US gallon	3.78 litres	1 litre	0.26 US gallon

Note: An American 'cup' = around 250ml or 0.25 litre.

Area

Imperial	Metric	Metric	Imperial
1 sq. in	0.45 sq. cm	1 sq. cm	0.15 sq. in
1 sq. ft	0.09 sq. m	1 sq. m	10.76 sq. ft
1 sq. yd	0.84 sq. m	1 sq. m	1.2 sq. yds
1 acre	0.4 hectares	1 hectare	2.47 acres
1 sq. mile	2.56 sq. km	1 sq. km	0.39 sq. mile

Note: An *are* is one-hundredth of a hectare or 100m^2.

Temperature

°Celsius	°Fahrenheit	
0	32	(freezing point of water)
5	41	
10	50	
15	59	
20	68	
25	77	
30	86	
35	95	
40	104	
50	122	

Notes: The boiling point of water is 100°C / 212°F.

Normal body temperature (if you're alive and well) is 37°C / 98.4°F.

Temperature Conversion

Celsius to Fahrenheit: multiply by 9, divide by 5 and add 32. (For a quick and approximate conversion, double the Celsius temperature and add 30.)

Fahrenheit to Celsius: subtract 32, multiply by 5 and divide by 9. (For a quick and approximate conversion, subtract 30 from the Fahrenheit temperature and divide by 2.)

Oven Temperatures

Gas	Electric	
	°F	°C
-	225–250	110–120
1	275	140
2	300	150
3	325	160
4	350	180
5	375	190
6	400	200
7	425	220
8	450	230
9	475	240

Air Pressure

PSI	Bar
10	0.5
20	1.4
30	2
40	2.8

APPENDIX E: **MAPS**

The map opposite shows the 17 autonomous regions and 50 provinces of Spain (listed below). The maps on the following pages show airports with scheduled services from the UK and Ireland (see **Appendix F**), high speed train (AVE) routes, and motorways and other major roads.

Galicia
1. A Coruña
2. Lugo
3. Pontevedra
4. Ourense

Asturias
5. Asturias

Castilla y León
6. León
7. Palencia
8. Burgos
9. Zamora
10. Valladolid
11. Soria
12. Salamanca
13. Avila
14. Segovia

Cantabria
15. Cantabria

La Rioja
16. La Rioja

País Vasco
17. Vizcaya
18. Guipúzcoa
19. Alava

Navarra
20. Navarra

Aragón
21. Huesca
22. Zaragoza
23. Teruel

Cataluña
24. Lleida
25. Girona
26. Barcelona
27. Tarragona

Extremadura
28. Cáceres
29. Badajoz

Castilla La Mancha
30. Guadalajara
31. Toledo
32. Cuenca
33. Ciudad Real
34. Albacete

Madrid
35. Madrid

Comunidad Valenciana
36. Castellón
37. Valencia
38. Alicante

Andalucía
39. Huelva
40. Sevilla
41. Córdoba
42. Jaén
43. Cádiz
44. Málaga
45. Granada
46. Almeria

Murcia
47. Murcia

Baleares
48. Baleares

Canarias
49. Santa Cruz de Tenerife
50. Las Palmas de Gran Canaria

REGIONS & PROVINCES

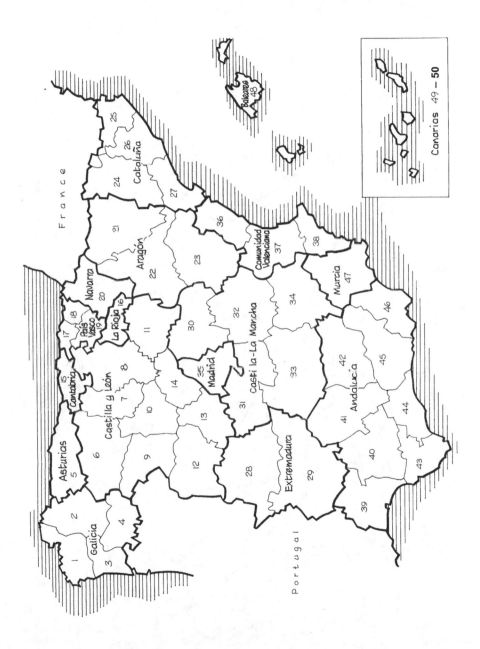

Motorways & Major Roads

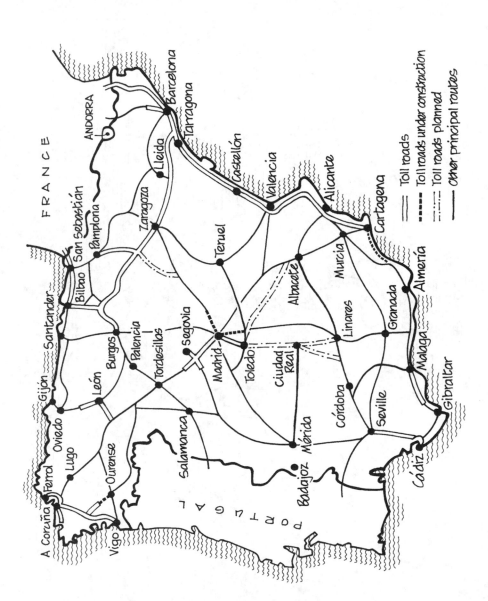

AVE Network

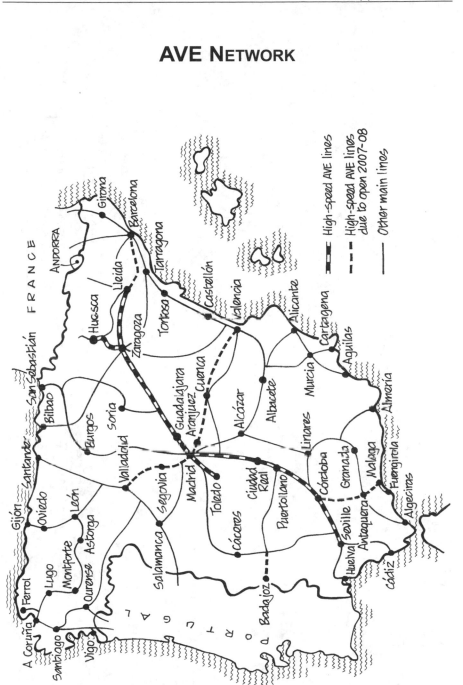

AIRPORTS

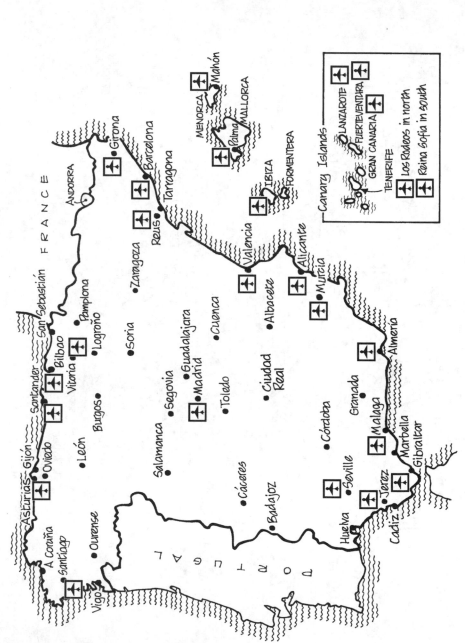

Appendix F: AIRLINE SERVICES

The following tables indicate scheduled flights to Spanish airports from the UK and Ireland. Details were correct in July 2006. Contact details for the airlines can be found on page 368. Contact telephone numbers for Spanish airports can be found on page 37 and contact telephone numbers for airports in the UK and Ireland on page 369.

Bear in mind that there are also many charter airlines (see page 36) serving the major Spanish airports from (approximately) April to October and year round in the Canaries.

Scheduled Flights

Alicante

Fly From	Airline(s)
Aberdeen	BMI
Belfast City	BMI, Easyjet, Excel Airways
Birmingham	Bmibaby, Flybe, Monarch
Blackpool	Jet2
Bristol	Easyjet, Excel Airways
Cardiff	Bmibaby, Excel Airways
Cork	Aer Lingus
Dublin	Aer Lingus, BMI, Spanair
Durham Tees Valley	BMI
Nottingham/East Mids	Bmibaby, Easyjet, Excel Airways
Edinburgh	Easyjet, Flyglobespan
Exeter	Flybe
Glasgow	Air Scotland, BMI, Easyjet, Excel Airways, Flyglobespan
Leeds/Bradford	Jet2
Liverpool	Easyjet
London Gatwick	Easyjet, Excel Airways, GB Airways, Iberia, Monarch
London Heathrow	BMI, Bmibaby
London Luton	Easyjet, Monarch
London Stansted	Easyjet
Manchester	Air Scotland, Bmibaby, Excel Airways, Jet2, Monarch
Newcastle	Easyjet, Excel Airways
Norwich	Flybe
Southampton	Flybe

Almería

Fly From	Airline(s)
Birmingham	Monarch
Dublin	Aer Lingus
London Gatwick	Easyjet
London Stansted	Easyjet, Ryanair
Manchester	Monarch

Asturias

Fly From	Airline(s)
London Stansted	Easyjet

Barcelona

Fly From	Airline(s)
Belfast City	Jet2
Birmingham	BA
Bristol	Easyjet
Dublin	Aer Lingus, Spanair
Edinburgh	Flyglobespan
Glasgow	Air Scotland, Flyglobespan
Leeds/Bradford	Jet2
Liverpool	Easyjet
London Gatwick	BA, Easyjet, Iberia
London Heathrow	BA
London Luton	Easyjet
London Stansted	Easyjet
Manchester	Air Scotland, Monarch
Newcastle	Easyjet

Bilbao

Fly From	Airline(s)
Cork	Aer Lingus
Dublin	Aer Lingus
London Stansted	Easyjet

Fuerteventura

Fly From	Airline(s)
Cardiff	Excel Airways
Dublin	Aer Lingus
Nottingham/East Mids	Excel Airways
Glasgow	Flyglobespan

London Gatwick	Excel Airways
Manchester	Excel Airways
Newcastle	Excel Airways

Gibraltar

Fly From	**Airline(s)**
London Gatwick	GB Airways
London Heathrow	GB Airways
London Luton	Monarch
Manchester	Monarch

Girona

Fly From	**Airline(s)**
Dublin	Ryanair
Nottingham/East Mids	Ryanair
Glasgow	Air Scotland
Glasgow Prestwick	Ryanair
Liverpool	Ryanair
London Luton	Ryanair
London Stansted	Ryanair
Manchester	Air Scotland
Newcastle	Air Scotland
Shannon	Ryanair

Granada

Fly From	**Airline(s)**
Liverpool	Ryanair
London Gatwick	Monarch
London Stansted	Ryanair

Ibiza

Fly From	**Airline(s)**
Nottingham/East Mids	Easyjet
Edinburgh	Flyglobespan
Glasgow	Flyglobespan
Leeds/Bradford	Jet2
Liverpool	Easyjet
London Gatwick	GB Airways
London Stansted	Easyjet
Manchester	Jet2
Newcastle	Easyjet

Jerez

Fly From
London Stansted

Airline(s)
Ryanair

Lanzarote

Fly From
Birmingham
Cardiff
Dublin
Edinburgh
Nottingham/East Mids
Exeter
Glasgow
Leeds/Bradford
London Gatwick
London Luton
Manchester
Newcastle

Airline(s)
Excel Airways, Monarch
Excel Airways
Aer Lingus, Spanair
Flyglobespan
Excel Airways
Excel Airways
Flyglobespan
Jet2
Excel Airways, GB Airways, Monarch
Monarch
Excel Airways, Monarch
Excel Airways

Las Palmas

Fly From
Bristol
Cardiff
Dublin
Nottingham/East Mids
Glasgow
London Gatwick
London Luton
Manchester
Newcastle

Airline(s)
Excel Airways
Excel Airways
Aer Lingus, Spanair
Excel Airways
Flyglobespan
Excel Airways
Monarch
Excel Airways
Excel Airways

Madrid

Fly From
Birmingham
Bristol
Dublin
Liverpool
London Gatwick
London Heathrow

Airline(s)
Iberia
Easyjet
Aer Lingus, Spanair
Easyjet
Easyjet, Iberia
Iberia

London Luton   Easyjet
Manchester   Iberia

Mahon

Fly From   **Airline(s)**
Birmingham   Monarch
Bristol   Easyjet
Edinburgh   Flyglobespan
Glasgow   Flyglobespan
Leeds/Bradford   Jet2
Liverpool   Easyjet
London Gatwick   Easyjet, GB Airways
Manchester   Monarch
Newcastle   Jet2

Malaga

Fly From   **Airline(s)**
Aberdeen   Monarch
Belfast City   Easyjet
Birmingham   Excel Airways, Flybe, Monarch
Blackpool   Jet2, Monarch
Bristol   Easyjet, Excel Airways
Cardiff   Excel Airways
Cork   Aer Lingus
Dublin   Aer Lingus, Ryanair, Spanair
Nottingham/East Mids Excel Airways
Edinburgh   Flyglobespan
Exeter   Flybe
Glasgow   Air Scotland, Easyjet, Flyglobespan
Humberside   Excel Airways
Leeds/Bradford   Jet2
Liverpool   Easyjet
London Gatwick   Easyjet, Excel Airways, Monarch
London Heathrow   GB Airways
London Luton   Easyjet, Monarch
London Stansted   Easyjet
Manchester   Air Scotland, Excel Airways, GB Airways, Jet2,
                      Monarch
Newcastle   Easyjet, Excel Airways
Norwich   Flybe
Shannon   Ryanair
Southampton   Flybe

Murcia

Fly From	Airline(s)
Belfast City	Jet2
Birmingham	Flybe, Monarch
Blackpool	Jet2
Bristol	Easyjet
Dublin	Ryanair
Nottingham/East Mids	Ryanair
Edinburgh	Flyglobespan, Jet2
Exeter	Flybe
Glasgow Prestwick	Ryanair
Liverpool	Ryanair
London Gatwick	Easyjet
London Luton	Ryanair
London Stansted	Ryanair
Manchester	Jet2
Norwich	Flybe
Shannon	Ryanair
Southampton	Flybe

Palma

Fly From	Airline(s)
Aberdeen	BMI
Belfast City	BMI, Easyjet
Birmingham	Bmibaby, Excel Airways, Monarch
Blackpool	Jet2
Bristol	Easyjet, Excel Airways
Cardiff	Bmibaby, Excel Airways
Dublin	Aer Lingus, BMI, Spanair
Durham Tees Valley	BMI, Bmibaby
Nottingham/East Mids	Bmibaby, Excel Airways
Edinburgh	Flyglobespan
Exeter	Flybe
Glasgow	Air Scotland, BMI, Easyjet, Flyglobespan
Leeds/Bradford	Jet2
Liverpool	Easyjet
London Gatwick	Easyjet, Excel Airways, GB Airways
London Heathrow	BMI, Bmibaby
London Luton	asyjet, Monarch
London Stansted	Easyjet, Excel Airways
Manchester	Air Scotland, BMI, Bmibaby, Excel Airways, Jet2, Monarch
Newcastle	Easyjet, Excel Airways

Reus

Fly From	Airline(s)
Dublin	Ryanair
Glasgow Prestwick	Ryanair
Liverpool	Ryanair
London Luton	Ryanair
London Stansted	Ryanair

Santander

Fly From	Airline(s)
London Stansted	Ryanair

Santiago de Compostela

Fly From	Airline(s)
London Stansted	Ryanair

Seville

Fly From	Airline(s)
Liverpool	Ryanair
London Gatwick	GB Airways
London Heathrow	Iberia
London Stansted	Ryanair

Tenerife

Fly From	Airline(s)
Belfast City	Jet2
Birmingham	Excel Airways, Monarch
Blackpool	Jet2
Bristol	Excel Airways
Cardiff	Excel Airways
Cork	Aer Lingus
Dublin	Aer Lingus, Spanair
Nottingham/East Mids	Excel Airways
Edinburgh	Flyglobespan
Glasgow	Excel Airways, Flyglobespan
Humberside	Excel Airways
Leeds/Bradford	Jet2
Liverpool	Flyglobespan
London Gatwick	Excel Airways, Monarch
London Luton	Monarch
London Stansted	Flyglobespan

Manchester   Excel Airways, Monarch
Newcastle   Excel Airways, Jet2

Valencia

Fly From	Airline(s)
Bristol	Easyjet
Dublin	Aer Lingus
London Gatwick	Easyjet, GB Airways, Iberia
London Stansted	Easyjet, Ryanair
Manchester	Jet2

Valladolid

Fly From	Airline(s)
London Stansted	Ryanair

Vitoria

Fly From	Airline(s)
London Stansted	Ryanair

Zaragoza

Fly From	Airline(s)
London Stansted	Ryanair

Airline Contacts

Airline	Telephone Number(s) & Website
Aer Lingus	☎ (Ireland) 0818-365 000
	☎ (Spain) 902-502 737
	🖥 http://www.aerlingus.com
Air Scotland	☎ (UK only) 0870-850 0958
	🖥 http://www.air-scotland.com
BA	☎ (UK only) 0870-850 9850
	🖥 http://www.ba.com
BMI	☎ (UK only) 0870-607 0555
	☎ (Spain) 902-999 262
	🖥 http://www.flybmi.com
Bmibaby	☎ (UK only) 0871-224 0224
	☎ (Spain) 902-100 737
	🖥 http://www.bmibaby.com

Easyjet   ☎ (UK only) 0871-244 2366
           ☎ (Spain) 902-299 992
           💻 http://www.easyjet.com

Excel Airways ☎ (UK only) 0870-169 0169
           💻 http://www.xl.com

Flybe   ☎ (UK only) 0871-700 0535
           💻 http://www.flybe.com

GB Airways   ☎ (UK only) 0870-850 9850
           ☎ (Spain) 902-111 333
           💻 http://www.gbairways.com

Globespan   ☎ (UK only) 0870-556 1522
           💻 http://www.flyglobespan.com

Iberia   ☎ (UK only) 0845-601 2854
           ☎ (Spain) 902-400 500
           💻 http://www.iberia.com

Jet2   ☎ (UK only) 0871-226 1737
           💻 http://www.jet2.com

Monarch   ☎ (UK only) 0870-040 5040
           ☎ (Spain) 800-099 260
           💻 http://www.flymonarch.com

Ryanair   ☎ (UK only) 0871-246 000
           ☎ (Ireland) 0818-303 030
           ☎ (Spain) 807 220 032
           💻 http://www.ryanair.co.uk

Spanair   ☎ (Spain) 902-929 191
           💻 http://www.spanair.com

Airport Contacts

Airport	Telephone Number	Website
Belfast City	☎ 028-9448 4848	💻 http://www.bial.co.uk
Blackpool	☎ 0870-027 3777	💻 http://www.blackpoolinternational.com
Birmingham	☎ 0870-733 5511	💻 http://www.bhx.co.uk
Bristol	☎ 0870-121 2747	💻 http://www.bristolairport.co.uk
Cardiff	☎ 01446-711111	💻 http://www.cial.co.uk

Cork	☎ 021-431 3131	💻 http://www.corkairport.ie
Dublin	☎ 01-814 1111	💻 http://www.dublinairport.ie
Durham Tees Valley	☎ 01325-332811	💻 http://www.teesside-airport-guide.co.uk
Nottingham/ East Mids	☎ 0871-919 9000	💻 http://www.eastmidlandsairport.com
Edinburgh	☎ 0870-040 0007	💻 http://www.edinburghairport.com
Exeter	☎ 01392-367433	💻 http://www.exeter-airport.co.uk
Glasgow	☎ 0870-040 0008	💻 http://www.glasgowairport.com
Glasgow Prestwick	☎ 0871-223 0700	💻 http://www.gpia.co.uk
Leeds/ Bradford	☎ 0113-250 9696	💻 http://www.lbia.co.uk
Liverpool	☎ 0870-129 8484	💻 http://www.livairport.com
London Gatwick	☎ 0870-000 2468	💻 http://www.gatwickairport.com
London Heathrow	☎ 0870-000 0123	💻 http://www.heathrowairport.com
London Luton	☎ 01582-405100	💻 http://www.london-luton.co.uk
London Stansted	☎ 0870-000 0303	💻 http://www.stanstedairport.com
Manchester	☎ 0161-489 3000	💻 http://www.manchesterairport.co.uk
Newcastle	☎ 0870-122 1488	💻 http://www.newcastleairport.com
Norwich	☎ 01603-411 923	💻 http://www.norwichairport.co.uk
Shannon	☎ 061-712 000	💻 http://www.shannonairport.com
Southampton	☎ 0870-040 0009	💻 http://www.southamptonairport.com

INDEX

N

O

P

LIVING AND WORKING SERIES

Living and Working books are essential reading for anyone planning to spend time abroad, including holiday-home owners, retirees, visitors, business people, migrants, students and even extra-terrestrials! They're packed with important and useful information designed to help you **avoid costly mistakes and save both time and money.** Topics covered include how to:

- Find a job with a good salary & conditions
- Obtain a residence permit
- Avoid and overcome problems
- Find your dream home
- Get the best education for your family
- Make the best use of public transport
- Endure local motoring habits
- Obtain the best health treatment
- Stretch your money further
- Make the most of your leisure time
- Enjoy the local sporting life
- Find the best shopping bargains
- Insure yourself against most eventualities
- Use post office and telephone services
- Do numerous other things not listed above

Living and Working books are the most comprehensive and up-to-date source of practical information available about everyday life abroad. They aren't, however, boring text books, but interesting and entertaining guides written in a highly readable style.

Discover what it's really like to live and work abroad!

Order your copies today by phone, fax, post or email from: Survival Books, PO Box 3780, YEOVIL, BA21 5WX, United Kingdom (☎/🖷 +44 (0)1935-700060, ✉ sales@survivalbooks.net, 🖳 www.survivalbooks.net).

BUYING A HOME SERIES

Buying a Home books, including *Buying, Selling & Letting Property*, are essential reading for anyone planning to purchase property abroad. They're packed with vital information to guide you through the property purchase jungle and help you **avoid the sort of disasters that can turn your dream home into a nightmare!** Topics covered include:

- Avoiding problems
- Choosing the region
- Finding the right home and location
- Estate agents
- Finance, mortgages and taxes
- Home security
- Utilities, heating and air-conditioning
- Moving house and settling in
- Renting and letting
- Permits and visas
- Travelling and communications
- Health and insurance
- Renting a car and driving
- Retirement and starting a business
- And much, much more!

Buying a Home books are the most comprehensive and up-to-date source of information available about buying property abroad. Whether you want a detached house, townhouse or apartment, a holiday or a permanent home, these books will help make your dreams come true.

Save yourself time, trouble and money!

Order your copies today by phone, fax, post or email from: Survival Books, PO Box 3780, YEOVIL, BA21 5WX, United Kingdom (☎/▤ +44 (0)1935-700060, ✉ sales@survivalbooks.net, ▢ www.survivalbooks.net).

OTHER SURVIVAL BOOKS

The Alien's Guides: *The Alien's Guides to Britain and France* will help you to appreciate the peculiarities (in both senses) of the British and French.

The Best Places to Buy a Home in France/Spain: The most comprehensive homebuying guides to France and Spain, containing detailed regional profiles.

Buying, Selling and Letting Property: The most comprehensive and up-to-date source of information on buying, selling and letting property in the UK.

Earning Money From Your Home: Essential guides to earning income from property in France and Spain, including short- and long-term letting.

Foreigners in France/Spain: Triumphs & Disasters: Real-life experiences of people who have emigrated to France and Spain, recounted in their own words.

Lifelines: Essential guides to life in specific regions of France and Spain. See order form for a list of current titles in the series.

Making a Living: Essential guides to self-employment and starting a business in France and Spain.

Renovating & Maintaining Your French Home: The ultimate guide to renovating and maintaining your dream home in France.

Retiring: Retiring Abroad is the most comprehensive source of practical information available about retiring to a foreign country. Retiring Abroad in Spain and Retiring Abroad in France provide up-to-date information on the two most popular retirement destinations.

Rural Living in France: The most comprehensive source of practical information available about life in rural France.

Shooting Caterpillars in Spain: The hilarious but compelling story of two innocents abroad in the depths of Andalusia in the late '80s.

Surprised by France: Even after living there for ten years, Donald Carroll finds plenty of surprises in the Hexagon.

Broaden your horizons with Survival Books!

Order your copies today by phone, fax, post or email from: Survival Books, PO Box 3780, YEOVIL, BA21 5WX, United Kingdom (☎/🖨 +44 (0)1935-700060, ✉ sales@survivalbooks.net, 🖳 www.survivalbooks.net).

ORDER FORM

Qty.	Title	Price (incl. p&p)			Total
		UK	Europe	World	
	The Alien's Guide to Britain	£7.45	£9.45	£12.95	
	The Alien's Guide to France	£7.45	£9.45	£12.95	
	The Best Places to Buy a Home in France	£14.45	£16.45	£19.95	
	The Best Places to Buy a Home in Spain	£14.45	£16.45	£19.95	
	Buying a Home Abroad	£14.45	£16.45	£19.95	
	Buying a Home in Australia & NZ	£14.45	£16.45	£19.95	
	Buying a Home in Cyprus	£14.45	£16.45	£19.95	
	Buying a Home in Florida	£14.45	£16.45	£19.95	
	Buying a Home in France	£14.45	£16.45	£19.95	
	Buying a Home in Greece	£14.45	£16.45	£19.95	
	Buying a Home in Ireland	£12.45	£14.45	£17.95	
	Buying a Home in Italy	£14.45	£16.45	£19.95	
	Buying a Home in Portugal	£14.45	£16.45	£19.95	
	Buying a Home in South Africa	£14.45	£16.45	£19.95	
	Buying a Home in Spain	£14.45	£16.45	£19.95	
	Buying, Letting & Selling Property	£12.45	£14.45	£17.95	
	Buying or Renting a Home in London	£14.45	£16.45	£19.95	
	Buying or Renting a Home in New York	£14.45	£16.45	£19.95	
	Earning Money From Your French Home	£14.45	£16.45	£19.95	
	Earning Money From Your Spanish Home	£14.45	£16.45	£19.95	
	Foreigners in France: Triumphs & Disasters	£12.45	£14.45	£17.95	
	Foreigners in Spain: Triumphs & Disasters	£12.45	£14.45	£17.95	
	Costa Blanca Lifeline	£12.45	£14.45	£17.95	
	Costa del Sol Lifeline	£12.45	£14.45	£17.95	
	Dordogne/Lot Lifeline	£12.45	£14.45	£17.95	
	Normandy Lifeline	£12.45	£14.45	£17.95	
	Poitou-Charentes Lifeline	£11.95	£14.45	£17.95	
	Provence-Côte d'Azur Lifeline	£12.45	£14.45	£17.95	
	Living & Working Abroad	£15.45	£17.45	£20.95	
	Living & Working in America	£17.45	£19.45	£22.95	
	Living & Working in Australia	£17.45	£19.45	£22.95	
	Living & Working in Britain	£17.45	£19.45	£22.95	
	Living & Working in Canada	£17.45	£19.45	£22.95	
	Living & Working in the European Union	£17.45	£19.45	£22.95	
	Total carried forward (see over)				

ORDER FORM

Qty.	Title	Total brought forward			Total
		UK	Europe	World	
	Living & Working in the Far East	£17.45	£19.45	£22.95	
	Living & Working in France	£17.45	£19.45	£22.95	
	Living & Working in Germany	£17.45	£19.45	£22.95	
	L&W in the Gulf States & Saudi Arabia	£17.45	£19.45	£22.95	
	L&W in Holland, Belgium & Luxembourg	£15.45	£17.45	£20.95	
	Living & Working in Ireland	£15.45	£17.45	£20.95	
	Living & Working in Italy	£17.45	£19.45	£22.95	
	Living & Working in London	£14.45	£16.45	£19.95	
	Living & Working in New Zealand	£17.45	£19.45	£22.95	
	Living & Working in Spain	£17.45	£19.45	£22.95	
	Living & Working in Switzerland	£17.45	£19.45	£22.95	
	Making a Living in France	£14.45	£16.45	£19.95	
	Making a Living in Spain	£14.45	£16.45	£19.95	
	Renovating Your French Home	£17.45	£19.45	£22.95	
	Retiring Abroad	£15.45	£17.45	£20.95	
	Retiring in France	£14.45	£16.45	£19.95	
	Retiring in Spain	£14.45	£16.45	£19.95	
	Rural Living in France	£14.45	£16.45	£19.95	
	Shooting Caterpillars in Spain	£10.45	£12.45	£15.95	
	Surprised by France	£12.45	£14.45	£17.95	
				Grand Total	

Order your copies today by phone, fax, post or email from: Survival Books, PO Box 3780, YEOVIL, BA21 5WX, United Kingdom (☎/▤ +44 (0)1935-700060, ✉ sales@ survivalbooks.net, ▤ www.survivalbooks.net). If you aren't entirely satisfied, simply return them to us within 14 days for a full and unconditional refund.

I enclose a cheque for the grand total/Please charge my Amex/Delta/Maestro (Switch)/MasterCard/Visa card as follows. (delete as applicable)

Card No. _ _ _ _   _ _ _ _   _ _ _ _   _ _ _ _   Security Code* _ _ _

Expiry date _____ Issue number (Maestro/Switch only) _____

Signature _____ Tel. No. _____

NAME _____

ADDRESS _____

_____

* The security code is the last three digits on the signature strip.